Y0-BZF-926
2126

FRIEND
MY FRIENDS
Ex Libris
A GOOD
I WOULD
IS LIKE
FOREVER
A BOOK
KEEP
From the André Sobel
Memorial Library

Convergences

Inventories of the Present

Edward W. Said. General Editor

MINOTAUR

POETRY AND THE NATION STATE

Tom Paulin

Harvard University Press
Cambridge, Massachusetts
1992

For Michael and Niall

Printed in Great Britain
10 9 8 7 6 5 4 3 2 1

Library of Congress Cataloging-in-Publication Data

Paulin, Tom,
Minotaur: poetry and the nation state / Thomas Paulin.
p. cm. — (Convergences)
ISBN 0-674-57637-3
1. English poetry—History and criticism. 2. American poetry—History and criticism. 3. Russian poetry—History and criticism.
I. Title. II. Series: Convergences (Cambridge, Mass.)
PR503.938 1992
821.009—dc20 91-34479
CIP

Contents

Author's Note

For their help and encouragement, I am indebted to Jillian Binns, John Cronin, Anne Cutts, Tony Crowley, Seamus Deane, Marianne Elliott, Kelvin Everest, Roy Foster, Seamus Heaney, John Kelly, John and Tina McClelland, Jamie McKendrick, Andrew Motion, David Murray, David Norbrook, Bernard O'Donoghue, Gerard Quinn, Xon de Ros, Edward Said, Judith Still, Norman Vance. I am also deeply grateful to my students at the University of Nottingham, particularly to those gifted enthusiasts with whom I have studied modern poetry.

Introduction

Hegel says, 'It is the way of God with the world that the state exists.' The state's energizing principle is the power of reason 'actualizing itself as will'. However, the state is 'no ideal work of art; it stands on earth and so in the sphere of caprice, chance and error; and bad behaviour may disfigure it in many respects'. Yet despite its limitations, the state has an 'affirmative factor', which is Hegel's theme in *The Philosophy of Right*. The state is more than the sum of its institutions; it exists through those institutions, but is also above and beyond them. It is power, propaganda, a climate of opinion, culture. It inhabits our minds, shaping our beliefs and desires.

Nietzsche attacks Hegel's idea of the state as 'this new idol' in *Thus Spake Zarathustra*, asserting that *state* is the name of the 'coldest of all cold monsters'. It was invented for 'superfluous people' and is a 'monster' that devours them. Attacking social contract theory in *The Genealogy of Morals*, he argues that the state originated not in an act of agreement, but in an act of violence. It therefore appeared as 'a ghastly tyranny, a grinding ruthless piece of machinery, which went on working, till this raw material of a semi-animal populace was not only thoroughly kneaded and elastic, but also moulded'. Nietzsche defines this monster in an angrily prophetic manner that mixes hatred with admiration: 'a herd of blonde beasts of prey, a race of conquerors and masters which with all its war-like organization and all its organizing power pounces with its terrible claws on a population, in numbers possibly tremendously superior, but as yet formless, as yet nomad'.

Nietzsche pitches his assertions against the Enlightenment's optimistic confidence in the nation state, a confidence that informs these lines from *The Prelude*:

How quickly mighty Nations have been formed,
From least beginnings; how, together locked
By new opinions, scattered tribes have made
One body, spreading wide as clouds in heaven.

Punning subconsciously on Locke as a pointer to Rousseau's theory of the social contract, Wordsworth identifies nature with spirit. He sees the French people from the depth of 'shameful imbecility uprisen, / Fresh as the morning star', and he celebrates their virtues of self-sacrifice, 'continence of mind, and sense of right'.

Wordsworth's language and cadencing are distinctively puritan – they are indebted both to Milton and Rousseau – but Nietzsche's modernist disillusion with the state is also rooted in Protestant culture, specifically in a belief in the supremacy of the individual conscience. This is one reason why his passionate anti-statism appealed so strongly to Yeats and Lawrence. In 'A General Introduction for my Work', Yeats denied that he was a nationalist, 'except in Ireland for passing reasons', and he dismissed 'State and Nation' as merely 'the work of the intellect . . . not worth the blade of grass God gives for the nest of the linnet'. His rejection of the nation state is a strategy which aims to identify poetry with an elemental simplicity:

I never bade you go
To Moscow or to Rome.
Renounce that drudgery,
Call the Muses home.

Seek those images
That constitute the wild,
The lion and the virgin,
The harlot and the child.

The primitive is offered as an alternative to political commitment in 'Those Images', but Yeats's rejection of the ideology of Soviet communism and Italian fascism is disingenuous: he was a dedicated nation-builder, the shadow of the gunmen who founded the Irish Free State. His writing is entangled with the ideology of romantic nationalism, even though he wants to identify his poems with the prehistorical, with myth and transcendence. He therefore dismisses the state by denying that it has any imaginative qualities: it is simply mechanical. Thus Yeats rejects Hegel's idea of the nation state as a version of the Greek *polis*.

Yeats's irrationalism is Nietzschean, but we can identify a great theme, or a great and very difficult *potential* theme, in Nietzsche's contemptuous dismissal of the state as that 'coldest of all cold monsters'. By offering us a metaphor, Nietzsche has moved the state out of a mechanically rational into an imaginative reality. This identification of the state with monstrosity was made much earlier by Mary Shelley in *Frankenstein*, a novel that mythologizes the idea of the modern nation state which began with the French Revolution. In 1818, Mary Shelley understood that the nineteenth century was to be, in Bagehot's phrase, the age of 'nation-building', and her haunted, cruel, ugly but somehow sympathetic monster is superior to all those notoriously inadequate definitions of the term 'nation'. As Chris Baldick shows in his exemplary critical study, *In Frankenstein's Shadow*, this imaginative monster is the offspring of Hobbes's image of the state as an 'Artificial Man'.

In 1820, Percy Shelley wrote *Oedipus Tyrannus or Swellfoot the Tyrant* in which Minotaur says:

> I am the Ionian Minotaur, the mightiest
> Of all Europa's taurine progeny –
> I am the old traditional Man-Bull;
> And from my ancestors having been Ionian,
> I am called Ion, which, by interpretation,
> Is JOHN; in plain Theban, that is to say,
> My name's JOHN BULL; I am a famous hunter,
> And can leap any gate in all Boeotia,
> Even the palings of the royal park,
> Or double ditch about the new enclosures;
> And if your Majesty will deign to mount me,
> At least till you have hunted down your game,
> I will not throw you.

The modern identification of Minotaur with state repression begins here. Before this the myth was used to illustrate the vice of bestiality.*

The state is an artifice that is founded on material reality, and therefore, as Hegel concedes, it is no ideal work of art. But this denial is itself imaginative, since it suggests that the state has an approximate relation to the aesthetic. At some deep, culturally inherited level, it would appear that the European imagination perceives a secret kinship between art and the state.† And if Mary Shelley's *Frankenstein* offers a modern myth of the nation state, then the classical myth of Minotaur and the Cretan labyrinth can be interpreted as a story of the occult relationship between art and the state. Miroslav Holub's poetry is dominated by Minotaur, both as an identified symbol and as an invisible monster. In 'The Minotaur's Thoughts on Poetry', the monster tries to puzzle out the nature of poetry:

> Certainly this thing exists. For
> on dark nights when, unseen,
> I walk through the snail-like windings of the street
> the sound of my own roar reaches me
> from a great distance.

The state respects poetry, rather like Stalin when he phoned Pasternak to ask his opinion of the dissident Mandelstam's poems.

For Holub, writing under the claustrophobic pressure of the Czechoslovakian communist state, there is no such person as the poet, no possibility of writing a transcendent or timeless lyric. Founded on an absolute denial of a personal or private life, his poems are written without hope, but with an obstinate integrity that

*A more benignly sexual interpretation of the myth is present in Picasso's drawings of Minotaur in the *Vollard Suite*.

†In *The Civilization of the Renaissance in Italy*, Jacob Burckhardt discusses the multitude of republican and despotic states in fourteenth-century Italy: 'In them for the first time we detect the modern political spirit of Europe, surrendered freely to its own instincts, often displaying the worst features of an unbridled egoism, outraging every right, and killing every germ of a healthier culture. But, wherever this vicious tendency is overcome or in any way compensated, a new fact appears in history – the state as the outcome of reflection and calculation, the state as a work of art.'

negates even as it creates. Dismissing morning and the lyric poem as 'the naïve light of songbirds' brains', he refuses the romantic nationalism that earlier this century charged Yeats with the desire to write a poem 'maybe as cold/And passionate as the dawn'. Trapped in a closed society dominated by the Soviet Union, Holub ironizes Icarus and designs an anti-poetry that is appropriate to post-war Europe. In 'Distant Howling', Holub narrates a *petite histoire* where Pasteur saves the nine-year-old Joseph Maister with his new vaccine:

Pasteur died of ictus
ten years later.
The janitor Meister
fifty-five years later
committed suicide
when the Germans occupied
his Pasteur Institute
with all those poor dogs.

Only the virus
remained above it all.

These laconic closing lines are aimed against the idea of critical disinterestedness and complete aesthetic autonomy – they remind us that there are no imaginative exits from history. In translation, and it is safe to assume in the original Czech too, the poem's language has a minimal simplicity that denies us the consolation of a final transcending image.

Yet so often it is transcendence we crave. In Larkin's phrase, its uplift is an 'arrow-shower sent out of sight' that seems to take us outside history and society into vision, into timelessness. This is Coleridge's strategy in 'Frost at Midnight', where he invokes an 'eternal language' that is both apparently natural – it is identified with clouds, lakes, shores, mountains – as well as being supernatural. It is the voice of God, the 'Great universal Teacher'. This eternal, universal language is in fact a rhetorical trope that enables Coleridge to assuage his own fears of a French invasion. Addressing his baby son, he utters this earnest prayer:

Therefore all seasons shall be sweet to thee,
Whether the summer clothe the general earth
With greenness, or the redbreast sit and sing
Betwixt the tufts of snow on the bare branch
Of mossy apple-tree, while the nigh thatch
Smokes in the sun-thaw; whether the eave-drops fall
Heard only in the trances of the blast,
Or if the secret ministry of frost
Shall hang them up in silent icicles,
Quietly shining to the quiet Moon.

The nimble sweetness of the verse-line builds the illusion of a voice that is present as we read. A voice that speaks to us here, now, always. Or so it seems. The cradled baby doubles for the reader, so the lines gain in immediacy and warmth. We are not being offered – or it seems that we are not being offered – a belief expressed in a series of printed signs. Rather the voice speaking to us *is* the belief. The poem aims to discard its existence as text in order to become pure voice.

This rejection of writing is made by Rousseau in his 'Essay on the Origin of Languages', where he argues that a written language will not retain its *vivacité* 'as long as one that is only spoken'. This is a version of Socrates' attack on writing as a system of external 'alien marks' (he tells the story of writing's invention in Plato's *Phaedrus*). St Paul also denigrates writing in the Second Epistle to the Corinthians, where he insists on the living, spiritual nature of speech – 'great plainness of speech'. Coleridge is therefore drawing on the long association of voice with authentic presence or parousia. When he states 'while the nigh thatch / Smokes in the sun-thaw', the image of immediate sunlight and sudden steamy condensation exactly fits the spontaneous vocal chiming of *thatch / thaw*. The intense orality of 'Smokes in the sun-thaw' overrides the normative iambic meter of the poem. As in 'Christabel', Coleridge is drawing on ballad rhythm in order to lift the cadence of his lines away from a predictable print-rhythm. The poem attempts to preserve an appearance of regularity for the eye-reader, but properly it needs to begin a new line after the arresting spondee, 'sún-tháw'. The line is effectively broken apart by the four heavy stresses in the invocatory: 'whéther the eáve-dróps fáll'. Coleridge wants to present us with an image which culminates in the doubly peaceful vision of icicles shining quietly in the quiet moonlight, but the eruptive ballad rhythm – a rhythm that embodies popular energy – works against the visual iambic frame of the lines. There is a gap, not in the text, but in the voice's movement, for the pause after 'sun-thaw' is too long and too emphatic to let the line continue. That it does continue after the semicolon – or at least try to – is because Coleridge wants to smooth over all possible threats and difficulties. He has to find a way of incorporating this rhythmic blip into the seamless prayer that is the poem's closing paragraph. But he has allowed the voice of the people to briefly toughen and disrupt the quieter Anglican tone of the poem.

If there is a disjunction here, it may be caused by the conflict between Coleridge's ambition to console his readers and his deeper awareness of the enormous social discontent in Britain and Ireland at that time. He wrote 'Frost at Midnight' in February 1798, a period of widespread revolutionary conspiracy and fierce government repression. Later that year there was a French invasion and a revolutionary uprising in Ireland (there had been a minor French landing near Fishguard in February 1797). In this violent context, the image of icicles hanging – being hung up – under the eaves can seem strangely proleptic. To suggest this is not to argue that there is a metaphoric suggestion of actual violence in the poem – gunsmoke, burning thatch, hangings – only to notice that this is a language that aspires to an innocence it cannot acquire. It is possible that Coleridge is remembering a speech in *Henry V* where the Constable of France laments the successes of the invading English army:

> And shall our quick blood, spirited with wine,
> Seem frosty? O, for honour of our land,
> Let us not hang like roping icicles
> Upon our houses' thatch, whiles a more frosty people
> Sweat droplets of gallant youth in our rich fields –
> Poor we call them in their native lords!

In order to overcome his fear of a French invasion of England, Coleridge subconsciously alludes to a successful English invasion of France.

In 'Frost at Midnight', Coleridge attempts to naturalize emotion, to evoke ye olde traditionalism of 'When icicles hang by the wall', but there is an abstract precision to the phrase 'secret ministry' that is intellectual, doctrinal, even sinister. Three years earlier, Coleridge had published a pamphlet in which he attacked Pitt's speeches as 'Mystery concealing Meanness, as steam-clouds envelope a dunghill'. The frost's 'secret ministry' makes a similar but much subtler connection between rural nature and the public world. The noun 'ministry' has specifically religious and political meanings which combine in Coleridge's usage to suggest an activity that is natural and spiritual, as well as emanating from the state. The word also means 'the condition or fact of being employed as executive agent or instrument', and that instrumentality is brought out in Kelvin Everest's analysis of the poem's opening line: 'The Frost performs its secret ministry', where the verb 'performs' is shown to reinforce the sense of a task that has to be done, 'a task that is at once lonely and isolated, introspective and wary, and yet very important, full of potential and implication; like the task of a secret agent'. The title of Everest's study, *Coleridge's Secret Ministry*, stresses the occult activism present in this and other poems. The term rises from Coleridge's subconscious to unite his sense of poetic vocation in a vision that merges several types of process – religious, political, educative, natural. At this time, he was involved in yet another process – that of shifting his opinions from radical to conservative. It is as if Coleridge intuitively knew Pitt's spies were watching him. But he was also doubting his earlier republicanism. The French invasion of Switzerland that February contributed to a disillusion with radical politics which led to his espousal of a conservative politics.

The disjunctive rhythm and the apparently reconciling frost image in the poem's closing lines signal Coleridge's political anxiety, but they do so only if we read them with a knowledge of their historical situation. It was part of Coleridge's strategy to offer the concept of aesthetic autonomy and transcendental vision as alternatives to the ash-film in the 'low-burnt fire'. The fluttering ash-film is the 'stranger' or 'sole unquiet thing' which portends danger and symbolizes Coleridge's historical consciousness. In the summer of 1798, at the height of the United Irish uprising, he wrote a poem which appears to celebrate the autonomous work of art, but whose orientalist and primitivist surface is disturbed by a sudden violent eruption:

> A mighty fountain momently was forced:
> Amid whose swift half-intermitted burst
> Huge fragments vaulted like rebounding hail,
> Or chaffy grain beneath the thresher's flail:
> And 'mid these dancing rocks at once and ever
> It flung up momently the sacred river.

Kubla Khan re-established the unity of the Chinese state, and an idea of the state is imaged in the labyrinthine river which runs 'through caverns measureless to man'. That state and its literal superstructure – the aesthetically pleasurable garden – are disrupted by an image of revolutionary violence which is given an emphatically temporal movement through the repeated adverb 'momently'. Coleridge wants to express the moment-by-moment movement – the current – of present political action, but he also wants to soften and distance such action historically and geographically. As a result, readings of this poem tend to stress its exoticism and the myth of its incompletion, rather than considering its situation in a decade of revolutionary struggle. But the ancestral voices that prophesy war in 'Kubla Khan' issue from the struggles of European states. It is their violence and their responsibility for war and empire which Coleridge seeks to offload on to this 'romantic chasm', this 'savage place'.

On the other hand, the poem exults in the disruption of the sacred river, and, as Carl Woodring has argued, the image of the caves of ice may have a radical tenor. Coleridge associated it with Russian despotism – he had a particular hatred for Catherine the Great – and he also saw pleasure gardens as symbols of tyranny. As Woodring notes, he employed a similar image two years later in this account of a debate between Pitt and Fox in the House of Commons:

Mr Pitt built up his periods, as usual, in all the stately order of rhetoric architecture; but they fell away at once before that true eloquence of commonsense and natural feeling which sanctifies, and renders human, the genius of Mr Fox. Like some good genius, he approached in indignation to the spell-built palace of the state-magician, and at the first touch of his wand, it sunk into a ruinous and sordid hovel, tumbling in upon the head of the wizard that had reared it.

Here, the energy of romantic authenticity overthrows Pitt's artificial rhetoric, which is identified with a magic palace. Yet in the closing lines of 'Kubla Khan' Coleridge dramatizes himself as the poet–prophet whose ambition it is to build the icy domes:

I would build that dome in air,
That sunny dome! those caves of ice!
And all who heard should see them there,
And all should cry, Beware! Beware!
His flashing eyes, his floating hair!
Weave a circle round him thrice,
And close your eyes with holy dread,
For he on honey-dew hath fed,
And drunk the milk of Paradise.

The poet and the poem are identified, the reader must bow down before them. From Coleridge's insistence on the mysterious to Pater's famous invocation to the enigma of the *Mona Lisa*, there is a common ambition to make the aesthetic unapproachably difficult. Our aesthetics are suffused with riddles and luminous mysteries.

One result of the Romantic deification of the artist – the poet as hero, the poem as icon – has been an oppositional denial of what has been clumsily termed the 'literarity' of literature. For more than a decade now, critics, teachers and students of literature have had to question the notion that a literary or poetic consciousness is 'a privileged consciousness, whose use of language can pretend to escape, to some degree, from the duplicity, the confusion, the untruth that we take for granted in the everyday use of language'. By 'we', Paul de Man means a certain type of academic literary specialist; by 'everyday', he probably means Heidegger's 'Gerede' –

idle talk, ordinary spiel. But unlike Heidegger, de Man does not wish to exalt the poet as a 'shepherd of Being'. He aims to make the critic into the equivalent of the artist, while denying there is such a thing as 'literary language'. That denial has contributed to the empowering of those various critical approaches to texts which are presently concealed by the unitary title 'critical theory'. No one involved in the study and teaching of literature over the past decade can fail to notice how deeply this sceptical view of literary language has infiltrated critical discussion. The writer, in Foucault's phrase, is no longer 'the rhapsodist of the eternal'. Curiously, the denial of a privileged literary language would appear to stem from a consideration of the type of issue raised by 'Frost at Midnight': the disjunction between voice and written or printed language.

As de Man notes, Rousseau asserted 'the primacy of voice over the written word', and in this he adhered to a myth of original innocence. Rousseau argues in his essay on the origin of languages that academies kill the spoken language, while Jacques Derrida criticizes the repression of written language by the 'logocentric' fallacy of favouring voice over writing. In his commentary on Derrida, de Man suggests that if we argue that Rousseau escapes 'from the logocentric fallacy precisely to the extent that his language *is literary*, then we are saying by implication that the myth of the priority of oral language over written language has always already been demystified by literature, although literature remains persistently open to being misunderstood for doing the opposite'. Romantic and much post-Romantic writing is based on a denial of literariness and an espousal of orality. Both Derrida and de Man challenge this deep-seated cultural myth of the priority of oral language.

One result of this challenge has been that antipathy to history which even the most cursory reader of literary theory is bound to notice. Here, Nietzsche's essay 'Of the Use and Misuse of History' would appear to be a crucial influence. In this essay, Nietzsche rejects a sense of history: 'there is a degree of sleeplessness, of rumination, of "historical sense", that injures and finally destroys the living thing, be it a man or a people or a system of culture'.

According to de Man, Nietzsche's polemic exemplifies the collision between a 'genuine impulse toward modernity' and the demands of 'a historical consciousness or a culture based on the disciplines of history'. Nietzsche, who was then a young philologist, had turned violently against 'the traditional foundations of his discipline'. His angry repudiation of that discipline reverberates in more recent arguments about the nature of literary criticism and the academic subject called English Literature.

De Man argues that in Nietzsche's essay modernity and history are opposed. By 'modernity', de Man means the 'temptation of immediacy', and he asks how it is that the desire for modernity, which is such a 'specific and important' feature of a literary consciousness, seems to lead 'outside literature into something that no longer shares this specificity, thus forcing the writer to undermine his own assertions in order to remain faithful to his vocation'. Though de Man does not say so, the answer to his question must surely be that the demand for immediacy – the nowness of the living spoken word – is the expression of Protestant culture. Nietzsche's closing insistence that 'sincerity' is a step towards 'true culture', his assertion that it may have the 'power to shatter a whole system of merely decorative culture', is deeply Lutheran and iconoclastic (Nietzsche came from a family of pastors). More attractively, it is this type of proenergetic iconoclasm – one of the private conscience's most distinctive reflexes – that inspires Milton's prose writings and underlies his defence of the republican nation state.

Many of the essays in the present volume consider literary texts in relation to Protestant or puritan ideas, not least that of orality with its accompanying hostility to what St Paul terms 'the bondage of the letter'. Though the deep structure of that dissenting imagination often dismays me with its single-minded, driven violence and ferocity, I recognize that these essays are also stages towards a work which would seek to complement Conor Cruise O'Brien's remarkable study of the Catholic imagination, *Maria Cross*. What haunts me is the desperate sleeplessness of the historical sense and a belief that it is criminal to try to banish it from the discussion of art. Nietzsche's fierce impulse towards modernity and immediacy, his wish to tear down the merely decorative, for me expresses a characteristically Protestant wish to break with the past and destroy the aesthetic.

De Man follows Nietzsche in rejecting history by denying that literary texts need to be located culturally and socially. Discussing Heidegger's commentaries on Hölderlin, de Man asks:

> Heidegger's need for a witness is understandable, then, but why must it be Hölderlin? There are, to be sure, secondary reasons, of a sentimental and national nature, in his favor. Heidegger's commentaries were thought out just before and during World War II, and are directly linked to an anguished meditation upon the historical destiny of Germany, a meditation that finds its echo in the 'national' poems of Hölderlin. But that is a side issue that would take us away from our topic.

The idea that Nazism, the Second World War, Heidegger's support for Hitler, are somehow a 'side issue' is both arrogant and sinister. Here the virus remains above it all, and here de Man's earlier complicity with Nazism ministers secretly to his many admirers. In an essay on Keats, his strategy of denial offers the argument that 'we are on very safe ground when we derive our understanding from the work itself'. This is the close reader as war criminal.

Reflecting on the essays gathered here, I have to consider why so much cultural and institutional attention is given to the critical act. Isn't the act of reading solitary and personal? Doesn't the critic merely help the reader? Trying to answer those questions takes me – the never entirely detribalized me – back to the experience of reading what must be one of the very earliest accounts of the centrality of hermeneutics to society, the Book of Daniel.

When Nebuchadnezzar captures Jerusalem he adopts certain of the most able children of Israel. Among them are Daniel, Hananiah, Mishael and Azariah, who are given the names Belteshazzar, Shadrach, Meshach and Abed-nego. Daniel has understanding 'in all visions and dreams' and Nebuchadnezzar finds him to be much more able than all the magicians and astrologers in his kingdom. Nebuchadnezzar is troubled by dreams and he commands the magicians and astrologers, the sorcerers and Chaldeans, to 'shew' him a dream he has forgotten. They are unable to describe or interpret it, but Daniel reveals that the dream was of a 'great image' – the metal statue with the feet of clay. He interprets this as a prophecy of the series of inferior kingdoms that will follow Nebuchadnezzar's reign. Daniel, Shadrach, Meshach and Abed-nego are rewarded with increased power. Shadrach, Meshach and Abed-nego survive the burning fiery furnace untouched; then Daniel interprets another of the King's dreams: 'thy dwelling shall be with the beasts of the field, and they shall make thee to eat grass as oxen, and they shall wet thee with the dew of heaven'. Daniel then interprets the writing on the wall for Nebuchadnezzar's son and successor. He becomes more and more powerful.

The biblical text is mainly known nowadays through a series of images that have become clichés: statue with the feet of clay, burning fiery furnace, the writing on the wall, the lions' den. I had been familiar with the story since childhood and had heard excerpts from it read out at primary and Sunday school, where I learnt parts of it off by heart, a process that was more than the apparently personal act of reading and rereading a text in order to memorize certain selected verses – it was the experience of being read into a narrative which is part of the tribal myth of the Protestant community in Ulster. Later on I was to doubt that myth, and then in November 1985 a significant political event took place in the North of Ireland – the British and Irish governments signed the Anglo-Irish Agreement. This agreement, the successor to the treaty which partitioned Ireland in 1921, gave the Irish government influence over the administration of the Northern Irish state in return for increased co-operation in the struggle against political terrorism. The implicit dilution of British sovereignty profoundly traumatized Ulster's loyalist community, and one of that community's leaders – Ian Paisley – ended a bitter attack on the British government for its 'betrayal' of the loyalists by stating: 'Like the three Hebrew children, we will not budge, we will not bend and we will not burn.'

Reading the Book of Daniel in the light of Paisley's citation of that text – and reading with that intense concentration which is like a type of underwater recognition – I found a narrative that viewed the critical act of interpretation as central to social life. This story of 'peoples, nations and languages' related hermeneutics to state authority, political power and nationhood. Nebuchadnezzar's Babylon was Britain in post-imperial confusion, Daniel was the loyalist imagination which sits 'in the gate of the king', identifies with the British sovereign and holds to a British identity. To read the story in this way was to read both personally and communally, but that process of recognition also carried an awareness that such an intensely direct interpretation was boxed-in and parochial; it could be of no interest to anyone outside a community that now felt it was a minority within Ireland. This sense of embattled provincialism deepened when I discovered that in the Apocrypha there is a series of verses which was inserted between verses 23 and 24 of Daniel chapter 3. This passage is known as 'The Song of the Three Holy Children', the 'Prayer of Azaria', the 'Hymn of the Three', and in it Azaria witnesses from the burning fiery furnace. Perhaps significantly, this canticle is used at feast days in the Catholic Church and is not regarded as being outside the scriptural canon (it appears in the Jerusalem Bible as part of the Book of Daniel).

Reading this non-canonical text – non-canonical, that is, from a Protestant point of view – I found a passage which speaks for the deep psychic wound that was reopened by the Anglo-Irish Agreement:

> For we, O Lord, are become less than any nation, and be kept under this day in all the world because of our sins.
>
> Neither is there at this time prince, or prophet, or leader, or burnt offering, or sacrifice, or oblation, or incense, or place to sacrifice before thee, and to find mercy.
>
> Nevertheless in a contrite heart and an humble spirit let us be accepted.

As I read it – that is, subjectively shape it in relation to a community – this is about the experience of being marginalized. These verses describe what it feels like to belong to a people – a tribe like the Ulster Protestants – but a people that is not a nation. To adapt Benedict Anderson's famous phrase, there is an underground 'imagined community' that is being invoked in these lines. This community is not internationally accepted: it is 'kept under' and has no leader or prophet, no place where it can feel secure to worship its God. To have no place to sacrifice is like a version of penal times when Irish Catholics were forbidden to celebrate mass and had to do so, fearfully, at 'mass rocks' out in the hills. This experience, this sense of being persecuted, is the result of a political process which aims to 'unlock' a tribe from a powerful nation.

Another loyalist leader said that the signing of the Agreement meant that 'We've been put out on the window-ledge.' This was another attempt to find an imaginative image for the sudden shock of being marginalized by two more powerful states. It is an image which rises out of the historical memory of European Protestantism, out of the loyalist sense of solidarity with Protestant experience in France, Germany and Central Europe, as well as in England and Scotland. The experience of being put out on a window-ledge is a reference to the Defenestration of Prague (23 May 1618) which began the Thirty Years War, a bloody conflict that broke up the Holy Roman Empire into a series of separate states. The historical memory of that war shapes Hopkins's *The Wreck of the Deutschland*, which is a prophecy of the imminent collision of the great nineteenth-century European nation states whose beginnings Wordsworth celebrates in *The Prelude*. Writing out of a Catholic experience of defeat and marginalization within England, Hopkins imagines the future 'wreck' of European civilization.

Like the loyalist leader who cited the Defenestration of Prague in order to express his anguished sense of being forced out of the British nation, I studied the history of the Thirty Years War within the Northern Irish system of state education. This necessarily conditions my reading of Hopkins. I say 'conditions' because with hindsight I can see that the school syllabus was designed to reinforce a Protestant identity and to submerge the Catholic population of the province within those dominant values. More than two decades later, I can appreciate that the essays in this collection are rooted in that social experience. They are attempts to combine immediacy with the historical sense Nietzsche and others have decried. They aim to explore the experience of marginality in relation to the nation state, as well as approaching certain questions raised by the oral and primitivist imaginations. Many of the writers I discuss – Southey, Coleridge, Arnold, Hopkins, Larkin, Hughes – are in some important ways prompted by Irish history and culture, by the long and difficult relationship between the two islands. Their works, like the Anglo-Irish Agreement, have a dual identity at various crucial moments. Southey may appear to be a deservedly neglected figure who is not worth any extensive critical attention, but his sojourn in Ireland reveals some of the tensions that underlie that dual identity. He lives again in Paul Muldoon's long poem, *Madoc: A Mystery* (1990), where his and Coleridge's political idealism, radical politics and essentially colonial outlook are subjected to enormous imaginative and ironic pressure. In the poem entitled '[Locke]', mind and perhaps a sovereign sense of nationhood dissolve away entirely:

> Not until he sees the great cloud-eddy
> renewing itself in a pond
> will Southey have even the faintest idea
> of what's happened.
>
> Until he hears
> the sobbing of a resinous plank
> that's already been shaved of its ears
> his mind's a total blank.

Where Wordsworth celebrates 'scattered tribes', unified into a single nation and 'spreading wide as clouds in heaven', Muldoon aims to deconstruct such a fictitious unity.

In a collection of critical essays devoted to poetry, the essay on *Great Expectations* may seem out of place, but it is an attempt to see Dickens's novel as an epic prose-poem whose vernacular and primitivist vision is shared by many of the poets I discuss – Elizabeth Bishop, for example. If these essays seem at times obsessively entangled with social and ideological questions, that is because they are intended to bring to the critical act at least the possibility of an historical method. They are attempts to locate 'the mists and intricacies of state', as Milton termed them, in sometimes apparently innocent texts. But they also try to follow the Joycean imperative to escape the labyrinth. 'You talk to me of nationality, language, religion,' Stephen Dedalus tells his friend, the limited but poignantly decent nationalist Davin, 'I shall try to fly by those nets.' Perhaps only by identifying the shadow those nets cast upon texts whose formal joys we return to again and again can we begin to go beyond the power-relations they embody.

Pure Primitive Divinity: The Republican Epic of John Milton

The dominant English attitude to Milton – a type of begrudging embarrassment – is deeply puzzling. Unlike Dante in Italy or Joyce in Ireland, he is not venerated – respected and admired, yes, but not everywhere, and not always. Many English undergraduates never study his poetry, let alone his prose, with the result that Milton the polemicist, the radical republican visionary and Protestant internationalist, is perceived as being almost a nuisance. *Paradise Lost* is viewed as a tedious work of theology, and there is no adequate selection of his prose currently in print.

Towards the end of his robustly eloquent defence of Milton and the English Revolution, Macaulay expresses regret that Milton's prose writings are 'so little read':

> They abound with passages compared with which the finest declamations of Burke sink into insignificance. They are a perfect field of cloth of gold. The style is stiff with gorgeous embroidery. Not even in the earlier books of the Paradise Lost has the great poet ever risen higher than in those parts of his controversial works in which his feelings, excited by conflict, find a vent in bursts of devotional and lyric rapture.

Macaulay's aesthetic vocabulary has an assertive grandiloquence that is clearly inadequate, and he almost confesses as much when he sidesteps a more extensive analysis of the prose by saying that although he had intended to dwell on the 'sublime wisdom' of *Areopagitica* and 'the nervous rhetoric of the Iconoclast', the length to which 'our remarks have already extended renders this impossible'. Conjuring at the very last moment the possibility of a poetics that might be applied to the prose, Macaulay folds himself in sentimental rhetoric, then disappears. We are left with the belief that the prose of the 'great poet and patriot' is a subject which requires our attention, but not now, not yet.

More than fifty years later, in his influential essay 'A French Critic on Milton' which was first published in 1877, Matthew Arnold disparaged Milton's prose and mocked Macaulay's style – a 'brilliant, metallic, exterior' style that alternated invective with eulogy and lacked 'the soft play of life'. By identifying Milton with his Whig eulogist, Arnold aimed to dismiss what he regarded as the crude provincial energies of dissenting culture and politics. Quoting Macaulay's praise of Milton's 'sedate and majestic patience', his freedom from 'asperity', Arnold exclaimed:

> If there is a defect which, above all others, is signal in Milton, which injures him even intellectually, which limits him as a poet, it is the defect common to him with the whole Puritan party to which he belonged – the fatal defect of *temper*. He and they may have a thousand merits, but they are *unamiable*. Excuse them how one will, Milton's asperity and acerbity, his want of sweetness of temper, of the Shakespearian largeness and indulgence, are undeniable.

Angrily, Arnold scorns Macaulay's view of the prose by quoting one of the rougher passages from *The Doctrine and Discipline of Divorce* which he derides in his typically exclamatory, dinner-table manner.

Turning to Edmond Scherer, the French critic he so admired, Arnold argues that while Milton is a great poet, he is also a tiresome controversialist who in Scherer's phrase resembles 'the serpent of Eden, eating the dust, the dust of dismal polemics'. Milton belongs, the implication is, in those earnest rain-lashed northern mill towns Arnold loathed. His essay clears the way for the attacks on Milton which Eliot and Leavis were to mount this century.

Arnold's criticisms stem from his personal antipathy to mid-Victorian nonconformism. Yet if there is something very shameful about the English attitude to Milton – something dismal and boneheaded and degrading – it could be argued that Milton is the victim of that famous modesty topos in the preface to Book II of *The Reason of Church Government* where he characterizes his prose as a 'cool element', calling it the work 'of my left hand'. Many later readers gladly dismissed the prose as the work of a gauche and embittered polemicist, but as James Turner argues in his vigorous essay in *Politics, Poetics, and Hermeneutics in Milton's Prose,* this gesture of modesty on Milton's part is self-invalidating. By describing his literary ambitions in the left-handed preface and by representing his mind 'at home in the spacious circuits of her musing' as he writes, Milton is deliberately abolishing the restrictions that are allegedly intrinsic to prose:

> Just as the free movement of prose vanquishes the restriction of verse in the early letter to Young, so here the constraining properties of prose are localized and transcended, not by deferring all hopes to an unattainable poetic vision, but by reconstituting spaciousness in the prose itself.

Milton's main concern, Turner argues, is not the hierarchy of verse over prose, but that of 'vitality over deadness', and although Turner doesn't say so, Milton is a mould-breaker who sets the egalitarian energies of the free market against an aristocratic formality he found 'brutish' and 'slavish'. His free orations, or what he termed 'an Asiatic exuberance of words', therefore cannot be assimilated within a critical approach that polarizes the aesthetic and the functional:

> The issue is whether the text manifests an intrinsic vigor and authority, not whether it is formally or intentionally poetic. On this scale of values, the text-in-the-world, the committed and end-directed text in whatever form, wins out over the text of aesthetic disengagement, sporting with Amaryllis in the shade.

The vehemence and vituperation which belong to the proenergetic, antirationalist tendency in the prose do not mar the text – rather, they are assigned 'an intense uplifting power' and represent a vitalistic engagement which may have generated rather than impeded Milton's epic vision.

Along with many of their fellow essayists, Turner and his co-editor David Loewenstein attack what they term the 'separatist aesthetics' which demote the prose by arguing that poetic achievement depends on a withdrawal from the immediate processes of history, particularly the pressures of political crisis. Exploring Milton's commitment to revolutionary republicanism, they argue for an activist conception of his imagination, though Stanley Fish, in a tedious, slippery, trivializing essay, argues that the energy of the prose will not be found in the 'historical particulars' to which Milton responds. Predictably, the source of that energy is to be located in certain Derridean 'obsessions' which afflicted Milton. Turner easily disposes of Fish's self-regarding nihilism, while Loewenstein shows that for Milton political discourse *was* aesthetic, a belief exemplified in the *Second Defense of the English People* where he presents Cromwell as 'libertatis auctor' – the author of liberty – and links his authority with 'the creativity of the revolutionary writer'.

Loewenstein's essay, 'Milton and the Poetics of Defence', is exhilarating, but his critical study of the prose writings, *Milton and the Drama of History*, is less confident in its address to this disgracefully neglected subject. Even so, this is the first book-length study of the prose, and we must be grateful to Loewenstein for attempting what is in effect an epic critical venture. Unfortunately, for a book of this title, its author has only a tenuous idea of history and, except for the execution of Charles I, neglects to mention any concrete historical event. His study is really a gathering of learned articles which lack the enabling concentration of the essay form and so fail to cohere into a developing argument. He sidesteps the controversy over the date of *Samson Agonistes* by failing to choose between William Parker's view that it is an apolitical tragedy written in the mid-1640s and Christopher Hill's compelling argument that it is a highly political late work. However, Loewenstein challenges orthodox views of *Paradise Lost* when he argues that Michael's prophecies in books 11 and 12 should not be regarded as inferior. The prophecies constitute Milton's most ambitious attempt to confront and examine historical causation. He situates the drama of national destiny – a major concern of the prose – within 'the full spectacle of tragic human history' which Michael unfolds to Adam. In narrating the Noah episode, Michael shows that God is also a creative iconoclast whose signs in fallen history are open to interpretation if Adam can be educated into becoming 'a kind of semiologist'.

But it is one thing to assert that the concerns of the prose and the poetry should not be separated, another to make connections between them which are critically viable. If the prose is not to be seen simply as a gloss on the poems, how do we approach it? Quoting Hayden White, who has suggested that there is a 'poetic element' in all historical writing, Loewenstein is yet unable to identify very clearly what that element is. In a critical climate hostile to 'literariness' such an attempt may seem foredoomed anyway, though somewhere there may be a narratologist or theorist capable of grappling with a subject that has been lying around ever since Macaulay signed off in 1825. It is a formidable task and one which – no modesty topos this – I'm greatly daunted by, but let me attempt to suggest a way of integrating the concerns of the prose and the poetry.

To begin with, we need to recognize that for all its impressive scholarship, Alastair Fowler's edition of *Paradise Lost* – the most elaborate modern edition – is deeply inadequate. Lost in a desert of numerological obsessions, Fowler is concerned to minimize the topicality of the epic and to link it chiefly with Milton's *De Doctrina Christiana*, rather than with his more important prose works. Although Turner and Loewenstein rightly insist that we should not view the prose as a mere repository of glosses on the poems, readers need to assemble a store of glosses in order better to appreciate Milton's verse and as a preliminary to the establishment of a poetics for the prose. We have as yet no such poetics, but one thing is certain: topicality – the dramatic intensity of the polemical Now – must be the life-blood of such an enterprise. That proenergetic topicality can be felt, for example, when Milton compares the rebel angels to the Egyptian army that God has destroyed on the coast of the Red Sea. The Israelites behold 'from the safe shore':

> their floating carcasses
> And broken chariot wheels, so thick bestrewn
> Abject and lost lay these, covering the flood,
> Under amazement of their hideous change.

Loewenstein links these lines with this passage from *Of Reformation*, where Milton remarks:

how to keep up the floating carcase of a crazy, and diseased monarchy, or state betwixt wind, and water, swimming still upon her own dead lees, that now is the deep design of a politician.

Loewenstein's gloss is helpful, but the floating bodies and broken chariot wheels must also be interpreted as a kind of montage that adapts the Book of Exodus to produce an image of a civil war battlefield which stands for the complete intellectual and military defeat of the royalist forces. The battle is imaged as both a land and a naval engagement, a significant conflation that draws on *Of Reformation*'s evocation of an earlier English victory where 'for us the northern ocean even to the frozen Thule was scattered with the proud ship-wracks of the Spanish Armado'.

In a later reference to Philip II of Spain, Milton claims that God's enemies have joined their plots with 'that sad intelligencing tyrant that mischiefs the world with his mines of Ophir, and lies thirsting to revenge his naval ruins that have larded our seas'. These celebrations of the defeat of the Spanish Armada have also a significant imaginative energy in these lines from *Samson Agonistes* where the chorus introduces Dalila:

> But who is this, what thing of sea or land?
> Female of sex it seems,
> That so bedecked, ornate, and gay,
> Comes this way sailing
> Like a stately ship
> Of Tarsus, bound for th'isles
> Of Javan or Gadire
> With all her bravery on, and tackle trim,
> Sails filled, and streamers waving,
> Courted by all the winds that hold them play.

Tarsus, as John Carey notes in his edition of *Samson Agonistes*, is probably Tartessus in Southern Spain, so the Spanish place-name must be keyed through 'Armado' to *Of Reformation*'s conclusion. Dalila, significantly, is presented as a 'thing of sea or land', and in the earlier passage from *Of Reformation* where a crazy and diseased monarchy is shown as a kind of cadaverous hulk or Egyptian chariot, floating between wind and water, Milton offers an alternative image of a Commonwealth which 'ought to be but as one huge Christian personage, one mighty growth, and stature of an honest man'. Samson is that Commonwealth, just as Milton is England withstanding the might of the royalist reaction. The prose and verse are interfused, nowhere more so than in those choric rhythms in *Samson Agonistes* where Milton uses sporadic end-rhyme almost like tacking stitches to give a certain stability to the strange, exploratory hesitancy of his longer and shorter lines. Abandoning the high, majestic, epic singing voice, he experiments with prose rhythms in the chorus, aiming for the tentative rawness and authenticity of vernacular speech. In doing so, Milton achieves the informality of what in *Areopagitica* he terms 'this free writing and free speaking'. He initiates the possibility of a new poetic – the free verse of Whitman and Lawrence which draws so strongly on his Utopian vision of nature.

But perhaps he is actually consolidating in *Samson Agonistes* a poetic he had first experimented with in the prose? If we treat his satanic characterization of Philip II as a form of free verse, we get:

> that sad intelligencing tyrant
> that mischiefs the world with his mines of Ophir,
> and lies thirsting to revenge his naval ruins
> that have larded our seas.

This is a verse movement in the prose, and there is an almost Frostian sentence-sound earlier in *Of Reformation* when Milton attacks those who fear the 'plain field' of the Scriptures: 'they seek the dark, the bushy, the tangled forest, they would imbosk'. The fricative, susurrating assonance has an oral relish that breaks down the barriers separating prose from verse:

> they seek the dark, the bushy, the tangled forest,
> they would imbosk.

The play of speech rhythm against the iambic paradigm is uniquely beautiful, particularly in the thorny bushiness of that last syllable.

This prose movement – a type of speech-pulse – has an impacted, layered quality that is the stylistic equivalent of Milton's complex allusiveness, his method of merging different historical periods, personalities and textual sources. That method can best be observed in his central image of the ideal Commonwealth as a paradisal garden inhabited by the tall and godlike Adam and Eve. Paradise is also 'pure primitive divinity', the primitive Church of God and 'happy isle' towards which we see Satan flying. That phrase 'happy isle' is adapted from John of Gaunt's famous speech in *Richard II* where England on the brink of civil war is this 'other Eden, demi-paradise'. The interwoven allusions do not stop here, because Milton is also drawing on a subtly suggestive moment in the *Second Defense of the English People* where he refers to an adulterous affair in Claude Salmasius's garden. It was in reply to Salmasius's *Defensio Regia* that Milton wrote his first *Defense of the English People*, a polemic that made him, as Hill demonstrates, into a European figure of 'heroic magnitude' and so allowed England to take her place intellectually among the nations of the world. Referring to the first *Defense*, Milton said, 'by God's grace I so routed my audacious foe that he fled, broken in spirit and reputation', and it's likely that he was remembering the international impact of his victory when he described Abdiel smiting Satan so hard that he recoils 'ten paces huge', causing consternation to the 'rebel thrones'.

In answer to Milton's *Defense*, a work called *Regii Sanguinis Clamor* appeared anonymously in 1652. Milton took this pamphlet to have been written by Alexander More, a classical scholar and professor of theology who was a protégé of Salmasius. His notorious philandering offered an easy target and in the *Second Defense*, which Milton wrote in reply to what he believed was More's pamphlet, he described how a young woman called Pontia who was a servant in Salmasius's household had been seduced by More:

> The neighbours had often noticed that they entered all by themselves a certain summerhouse in the garden. Not quite adultery, you say. He could have done anything else in the world. Certainly. He might have talked to her, no doubt about matters horticultural, or he might have drawn from the subject of gardens (say those of Alcinous or Adonis) certain of his lectures

for this woman who had perhaps a smattering of knowledge and a willing ear.

Satan squatting like a toad at Eve's ear, his temptation of her, draw on this passage which allows us to glimpse the lecherous royalist theologian who is one of Satan's many embodiments. Another immediate, topical source for Satan's character is to be found in Milton's attack on the Earl of Strafford in *Eikonoklastes* as one of the 'boldest and most impetuous instruments that the King had to advance any violent or illegal design'. Satan's 'immortal vigour', his risky lunging hyperborean opportunism, derives in part from Strafford's ruthless character, his eloquence and links with the 'false North' Milton hated so strongly. When Satan is compared to a 'black mist low creeping', as he holds intently to:

> His midnight search, where soonest he might find
> The serpent: him fast sleeping soon he found
> In labyrinth of many a round self rolled,
> His head the midst, well stored with subtle wiles

Milton designs a resonant, rather Spenserian image that is very close to being a Minotaur. The serpent curled within his own self-involved maze is an anti-royalist and anti-papal symbol of the 'labyrinth of servitude' Milton attacks in *Eikonoklastes* and elsewhere in the prose. We need to link the persistent image of Satan as mist with the 'mists and intricacies of State' in *Eikonoklastes* and the 'thick mist' that Charles I took advantage of in order treacherously to ambush the parliamentary forces waiting at Brentford in expectation of a treaty.

Milton's insistent topicality shows in this eerily lavish description of Satan's snaky movement:

> on his rear
> Circular base of rising folds, that towered
> Fold above fold a surging maze, his head
> Crested aloft, and carbuncle his eyes;
> With burnished neck of verdant gold, erect
> Amidst his circling spires, that on the grass
> Floated redundant.

The 'circling spires' allude to an earlier moment where Satan is compared to a scout who sees from a hill 'some renowned metropolis / With glistering spires and pinnacles adorned, / Which now the rising sun gilds with his beams'. Satan is a conflation of Rome, whose 'glittering spires' are mentioned in *Paradise Regained*, and of royalist Oxford where Charles summoned an anti-Parliament in 1644 (his snakelike 'subtle and unpeacable designs' are associated with the city in *Eikonoklastes)*. Milton refers to that anti-Parliament in *The Ready and Easy Way to Establish a Free Commonwealth*, and he had personal reasons for associating Oxford with malevolent royalism through his first wife's family, the scheming and improvident Powells who lived in a village near the city. Again, that famous phrase in *The Ready and Easy Way* about the imminent restoration of monarchy being like choosing 'a captain back for Egypt' is caught up in Michael's prophecy that the 'race elect' will advance through the desert 'not the readiest way' lest fear returns them 'back to Egypt'. To gloss this passage in the poem by means of the prose is to substantiate the important point Loewenstein makes in *Milton and the Drama of History*: that Michael's prophecies confront the historic destiny of the English nation. That destiny can be felt in the description of how those 'inviolable saints', the good angels, 'in cubic phalanx firm advanced entire', like the psalm-singing soldiers of the New Model Army.

There are many more connections that can be made between the prose and the poetry, and I have drawn attention to some of them because they are not listed in the detailed notes to Fowler's edition of *Paradise Lost*. What is required is an edition that is historically grounded and that pays proper attention to those extraordinary prose works no one seems to think worth publishing a decent selection from. The reclamation of Milton initiated by Christopher Ricks and by Hill, but prophesied by Herbert Grierson's *Milton and Wordsworth* in 1937, can then be taken a stage further.

To propose this is still to avoid addressing Loewenstein's suggestion that we need to identify the poetic element in Milton's prose. In the absence of a poetics for prose, we could analyse its rhetorical structures, but this, like the metrical analysis of verse, would only be a preliminary exercise. Metrical analysis crucially depends on identifying departures from normative structures, but great prose is such an altogether more provisional and unfixed series of strategies that to advance beyond a dead taxonomy of rhetorical terms will be difficult (though Hazlitt does so effortlessly in his seminal essay 'On the Prose-Style of Poets'). Pointing the way forward Susanne Woods argues that Milton's elective poetics frees readers to choose 'among multiple meanings'. By using interrogative syntax, litotes, clusters of association, and scripture to 'discredit tradition', Milton avoids the rhetorical thundering and 'semantic diffusion' of an appositional style. Arguing that *Considerations Touching the Likeliest Means to Remove Hirelings* has the virtues of good plain-style poetry which we tend to associate with Jonson and Herbert, Woods begins very helpfully to map out possible approaches to the prose.

A criticism adequate to Milton's intellectual and imaginative processes – to 'the diligent alacrity of our extended thoughts', as he terms them – might begin with the passage which precedes that phrase in *Areopagitica*:

> Behold now this vast city; a city of refuge, the mansion-house of liberty, encompassed and surrounded with his protection; the shop of war hath not there more anvils and hammers waking to fashion out the plates and instruments of armed justice in defence of beleaguered Truth than there be pens and heads there, sitting by their studious lamps, musing, searching, revolving new notions and ideas wherewith to present, as with their homage and their fealty, the approaching Reformation; others as fast reading, trying all things, assenting to the force of reason and convincement.

Milton was fascinated by what he termed 'the natural heat of government and culture' – ideas in production, we might call it now – and he identified that process of expansion in its creative immediacy with 'all the happy enjoyments of a potent and flourishing republic'. Trade flourishes best, he insisted, in the free commonwealths of Italy. This is the mercantilist Milton speaking in a type of free writing that articulates an early vision of the ideal bourgeois republic.

With hindsight we can see that the mansion-house of liberty

passage in *Areopagitca* reads like an anticipation of Whitman's *Song of Myself*:

Many sweating, ploughing, thrashing, and then the chaff for
payment receiving,
A few idly owning, and they the wheat continually claiming.

This is the city and I am one of the citizens,
Whatever interests the rest interests me, politics, wars, markets,
newspapers, schools,
The mayor and councils, banks, tariffs, steamships, factories,
stocks, stores, real estate and personal estate.

The Whitman who hears 'all sounds running together, combined, fused or following' is true to the social relatedness of different individual activities which Milton sings in the prose. Especially at the close – 'others as fast reading, trying all things' – Milton sounds almost uncannily like Whitman democratically trying to pack every last rapid action in.

Both poets share an ecstatic primitivism ('Smile O voluptuous cool-breath'd earth!') that can also be a figure for the procreant urge of the market: 'millions of spinning worms,/That in their green shops weave the smooth-haired silk'. However, Milton's commitment to the busy hum of mercantile republics is not entirely wholehearted, for he assigns this vision of productive 'natural' labour to Comus, the tempter. It is therefore more than simply rhetorical to ask, has nature thronged the sea 'with spawn innumerable,/But all to please and sate the curious taste?' An idea of hectic consumerism is glanced at here, but the uncertainty in Milton's imagination is over-ridden by the sensuous delight of the imagery. The essential reason for this is the daring challenge he is offering to those writers who argue that monarchical societies are somehow organic. The 'green shops' of *Comus*, the busy workshops of *Areopagitica*, are celebrations of republican industry allied to and enmeshed with natural, benign, primitive energies. This is the 'natural heat' of government and culture which suffuses Milton's ennobling idea of *civitas*:

Now, surrounded by such great throngs, from the Pillars of Hercules all the way to the farthest boundaries of Father Liber, I seem to be leading home again everywhere in the world, after a vast space of time, Liberty herself, so long expelled and exiled. And, like Triptolemus of old, I seem to introduce to the nations of the earth, a product from my own country, but one far more excellent than that of Ceres. In short, it is the renewed cultivation of freedom and civic life that I disseminate throughout cities, kingdoms, and nations.

Milton's egotism, like Whitman's, has a generous, wonderfully innocent optimism that springs from their absolute confidence in the liberating possibilities of the free individual conscience.

By comparing Milton and Whitman, we start to see the republican poetics that structures the prose. Whitman asserts, 'Not words of routine this song of mine', and Milton is constantly striving to break down inert routines in order to free the imagination from 'linen decency', 'a gross confirming stupidity, a stark and dead congealment'. To adapt Hazlitt's terms, the 'momentum' and 'elasticity' of this republican style gives the prose an ever-expanding, infinitely capacious visionary force which confidently insists that of all governments a Commonwealth aims 'most to make the people flourishing, virtuous, noble and high-spirited'. It seems appropriate that scholars working in the United States should invite readers congealed in the royalist kitsch of present-day Britain to remember and admire this great servant of human liberty.

Southey Landing

Written Immediately after Reading
the Speech of Robert Emmet,
on his Trial and Conviction for High Treason,
Sept. 1803

'Let no man write my epitaph; let my grave
Be uninscribed, and let my memory rest
Till other times are come, and other men,
Who then may do me justice.'*
Emmet, no!
No withering curse hath dried my spirit up,
That I should now be silent, . . . that my soul
Should from the stirring inspiration shrink,
Now when it shakes her, and withhold her voice,
Of that divinest impulse never more
Worthy, if impious I withheld it now,
Hardening my heart. Here, here in this free Isle,
To which in thy young virtue's erring zeal
Thou wert so perilous an enemy,
Here in free England shall an English hand
Build thy imperishable monument;
O . . . to thine own misfortune and to ours,
Be thine own deadly error so beguiled,
Here in free England shall an English voice
Raise up thy mourning-song. For thou hast paid
The bitter penalty of that misdeed;
Justice hath done her unrelenting part,
If she in truth be Justice who drives on,
Bloody and blind, the chariot wheels of death.

*These were the words in his speech: 'Let there be no inscription upon my tomb. Let no man write my epitaph. No man can write my epitaph. I am here ready to die. I am not allowed to vindicate my character; and when I am prevented from vindicating myself, let no man dare to calumniate me. Let my character and my motives repose in obscurity and peace, till other times and other men can do them justice. Then shall my character be vindicated; then may my epitaph be written. I HAVE DONE.'

So young, so glowing for the general good,
Oh what a lovely manhood had been thine,
When all the violent workings of thy youth
Had pass'd away, hadst thou been wisely spared,
Left to the slow and certain influences
Of silent feeling and maturing thought.
How had that heart, . . . that noble heart of thine,
Which even now had snapt one spell, which beat
With such brave indignation at the shame
And guilt of France, and of her miscreant Lord,
How had it clung to England! With what love,
What pure and perfect love, return'd to her,
Now worthy of thy love, the champion now
For freedom, . . . yea, the only champion now,
And soon to be the Avenger. But the blow
Hath fallen, the indiscriminating blow,
That for its portion to the Grave consign'd
Youth, Genius, generous Virtue. Oh, grief, grief!
Oh, sorrow and reproach! Have ye to learn,
Deaf to the past, and to the future blind,
Ye who thus irremissibly exact
The forfeit life, how lightly life is staked,
When in distempered times the feverish mind
To strong delusion yields? Have ye to learn
With what a deep and spirit-stirring voice
Pity doth call Revenge? Have ye no hearts
To feel and understand how Mercy tames
The rebel nature, madden'd by old wrongs,
And binds it in the gentle bands of love,
When steel and adamant were weak to hold
That Samson-strength subdued!
Let no man write
Thy epitaph! Emmet, nay; thou shalt not go
Without thy funeral strain! O young and good
And wise, though erring here, thou shalt not go
Unhonour'd nor unsung. And better thus
Beneath that indiscriminating stroke,
Better to fall, than to have lived to mourn,
As sure thou wouldst, in misery and remorse,
Thine own disastrous triumph; to have seen,
If the Almighty at that aweful hour
Had turn'd away his face, wild Ignorance

Let loose, and frantic Vengeance, and dark Zeal,
And all bad passions tyrannous, and the fires
Of Persecution once again ablaze.
How had it sunk into thy soul to see,
Last curse of all, the ruffian slaves of France
In thy dear native country lording it!
How happier thus, in that heroic mood
That takes away the sting of death, to die,
By all the good and all the wise forgiven,
Yea, in all ages by the wise and good
To be remember'd, mourn'd, and honour'd still.

Keswick
Robert Southey

Robert Southey landed at Balbriggan, Co. Dublin, in mid-October 1801. The Act of Union had come into force on 1 January and Southey had secured an appointment as secretary to Isaac Corry, a politician who was widely regarded as a renegade – he had played a distinguished part in the Volunteer movement, but had been bought over from the popular side by the Marquis of Buckingham and appointed surveyor-general of the ordnance in 1788. After the suppression of the 1798 rebellion, Corry was made chancellor of the Irish exchequer and in the Union debates he was the chief government spokesman against Grattan, with whom he fought a duel. Corry was not wealthy and was a purely professional politician whose career, paradoxically, would be destroyed by the Union.

Southey had been appointed through the influence of his friend John Rickman, who was employed by Charles Abbot as secretary in preparing the first census act. When Abbot was appointed chief secretary for Ireland in 1801, Rickman accompanied him and was made deputy keeper of the privy seal. Rickman had held 'very seditious' opinions in his youth and been an opponent of Pitt. He became a distinguished statistician, was friendly with the engineer Thomas Telford, and, like Southey, developed into a convinced Tory.

Landing in Ireland that autumn, a young English Protestant with waning republican principles, Southey was disconcerted by the treeless landscape: 'The country that I passed is destitute of trees as if there existed an instinctive dread of the gallows in the people. Indeed most of the young trees in the kingdom had been cut down to make pikes.' Half of Southey's salary of £400 Irish was for travelling expenses and he regarded his position as a promising one – like Bunyan's Christian he saw himself 'in the road to a future, a *clear* road . . . and not a very long way'. With a characteristically Protestant sense of manifest destiny, he reflected that the road lay through a country whose people 'will be difficult to civilize':

> An Irishman builds him a turf stye, gets his fuel from the bogs, digs his patch of potatoes, and then lives upon them in idleness: like a true savage, he does not think it worthwhile to work that he may better himself. Potatoes and butter-milk – on this they are born and bred; and whiskey sends them to the third heaven at once. If Davy had one of them in his laboratory, he could analyze his flesh, blood, bones into nothing but potatoes, and butter-milk, and whiskey; they are the primary elements of an Irishman. Their love of 'fun' eternally engages them in mischievous combinations, which are eternally baffled by their own blessed instinct of blundering. The United Irishmen must have obtained possession of Dublin but for a bull. On the night appointed, the mail-coach was to be stopped and burnt, about a mile from town, and that was the signal; the lamplighters were in the plot; and oh! to be sure! the honeys would not light a lamp in Dublin that evening, for fear the people should see what was going on. Of course alarm was taken, and all the mischief prevented.

The reference to Humphry Davy suggests that Southey viewed the Irish not simply as comic savages, but as the subjects of a great experiment in social science or engineering. Meeting his, and Thomas Telford's, friend Rickman in Dublin that October, Southey took his place in a mission designed to civilize a people who were, he told his friend Charles Danvers, 'filthy – beastlily filthy. I cannot like them, and yet they are a people of genius.' And he adds characteristically: 'I have room for a Bull which Rickman heard.'

Writing to Coleridge and other friends, he recounts examples of 'Paddyisms' and in a letter to Grosvenor Bedford (Dublin, 20 October 1801) mentions: 'It is the opinion of Coleridge that the Irish are descended from certain aboriginals who escaped the deluge in a cock-boat that rested upon Mount Taurus. My own idea is that they are of Cretan race – the descendants of Pasiphae.' Southey's view of the Irish as part 'bull', part human, makes them into a dangerous herd of minotaurs which must be contained within the state-labyrinth.

Southey revised his long poem *Madoc* in Dublin and left after a fortnight. He never returned to Ireland, though throughout his life he maintained an interest in the country's history and politics. His commonplace books contain a great deal of Irish material and in his essays Southey draws heavily on these entries. His attitude to Ireland evidences a strong sense of racial superiority* combined with a paternalist concern which sometimes reveals fundamental feelings of guilt – a guilt that can give way to an angry desire to completely reshape Ireland. Thus in 1805 he remarks: 'England *was* free from the reproach of national cruelty till the accursed proceedings in Ireland.' Two years later he states that nothing can redeem Ireland but such measures as 'none of our statesmen – except perhaps Marquis Wellesley – would be hardy enough to adopt – nothing but a system of Roman conquest and colonization – and shipping off the refractory savages to the colonies'. And in 1828 he remarks menacingly that Spenser 'was not less highly endued with political sagacity than with poetical genius'.

During his brief stay in Dublin, Southey became friendly with someone who was a close friend of Robert Emmet. Leon Ó Broin suggests that this friend was either Tom Moore or 'young Curran', and Southey appears to have felt that his conversations with Emmet's intimate friend were a kind of privileged knowledge which virtually amounted to a personal friendship or tie with Emmet himself. Like Coleridge, he felt a strange kinship with Emmet – the Irish revolutionary was everything the two radical poets might have become had they been born in Ireland.

Southey's sense of racial superiority shows in his reactions to the Catholic Irish, but he appears to have been challenged and disconcerted by the United Irishmen whose origins were Protestant and

*'A journey in Ireland has, also, the great advantage of enabling us to study savage life.' Letter to Samuel Taylor Coleridge, Dublin, 16 October 1801.

republican. Writing from Portugal in 1800, a year before his Irish visit, he comments on the Portuguese refusal to accept the United Irish leaders whom the British government had banished there. Some of these republicans are 'virtuous and enlightened men; who have indeed erred grievously in their contracted spirit of patriotism, but who have acted however erringly, from the purest of motives. For such sedition as theirs change of climate is an effectual cure, and any where except in Ireland they would be among the best and most valuable members of society.' This attitude of mingled admiration, criticism and something that looks like an embarrassed guilt is expressed again in 1809:

England, indeed, may contemplate the sister-country with sorrow, and painfullest shame, and deep humiliation, but not with fear. The time of danger is gone by. A French army, with the lying invitation of liberty upon its banners, would once have been joined by men, formidable for their talents, and virtues, and enthusiasm. Some of these have expiated their errors by death, others are living peaceably in America . . . men to be blamed for these errors only, and fit to be the ornaments of any country, except their own.

Elsewhere in this essay, Southey cries, 'Peace to the spirit of Robert Emmett!' and it would seem that both he and Coleridge were haunted by Emmet's spirit.

Emmet was executed on 20 September 1803. Eight days later, in a letter to John King from Keswick, Southey wrote:

Poor young Emmet! I knew much of him from many conversations with his most intimate friend at Dublin. He was an admirable man. God Almighty seldom mixes up so much virtue and so much genius in one, or talents as ennobled. In the last rebellion he escaped by excavating a hiding-place under the study in his father's house. There he lived six weeks, having food, books, and a light, by night going out into the Park for exercise. And thus he continued till he found means for escaping. And now, – the stony hearts and the leaden heads that manage this poor world! as if the fear of death ever deterred any man from treason who could make treason dangerous! I would send Wm. Taylor this story of his hiding-place, for he, I know, will write his Eulogium in the 'Iris'; but it must not be published lest some other poor fellow may now be in the same asylum. To have spared that young man's life would have indeed strengthened the government. Had they said to him, 'Promise to plot no more and you shall be free', such a man would have been as safe under such a promise as in the grave. But so it is; the king has no heart for pardon: he wants goodness, and his counsellors want understanding. If they mean to extirpate disaffection in Ireland by the gallows, they must sow the whole island with hemp.

It is clear that Southey was profoundly affected by Emmet's life and execution, and his impassioned letter was followed rapidly by a poem whose public rhetoric aims ultimately to formalize and dispel the volatile emotion of the private letter.

Southey's poem is entitled 'Written Immediately after Reading the Speech of Robert Emmet, On His Trial & Conviction for High Treason, Sept. 1803', and he begins by versifying the conclusion to the speech which Emmet gave from the dock and which is cited in a footnote to the poem (this conclusion is not the romantic 'nations of the earth' version which is referred to, for example, in *Ulysses*). Having established his credentials as a sensitive and sympathetic onlooker, Southey then attempts a balanced assessment of Emmet's actions. The impression of balance is superficial because Southey's reaction is on one level apparently immediate and sincere, but on a deeper level is concerned to vindicate England of guilt: 'Here in free England shall an English hand/Build thy imperishable monument'. England, he insists, is a 'free isle' to which Emmet's 'erring zeal' was 'so perilous an enemy'.

Southey's 'mourning-song' expresses an uncertainty about the justice of Emmet's fate and imagines what might have happened if his 'lovely manhood' had been spared. He exclaims upon Emmet's future prospects had he been left to 'the slow and certain influences/Of silent feeling and maturing thought', and suggests how completely his heart might have 'clung to England'. It is the familiar argument for commonsense, for experience not theory, and it imagines a process by which Emmet might have aged into an Englishman. Instead of being simply bought by the government, as Southey's ex-employer Isaac Corry had been, Emmet might have been transformed into an upholder of the Union (by contrast, Shelley's poem of 1812, 'On Robert Emmet's Tomb', does not impose a ruling English style, instead it draws on Moore's melodies in order to pay a republican tribute which is sincere and unpatronizing). For Southey, Emmet's transformation into a sober, middle-aged Englishman would have created a true union of hearts – a bond of mutual kinship – and here there is an anticipation of the later Southey's paternalism, his feudal-conservative dislike of liberal economic individualism and his firm belief in state welfare. If the idea of 'clinging' to England seems merely demeaning, it should also be noted that Southey's essentially compassionate nature made him one of the early prophets of collectivism.

With a desperate sub-Wordsworthian eloquence, Southey insists that he must write Emmet's epitaph, and he concludes by arguing that it was better for Emmet to have died than to have lived to witness the inevitable results of his 'disastrous triumph' – i.e. 'the ruffian slaves of France / In thy dear native country lording it'. It was 'happier' (i.e. both luckier and more pleasant) for Emmet to have died in 'that heroic mood / That takes away the sting of death':

> By all the good and all the wise forgiven,
> Yea, in all ages by the wise and good
> To be remember'd, mourn'd, and honour'd still.

Yet Southey's poem is less a tribute than a vulnerable and revealing piece of self-exculpation which serves finally to vindicate political necessity and colonial rule.

Coleridge, who was sharing Gretta Hall with Southey in 1803, appears to have reacted to contemporary political events both physiologically and intellectually, and the impact on him of Emmet's execution first shows in this notebook jotting: 'Emmet = mad Raphael painting Ideals of Beauty on the walls of a cell with human Excrement.' Coleridge's editor comments that this is a supposition as to what Raphael might have done had he been mad, 'an image for the extremes meeting in Emmet, eloquent idealism and fanatical violence'. It is possible that this interpretation projects a typically Yeatsian, and necessarily anachronistic, tension into the note, and that the human excrement is Coleridge's symbol for the people whom he and Southey dismissed as 'savages'.* It may also be

*Cp. Southey's remark, 'the very dregs and faeces of the most corrupt Catholicism', in 'On the Catholic Question' (1809), *Essays, Moral and Political.*

significant that Coleridge's Protestant imagination transforms the Protestant Emmet into a Catholic, hypothetically insane, artist. As Seamus Deane has shown in *Civilians and Barbarians*, the wisdom of Coleridge and other English commentators on Irish affairs 'has always been vitiated by the assumption that there is some undeniable relationship between civilization, the Common Law and Protestantism'. By breaking the law, Emmet ceased for Coleridge to be either Protestant or civilized.

Two days after Southey's letter to John King, Coleridge addressed an extraordinary letter to his new aristocratic friends, Sir George and Lady Beaumont. It is a hysterical and phantasmagoric reflection on Emmet's execution which begins with an expression of gratitude to the Beaumonts for their 'kind Letter' of that afternoon. Coleridge then gives an account of a severe toothache, analyses the effects of his new gout medicine (at this point he writes with the medicine instead of ink), and expresses a fear that a hot climate may be his only medicine, though 'it seems better to die than to live out of England'. Having established his gratitude, physical suffering and fundamental patriotism, Coleridge moves immediately from the idea that he would be better off dead in England to this statement: 'I have been extremely affected by the death of young Emmett – just 24! – at that age, dear Sir George! I was retiring from Politics, disgusted beyond measure by the manners & morals of the Democrats, & fully awake to the inconsistency of my practice with my speculative Principles.' Carefully, Coleridge mentions that his speculative principles were 'perfectly harmless – a compound of Philosophy and Christianity'. Then, in an apparently uncontrolled tone of hysteria and self-pity, he attacks those who attacked his youthful opinions and admits that he 'aided the Jacobins, by witty sarcasms & subtle reasonings & declamations'. But even as he makes this admission he apologizes for those declamations and adds that, fortunately, the government appears to have known that he and Southey 'were utterly unconnected with any party or club or society', and in an enormous parenthetical aria he adds: '(and this praise I must take to myself, that I disclaimed all these Societies, these Imperia in Imperio, these Ascarides in the Bowels of the State, subsisting on the weakness & diseasedness, & having for their final Object the Death of that State . . .' Then Coleridge imagines what might have happened if he had been imprisoned during his youthful and supposedly brief seditious phase. It is a long passage, but it is worth quoting in its entirety:

my health & constitution were such as that it would have been almost as certain Death to me, as the Executioner has been to poor young Emmett. Like him, I was very young, very enthusiastic, distinguished by Talents & acquirements & a sort of turbid Eloquence; like him, I was a zealous Partisan of Christianity, a Despiser & Abhorrer of French Philosophy & French Morals; like him, I would have given my body to be burnt inch by inch, rather than that a French Army should have insulted my native Shores/ & alas! alas! like him I was unconsciously yet actively aiding & abetting the Plans, that I abhorred, and the men, who were more, far more unlike me, in every respect, in education, habits, principles & feelings, than the most anathematized Aristocrat among my opponents. Alas! alas! unlike *me*, he did not awake! the country, in which he lived, furnished far more plausible arguments for his active Zeal than England could do; the vices of the party, with whom he acted, were so palpably the effect of darkest Ignorance & foulest oppression, that they could not disgust him/the worse the vices & the more he abhorred them, the more he loved the men themselves, abstracting the men from their vices, the vices from the men, & transferring them, with tenfold Guilt, to the state of Society & to the Orange Faction holding together that State of Society, which he believed to be the cause of these Vices! Ah woe is me! & in this mood the poor young Enthusiast sent forth that unjustifiable Proclamation, one sentence of which clearly permitted unlimited assassination – the only sentence, beyond all doubt, which Emmett would gladly have blotted out with his Heart's Blood, & of which at the time he wrote it he could not have seen the Import – & the only sentence, which was fully realized in action – ! This moment it was a few unweighed words of an empassioned Visionary, in the next moment it became the foul Murder of Lord Kilwarden! – O my heart give praise, give praise! – not that I was preserved from Bonds, or Ignominy or Death! But that I was preserved from Crimes that it is almost impossible not to call Guilt! – And poor young Emmet[t!] O if our Ministers had saved him, had taken his Oath & word of honor, to have remained in America or some of our Colonies for the next 10 years of his Life, we *might* have had in him a sublimely great man, we assuredly sh[ould] have had in him a good man & heart & soul an *Englishman*! – Think of Lord Mansfield – About the Age of poor Emmett he drank the Pretender's Health on his Knees & was obnoxious to all the pains & penalties of high Treason. And where lies the

Difference between the two? Murray's Plot had for it's object a foul Slave[ry] under the name of Loyalty; Emmett's as foul a Slavery under the nam[e of] Liberty and Independence. – But whatever the Ministers may have done, Heaven h[as] dealt kindly with the young man. He has died, firm & in the height & heat of his Spirit, beholding in his Partizans only the wickedly oppressed, in his enemies the wicked oppressors. – O if his mad mad Enterprize had succeeded/! – Thou most mistaken & bewildered young Man, if other Punishment than the Death thou hast suffered, be needful for thy deadly Error, what better Punishment, what fitter Purgatory can be imagined, than a Vision presented to thee & conceived as real, a Vision of all the Massacres, the furious Passions, the Blasphemies, Sensualities, Superstitions, the bloody Persecutions, and mutual Cannibalism of Atheist & Papist, that would have rushed in, like a Torrent of Sulphur & burning Chaos, at the Breach which thou thyself hadst made – till thou, yea, even thou thyself hadst called out in agony to the merciless Gaul, & invoked an army of Slave-fiends to crush the more enormous evil of a mob of Fiends in Anarchy. – My honored Friends! as I live, I scarcely know what I have been writing; but the very circumstance of writing to *you,* added to the recollection of the unwise & unchristian feelings, with which at poor Emmett's Age *I* contemplated all persons of *your* rank in Society, & *that* recollection confronted with my present Feelings towards you – it has agitated me, dear Friends! and I have written, my Heart at a full Gallop adown Hill. – And now, good night – I will finish this Letter tomorrow morning.

As he contemplates his radical youth, Coleridge seems to melt into the figure of Emmet, then to emerge as a courtier who addresses his aristocratic friends in order to put behind him both Emmet's views and his own early opinions. Intellectual autobiography becomes a mixture of flattery, self-pity, pathological bigotry and hypochondria, and the medicinal ink clears the way for the emergence of the mature conservative sage. Thus while Emmet becomes an influential figure in the martyrology of romantic nationalism in Ireland, he also, quite inadvertently, helped to inspire a conservative English nationalism. Both interpretations of his career distort him for their own purposes.

In *Coleridge's Secret Ministry,* Kelvin Everest has persuasively traced the falsifications, inconsistencies, confusions and strategies which fill this letter. In it we can sense both a deep personal anxiety and the public alarm at the prospect of a Napoleonic invasion. And behind Coleridge's professed pity and admiration for Emmet, there lies an ambitious strategy which was to take him from Jacobin heresy to the organic consolations of Anglican clerisy. Like Southey, he came to believe that the Church of England had to be preserved at all costs. Along with Arnold's and Eliot's literary and social criticism, Coleridge's lavishly edited complete works may be regarded as influential propaganda for the state Church, and it is necessary to determine how extensively committed to such a concept English literary criticism is.

It can be argued that some of its fundamental principles derive from polemical, counter-revolutionary attitudes to French and Irish republicanism. Arnold, Eliot and Leavis share with the later Southey and the later Coleridge a conservative outlook which is often ethnically biased and which is profoundly influenced by Burke's *Reflections*. In Britain, now, many radical critics and scholars are engaged in a reassessment of traditional critical practice which often reveals its insidiously biased and reactionary nature. Chris Baldick's *The Social Mission of English Criticism* exposes the essentially imperialistic and nationalistic attitudes which informed both English literary criticism and the establishment of English literature as an academic discipline between 1848 and 1932. Baldick quotes from Macaulay's speech 'The Literature of Britain', where the Whig historian looks forward to the conscious propagation of 'that literature before the light of which impious and cruel superstitions are fast taking flight on the banks of the Ganges . . . And, wherever British literature spreads, may it be attended by British virtue and British freedom!' Baldick's outlook is post-imperial – noting this, is it possible to contemplate in Ireland a critical attitude which is both open as to its political ideology and distinctively post-colonial? This cannot happen if we attempt to make a false separation between literature and politics. If we want to make such a separation, then we ought to be honest about our motives. Coleridge was. In a letter to his publisher, Joseph Cottle, he discussed ways of increasing the sales of a new edition of his poems: 'by omitting every thing political, I widen the sphere of my readers'. This strategic omission is similar to that gesture of 'wounded withdrawal' from the public world which Matthew Arnold, as Baldick shows, was later to perfect. The result is an idea of balance, disinterestedness and objectivity which can be seen, for example, in the myth of Shakespeare as, in David Norbrook's words, 'completely impartial and therefore necessarily a supporter of the Church of England'.

Arnold's criticism shows a persistent interest in Irish politics. The day after the Clerkenwell bomb (13 December 1867) he wrote to his mother from the Athenaeum:

I have never wavered in saying that the Hyde Park business eighteen months ago was fatal, and that a Government which dared not deal with a mob, of any nation or with any design, simply opened the flood-gates to anarchy. You cannot have one measure for Fenian rioting and another for English rioting, merely because the design of Fenian rioting is more subversive and desperate; what the State has to do is to put down *all* rioting with a strong hand, or it is sure to drift into troubles. Who can wonder at these Irish, who have cause to hate us, making war on a State and society which has shown itself irresolute and feeble?

And in *Culture and Anarchy* Arnold deploys the figure of an Irish Fenian strategically, even sympathetically, in order to ironize liberal individualism (the freedom to do as one likes), and to express his own distaste for British industrial society:

There are many things to be said on behalf of this exclusive attention of ours to liberty, and of the relaxed habits of government which it has engendered. It is very easy to mistake or to exaggerate the sort of anarchy from which we are in danger through them. We are not in danger from Fenianism, fierce and turbulent as it may show itself; for against this our conscience is free enough to let us act resolutely and put forth our overwhelming strength the moment there is any real need for it. In the first place, it never was any part of our creed that the great right and blessedness of an Irishman, or, indeed, of anybody on earth except an Englishman, is to do as he likes; and we can have no scruple at all about abridging, if necessary, a non-Englishman's assertion of personal liberty. The British Constitution, its checks, and its prime virtues, are for Englishmen. We may extend them to others out of love and kindness; but we find no real divine law written on our hearts constraining us so to extend them. And then the difference between an Irish Fenian and an English rough is so immense, and the case, in dealing with the Fenian, so much more clear! He is so evidently desperate and dangerous, a man of a conquered race, a Papist, with centuries of ill-usage to inflame him against us, with an alien religion established in his country by us at his expense, with no admiration of our institutions, no love of our virtues, no talents for our business, no turn for our comfort! Show him our symbolical Truss Manufactory on the finest site in Europe, and tell him that British industrialism and individualism can bring a man to that, and he remains cold! Evidently, if we deal tenderly with a sentimentalist like this, it is out of pure philanthropy.

Rather like Coleridge, Arnold appears briefly to assume the identity of an Irish revolutionary; it is curious to observe a critic speaking for English high culture through the symbolic mask of an Irish terrorist. Arnold is here concealing himself behind a bomber in order to express his disgust at the British middle class. This anticipates the subversive irony and radical disgust of Wilde, but with Arnold it is a temporary strategy rather than a consuming ideological commitment. Arnold is arguing the case both for his own good taste and for tough measures against English 'roughs'. He is in love with the idea of a classical discipline, while Wilde is an anarchist and Fenian-sympathizer.

Arnold's strategy of using Irish politics as a lever for changing attitudes within England is evident in the preface to *Irish Essays* (1882):

English people keep asking themselves what we ought to do about Ireland. The great contention of these essays is, that in order to attach Ireland to us solidly, English people have not only to *do* something different from what they have done hitherto, they have also to *be* something different from what they have been hitherto. As a whole, as a community, they have to acquire a larger and sweeter temper, a larger and more lucid mind.

For Arnold, Ireland ought somehow to produce a significant change in the British national character, but it is hard to credit what would be a cross between an imperialistic value system and an open-minded, lucid, sweetly intelligent, necessarily post-imperial outlook on the world. And Arnold's innate conservatism shows in his remarks on the Irish Land Act, which he opposed because it would disturb 'the accepted and ordinary and constitutive characters of property'.

Southey, Coleridge and Arnold all see various facets of the British national character reflected in an Irish mirror, and the contemplation of these self-images makes them sometimes uncomfortable, sometimes impatient. Are the images cracked? Or the mirror? Or both? None of these writers is quite certain, but they are all haunted by a history that bumps around uneasily near the foundations of their world view.

Although their attitudes are in various ways vulnerable, all three share a sense of being disconcerted by the history they are commenting on. They attempt to occupy a critical middle ground, but it is an unstable, even anguished position. Like Hopkins, who was to find himself marooned in Ireland at the height of the agitation for Home Rule, they write in a manner that is bruised by current events. Although their writing is informed by many of the values of a hugely powerful state and by a fundamental belief in *raison d'état*, at times they appear to glimpse that state, not its colonized subjects, as Minotaur, the monster that hides deep in the labyrinth of official lies, inert language and myths of national destiny.

John Clare in Babylon

John Clare wrote before the long ice age of standard British English clamped down on the living language and began to break its local and vernacular energies. The damage to English liberty for which that change in the cultural climate is responsible has yet to be assessed, but from Tennyson to the poets of the Movement and beyond we can see how a dead official language and a centralizing conformity have worked to obliterate individual speech communities. Now, as the hegemony of Official Standard relaxes, Clare's poetry emerges like a soodling stream. Listening to his unique and delicate sound-patterns the reader is caught in the blow-back of an immense historical suffering, and glimpses what happens when an oral culture is destroyed by the institutions of law, order, printed texts. Clare ought to have been the English Burns, but as John Lucas has remarked he is a great poet who has for a long time 'been more or less invisible'. He is a non-person, as anonymous as the grass he identified his social class, himself and his language with:

> – So where old marble citys stood
> Poor persecuted weeds remain
> She feels a love for little things
> That very few can feel beside
> & still the grass eternal springs
> Where castles stood & grandeur died

The closing lines of 'The Flitting' are partly Clare's reply to those critics who believed he had coined words which were instead 'as common around me as the grass under my feet'. Though ostensibly a poem about the personal trauma of moving house, it speaks for the experience of being evicted by the economic and legal force of what E. P. Thompson calls, in his account of the effect of Enclosure on the field labourers, 'an alien culture and an alien power'. We wrong

Clare's writing if we regard it as the timeless lyric product of purely personal experience – his language is always part of a social struggle, entangled with and pitched against Official Standard.

Clare emerges for readers in this society as a displaced, marginalized poet whose reputation is being gradually rehabilitated – as Mandelstam's is in the Soviet Union. It may be many years, though, before his name is given the kind of official recognition which is accorded Wordsworth and Keats, and only when social readings of poetic texts have become generally accepted is it likely that his work will be widely read and studied. But it could be that Clare – shy, feral, intensely gifted – will never be redeemed from all the neglect and mutilation he has suffered. Like Mad Sweeney in Seamus Heaney's *Sweeney Astray*, he is a persecuted and derelict figure, a refugee in his own country:

> fallen almost through death's door,
> drained out, spiked and torn,
> under a hard-twigged bush,
> the brown, jaggy hawthorn.

Clare's suffering is both personal and social because he speaks for all those victims of the Enclosure Acts which transformed rural England in the early decades of the last century. He compares Enclosure to a 'Buonoparte' intent on destroying everything; like Stalin's collectivization of agriculture, Enclosure was a form of violent and centrally-directed social engineering. It was the Great Displacement – the crushing of a social class by market forces and political interests.

The social forces that were to lift Clare up and then destroy him are prefigured in that flattered sense of alienation he describes five days after the publication of his first book, *Poems Descriptive of Rural Life and Scenery*. Writing to his friend Octavius Gilchrist on 21 January 1820, Clare includes an 'Address to a Copy of "Clares Poems" Sent O. Gilchrist Esqr' – a piece of light verse in which he imagines *Poems Descriptive* being given a gold-tooled binding. The actual volume is 'plain & simple' like its author, but the 'gilded coat' it may receive will elevate it beyond Clare's social position, rather like an upwardly mobile son leaving his illiterate labouring father behind. Clare's father, like his mother and his wife, was illiterate, but the literate Clare is recognizing here that he is just as trapped as they are. Addressing his printed text, he says:

> L—d knows I couldnt help but laugh
> To see ye fixt among yer betters
> Upon the learned shelves set off
> & flasht about wi golden letters

and he concludes by saying that if he and this sparky, proud volume happened to meet, the gilded book would 'turn thy nose up wi' disdain/& thinkt disgrace thy dad to own'. This means that his reputation – symbolized by the notional gold binding – must always run ahead of him while he stays stuck where he is. He is not worthy of his own work and must always be a stranger in the society which has created his reputation. He is therefore writing against himself. (There is a similar recognition in Heaney's 'Digging' that the process of writing and publication necessitates a break with the ancestral agrarian society.) Oral tradition enters the metropolitan world of printed texts, but for Clare nothing is changed – the fruit of his labour disowns him, and he exists only as a type of abject advertisement for a commodity labelled *Poems Descriptive of Rural Life and Scenery*. The good, the great and the chic may come to visit him: 'they will not let me keep quiet as I usd to be – they send for me twice & 3 times a day out of the fields & I am still the strangers poppet Show   what can their fancys create to be so anxious & so obstinate of being satisfied   I am but a man (& a little one too) like others'. But Clare feels lacerated by their attentions, a puppet knocked about by audience, publishing industry and the reactions of the local community to his sudden fame. His gift has taken him away from that community and he begins to lose his sense of dwelling in the world – that 'essence of dwelling' which Heidegger discusses in his essay 'Building Dwelling Thinking'. It is this ontological theme that Clare shares with Emily Dickinson and Elizabeth Bishop.

As Edward Storey demonstrates in his biography of Clare, the Stamford bookseller Edward Drury helped to initiate the process of

Clare's alienation. Drury was among the first people to notice Clare's talent, and he took a bluntly practical view of the commodity-value of his poems. Writing to his cousin, the publisher John Taylor, Drury said in June 1819 that he regarded Clare's manuscript poems 'as wares that I have bought which will find a market in the great city. I want a broker or a partner to whom I can consign or share the articles I receive from the manufacturer.' Six months later, on 16 January 1820, *Poems Descriptive of Rural Life and Scenery* went on sale and Clare was propelled into polite society. It is painful to watch his spirit being racked by that terrible numbing English deference. Writing letters to the educated and powerful, he concludes, 'I am Respected Sir Your Gratful Servant John Clare'. He calls himself a 'Pheasant' and a 'Clown' and trembles under the mind-blowing attentions of bishops and aristocrats: 'I send you some of the principal Subscribers which I have procured lately: the first of which is a Baronet!!!'

This is the opening sentence of Clare's first extant letter, and those stunned exclamation marks point to the spiked trap Clare fell into – his success set him apart from his own community, while the system of patronage and publishing which created him could offer nothing but a fitfully marketable public image. The bare, nervous human being experienced this public attention as 'all the cold apathy of killing kindness that has numbed me'. It is little wonder the strain destroyed him. Like the badger in one of his finest poems, Clare felt hunted, torn and persecuted, a harmless victim of social violence.

To approach Clare's experience we need to see the English class system as a type of apartheid, a form of segregation which made Clare feel like a black slave chained in a plantation. Clare believed that slavery was 'disgraceful to a country professing religion', and it would seem that at some level he felt himself to be a slave who had mistaken the brief kiss of fame for a lasting manumission. But Clare was initially no radical – 'I am as far as my politics reaches "King & Country"' – and it is clear that he tried to square his conservatism with the upsetting facts of his social experience. He became obsessed by an episode in which he had addressed a stranger in Drury's bookshop as he might anyone else. The stranger turned out to be the

Marquis of Exeter and Clare transformed their terse, equal speech-encounter into a 'cursed blunder', a shocking solecism that haunted him like damnation.

The agrarian unrest of the 1830s seriously disturbed Clare, and in January 1831 he praised Viscount Althorp, the leader of the House of Commons and one of the chief supporters of the Reform Bill. Clare hoped that the government might be able to 'find out the way to better the unbearable oppressions of the labouring classes', and he was divided between a fear of revolution and his identification with his own class. He tells Taylor that 'the "people" as they are called were a year or two back as harmless as flies – they did not seem even to be susceptible of injustice but when insult began to be tried upon them by the unreasonable & the proud their blood boiled into a volcano & the irruption is as certain as death if no remedy can be found to relieve them'. Tennyson was at this time an undergraduate at Cambridge, where he paraded armed with a club and helped put out fires that had been started by rebellious labourers. Yet it would be wrong to see Clare and Tennyson as being politically very far apart – both believed in reform, and they shared a similar patriotism. However, they were thousands of miles apart *socially*, and it is the sense of an absolute social divide which weighs on Clare in his letters. That divide is the real *néant*, a 'bottomless' void between the classes which the 'clown' stared into and was destroyed by.

Clare lived through and was spiritually damaged by the change from the free space of the open-field system to the reticulated, boxed-in pattern of fields which Enclosure created. Two million acres of wild land were also enclosed, and this seizure of 'the common heath' traumatized Clare. It is difficult for us nowadays to register that shock, but a visit to the village of Laxton in Nottinghamshire, the last surviving example of the feudal open-field system, does help towards an understanding of the great change that hit Clare's community. To walk along a wide chalky track through gently sloping, hedgeless ploughland is to step out of the owned space of fenced and protected private property into what feels like a free, almost floating environment. You are in touch with land and space and sky, and that sense of natural freedom depends on the absence of barriers and partitions. Here you can sense what England used to be like – there is a kind of hum or buzz in the place that feels very precious and fragile. Once out of it you are pushed back against that artificially 'natural' world of thick hedges and rectangles which our ordinary experience tells us has been there always, eternally. The transition back into the enclosed world brings with it a certain sense of glumness and suffocation that is like the last memory-trace of a deep social trauma.

During his years in Northampton General Lunatic Asylum, Clare saw himself as being locked in the 'purgatoriall hell & French Bastile of English liberty', and from his corner of that hell the Ranter convert denounced 'English priestcraft & english bondage more severe then the slavery of Egypt & Affrica'. For all the tough, desperate moderation of Clare's professed social opinions in the pre-asylum years, his political subconsciousness is a territory of primal hurt and bondage where something wild – some uniquely sensitive spirit – tries to jeuk away from all institutions. With its lack of punctuation, freedom from standard spelling and its charged demotic ripples, Clare's writing becomes a form of Nation Language beating its head against the walls of urbane, polished Official Standard. This is apparent in a letter to Taylor where Clare first strategically praises his publisher's editorial improvements and then adds, 'you cross'd "*gulsh'd*" I think the word expressive but doubt its a provincialism it means tearing or thrusting up with great force take it or leave it as you please'. Between 'gulsh'd and 'gushed' there is a wide social gap that is like the distinction between hollow charm and a real social force, one that desperately wants to burst through all types of barriers and enclosures. Clare's ambition is Joycean – flying through the nets of class, race, religion, monolingualism – and it is a strange coincidence that Clare and James Joyce's daughter Lucia should both have ended their days in that asylum in Northampton.

Ten years after his attempt to protect 'gulsh'd' from extinction, Clare wrote to Taylor that he was 'astonied' at finding words in 'chaucer that are very common now in what is called the mouths of the vulgar'. This is the reverse perception of that gold binding which

Clare had imagined for *Poems Descriptive* and it shows him beginning to feel a confidence in his own language that Chaucer as literary institution, a well of ethnically pure English, had previously helped rob him of. Clare's identity is created in and through the language he uses, and is then distorted by the changes forced on him by the need to tame that language in order to sell the poems it speaks.

Lord Radstock and other patrons insisted that Clare rid his poems of 'radical slang' and ungrateful social sentiments, so the battle between the two nations is fought out in business correspondence about Clare's grammar and use of common speech. Taylor edits, shapes and sometimes rewrites Clare's poems, sends them back, and Clare replies, 'your verse is a develish puzzle I may alter but I cannot mend grammer in learning is like Tyranny in government'. His identification of this unfettered but precise language with English liberty is sometimes made through the figure of William Cobbett, whose writings Clare admired and to whose *Grammar of the English Language* he often referred. When we consider contemporary reactions to Clare's language we can see that every non-standard word he used could provoke a class anxiety and fear. That sense of threat is apparent in a reviewer's reaction to *The Shepherd's Calendar*:

> We had not, however, perused many pages before we discovered that our self-suspicions were wholly groundless. Wretched taste, poverty of thought, and unintelligible phraseology, for some time appeared its only characteristics. There was nothing, perhaps, which more provoked our spleen than the want of a glossary; for, without such an assistance, how could we perceive the fitness and beauty of such words as – *crizzling* – *sliveth* – *whinneys* – *greening* – *tootles* – *croodling* – *hings* – *progged* – *spindling* – *siling* – *struttles* – &c. &c.

Those words have a beautifully intimate quality; each is a unique subversion of the uptight efficiency of Official Standard, and the reviewer rejects them in an angrily institutional manner, crushing them savagely under his heels like so many snails.

This constriction of language was paralleled by the enclosure of the countryside, and several years before mental illness set in Clare is already imagining himself trapped in Babylon. He encloses an imitation of the 137th Psalm in a letter to Taylor:

> By Babels streams we sat & sighed
>   Yea we in sorrow wept
> To think of Sions former pride
>   That now in ruin slept
>
> Our Harps upon the willows hung
>   Cares silenced every string
> Our woes unheeded & unsung
>   No hearts had we to sing
>
> For they that made us captive there
>   & did us all the wrong
> Insulted us in our despair
>   & asked us for a song

In Psalm 114 the psalmist begins by remembering how Israel 'went out of Egypt, the house of Jacob from a people of strange language', and in the psalm which Clare imitated he asks, 'How shall we sing the Lord's song in a strange land?' Although Clare tactically avoids rendering that question in his version of Psalm 137, it is fundamental to the Babylonian experience he underwent. That experience is similar to the historical anger and suffering which beats through the poems in James Berry's anthology of West Indian–British poetry, *News for Babylon*.The common cultural root is Bible Protestantism – that driven, exalted, desperate identification with the scriptures to which Clare gained access through his early interest in Dissenting groups and when he joined the Ranters in 1824. It is hard to convey the intensity of such experience to those nurtured in more 'balanced' or more theologically coherent cultures; similarly, the term 'culture shock' is inadequate to describe a torn speech struggling in its homelessness against the dead letter.

Clare's madness was therefore nothing less than his manner of living his society's history, and his idea of himself as black slave, prizefighter, Bastille prisoner, captive of the Babylonians, combines images of social injustice with a symbol of individualistic escape from a rural slum (Jack Randall the prizefighter). His oral writing speaks for and to all those who dream of unlocking a frozen language and redeeming an unjust society.

Citizen Clough

These lines from *The Bothie of Tober-Na-Vuolich* appear to exult in the natural, the elemental:

How under Linn of Dee, where over rocks, between rocks,
Freed from prison the river comes, pouring, rolling, rushing,
Then at a sudden descent goes sliding, gliding, unbroken,
Falling, sliding, gliding, in narrow space collected,
Save for a ripple at last, a sheeted descent unbroken, –
How to the element offering their bodies, downshooting the fall, they
Mingled themselves with the flood and the force of imperious water.

Only the adjective 'imperious' suggests a human reference, though it may be just a deliberate use of the pathetic fallacy. Yet if we read these lines knowing that Clough wrote them in 1848, they inevitably take on the excitement of that year of revolutions. Clough was fascinated by events in Europe and followed them closely. A reading of his poetry must begin with a plunge into that history.

On 12 January 1848 the people of Palermo in Sicily rebelled against Ferdinand II of Naples. Riots spread through the Italian cities. In Paris, a month later, the liberal opposition to the conservative government of Guizot cut the government's majority to only forty-three and proclaimed their intention of holding a propaganda banquet on 22 February. The government banned the banquet, the people of Paris demonstrated and barricades went up. Louis Philippe, the French King, decided to dismiss Guizot and his ministry, but he lost the support of the National Guard after a company of regular soldiers fired on a crowd of demonstrators. On 24 February, Louis Philippe abdicated and fled to England. Under the leadership of the poet Lamartine, a group of liberal parliamentarians formed a provisional government. France became a republic once again. Later that year a French translation of *The Communist Manifesto* was published in Paris (the German text was printed in London earlier in 1848). Disturbances spread through Germany and the Austrian Empire; in Ireland there was a failed insurrection, in Britain riots and demonstrations. With the recent invention of the electric telegraph, communication was rapid, and on the morning of 7 March readers of the London *Times* were able to learn of the riots which had taken place in Glasgow the previous afternoon: 'A Chartist mob is at this moment creating serious disturbances in our city. They have broken into many gun-shops, and among them that adjoining the Electric Telegraph-office. Thus many of them are provided with arms, and these they flourish like madmen or drunkards, shouting "Down with the Queen".' In Halifax, the *Halifax Guardian* reported on 6 April, 5,000 Chartists marched to the railway station accompanied by a brass band and carrying a tricolour flag. 'France has the Republic, England shall have the Charter' became the national slogan.

In early May, Clough left England for Paris to observe the Revolution there. On 14 May he wrote to his friend A. P. Stanley:

> I do little else than potter about under the Tuileries Chestnuts and here and there about bridges and streets, pour savourer la republique. I contemplate with infinite thankfulness the blue blouses, garnished with red, of the garde mobile; and emit a perpetual incense of devout rejoicing for the purified state of the Tuileries, into which I find it impossible, meantime, to gain admittance. I growl occasionally at the sight of aristocratic equipages which begin to peep out again, and trust that the National Assembly will in its wisdom forbid the use of livery servants.

The next day the newly elected National Assembly was invaded by left-wing demonstrators angered by the results of the elections which had been held in late April. Led by two revolutionaries, Auguste Blanqui and Armand Barbès, the socialist clubs attempted a second revolution against the huge majority of conservatives and liberals in the National Assembly. The new *garde mobile*, which had been formed by the middle classes to protect property, cleared the demonstrators from the Assembly and arrested Blanqui and Barbès.

Clough's reaction to these events is couched in a facetiously

Carlylean style that expresses his antipathy to the new bourgeois order. Writing to Stanley on 19 May, he laments:

Ichabod, Ichabod, the glory is departed. Liberty, Equality, and Fraternity, driven back by shopkeeping bayonet, hides her red cap in dingiest St. Antoine. Well-to-do-ism shakes her Egyptian scourge to the tune of Ye are idle, ye are idle; the tale of bricks will be doubled, and Moses and Aaron of Socialism can at best only pray for plagues, – which perhaps will come – paving stones for vivats, and emeutes in all their quarters.

Meantime the glory and the freshness of the dream is departed. The very garde mobile has dropped its dear blouse and red trimmings for a bourgeoisie-praetorian uniform with distinctive green hired-soldier epaulettes.

Typically, Clough is excited by the fast-changing current of events. He immerses himself in its procreant urges, noting that the socialist clubs have been silenced and Barbès arrested. Where a few days before it was 'rather pointed' to be seen wearing gloves, the world now begins to 'draw on its kid gloves' and millionaires' carriages appear on the streets again. The golden age of the Republic displays itself as 'a very vulgar parcel-gilt era'. Visiting semiotician and political tourist, Clough expertly analyses the ideological meanings signalled by the *garde mobile*'s new uniform. His sympathies are with the working class of Paris, just as the following year he will identify with the Roman republicans in their struggle against Louis Napoleon's army.

It is this radicalism which led Clough to sketch out a rather Hegelian view of political action:

Yet Politics I will confess it,
Yes, my political friends, I recant and acknowledge, have something
Generous – something organic Creative and Art-like in them;
Something at some great times which a man forgetting all else and
Casting to moles and to bats his idols of thought and self knowledge,
Losing his soul for the gospel, with joy could embrace and could die in –
Could as it were with quick fingers extinguish the light in the chamber,

Enter the great bridal bed of the combat and conflict of men, and
Know not, nor ask, whether morning should ever return to awake
him.

These lines are from a cancelled passage in the manuscript of *Amours de Voyage*, and although Claude – the chief character in the poem – immediately dismisses the sentiment they express as a 'delusion', there is an analytic glint here which signals the ambitious nature of Clough's imaginative enterprise. He refuses the manichean view of political reality as second-rate and inferior, arguing through Claude that it is 'good and the purpose of Nature'.

Yet to fully comprehend this view involves making a commitment – it means entering politics totally, like Lamartine, and refusing to set art or love above the turmoil of history. Claude is unable to make that commitment, while Philip Hewson's emigration to New Zealand is presented as an amusing cop-out. Both Hewson – the central male character in *The Bothie* – and Claude are effortlessly fluent spielers, whose verbal gifts have the effect of sidelining their intellects. It is their very self-consciousness – that mistaken fidelity to 'idols of thought and self knowledge' – which makes them superfluous men. Even so, there is more to their marginality than this might suggest.

Clough's dream is of an ideal vernacular, an ideal vernacular republic. Writing *The Bothie* in the autumn of 1848 after he had resigned his Oxford fellowship, he longs to release the language of poetry from the bondage of traditional rhythms. Oxford and the obligatory subscription to the Thirty-nine Articles which all college fellows had to make are rejected in favour of an Emersonian optimism. Clough met Emerson daily during his stay in Paris, and this must have influenced his attitude to the traditional order. With its lovely lithe fluency, his vernacular verse-line anticipates Whitman and echoes Christopher Smart's wildly visionary afflatus. It sings the idea of a new, generous, social order: 'L'Ere Nouvelle – La Liberté, – La Reforme, La Republique – la Vraie Republique', as Clough phrases it in his 19 May letter to Stanley.

In Smart's *Jubilate Agno*, this democratic style is a released language of exultation: 'Let Asaph rejoice with the Nightingale – The musician of the Lord! and the watchman of the Lord!' The split-second, all-off-the-top-of-the-head newness and nowness of this is rooted in the Authorized Version and the raw new poetry of consciousness which was enabled by Faustus's final soliloquy: 'See see where Christs blood streames in the firmament.' If this style begins in the extremist agonies of the private conscience as a type of Protestant baroque or intense vernacular excitement, it can also carry an overwhelming sensuousness which is sunny, witty, Hellenic. As an inspiration and an aesthetic, it seeks to free itself from Christian guilt and the iambic pentameter, so that the whole world leaps into being, as though a benign irenic consciousness has that instant created it: 'The earth good and the stars good, and their adjuncts all good.' Whitman's spondees build that ennobling, democratic universe in a line whose texture is somehow simultaneously classical and biblical. For Whitman, as for Clough, sexuality and material reality become natural symbols of the Good: everywhere there is ecstasy and celebration, a visionary concreteness charged with an erotic current.

This is the inspiration behind Clough's 'Natura Naturans' where he imagines making love to the young working-class woman who is seated beside him in a railway compartment:

> Yet owned we, fused in one,
> The Power which e'en in stones and earths
> By blind elections felt, in forms
> Organic breeds to myriad births;
> By lichen small on granite wall
> Approved, its faintest feeblest stir
> Slow-spreading, strengthening long, at last
> Vibrated full in me and her.

His randiness, her imputed or conscious sexiness, the mechanical vibrations of the train become aspects of the life force, but with an emphatic parodic disengagement that is felt in the hectic rhythm and use of the double rhymes found in some ballads and bawdy poems ('The figurehead was a nude in bed' etc.). This is not a released language: instead, it has a campy consciousness of its second-hand staleness that Clough pushes towards a primitivist intensity:

Flashed flickering forth fantastic flies,
   Big bees their burly bodies swung,
Rooks roused with civic din the elms,
   And lark its wild reveillez rung;
In Libyan dell the light gazelle,
   The leopard lithe in Indian glade,
And dolphin, brightening tropic seas,
   In us were living, leapt and played.

Deliberately routine alliteration, like the big, bold eyes in a naïve portrait, can communicate that 'sinless' Edenic vision where he and she combine in 'the primal prime embrace'. Naturally there is an ideology present here, because as a convinced republican Citoyen Clough is imagining a lush Miltonic paradise where they both walk the garden paths naked, 'unconscious, unashamed'.

Railway travel, Asa Briggs shows in *The Age of Improvement,* broke down class barriers as people were casually thrown together. Here, Clough typically conflates sex and ideology by centring his poem on one of the many working-class women who were to engage his imagination. There is often something cloying, patronizing, possessive in his attitude: the Highland lassie, 'my' Highland lassie in 'ὁθεὸς μεγὰ σοῦ', becomes a yukky symbol of democracy (she has 'pure and democratic lips' in one manuscript), while Clough presents himself as an Antaeus figure who wants 'strong root in blackest earth to strike'. There is a sinister voyeurism and sexual acquisitiveness in this condescending address to a woman who, instead of being named, is given the embarrassingly routine label, 'lassie'.*

*Clough's work influenced that 'connoisseur' of working-class women Arthur Munby, who described Hannah Cullwick, the woman he later married, as: 'A robust hardworking peasant lass, with the marks of labour and servitude upon her everywhere: yet endowed with a grace and beauty, an obvious intelligence, that would have become a lady of the highest.'

This weakness infiltrates Philip Hewson's remark in *The Bothie of Tober-Na-Vuolich*:

Chanced it my eye fell aside on a capless, bonnetless maiden,
Bending with three-pronged fork in a garden uprooting potatoes.
Was it the air? who can say? or herself, or the charm of the labour?
But a new thing was in me; and longing delicious possessed me,
Longing to take her and lift her, and put her away from her slaving.

The young female labourer partly symbolizes a Carlylean work-ethic that contrasts with the 'dreary botanical titles' of those Lady Augustas and Floras who are ignorant of 'the grace, the attraction/ Labour, and labour alone, can add to the beauty of women'. Superficially, the class system and traditional gender roles are being challenged here, but behind the apparent polemic a predictably chivalrous attitude is firmly in place. Indeed it is reinforced by a sexual connoisseurship and apparently enlightened tone that anticipates the condescensions of the Bloomsbury accent.

The discontent that provokes Clough's rejection of what, in an MS draft of 'ὁ θεὸς μεγὰ σοῦ', he calls 'the lies of breeding, birth and rank' is partly a protest against the narrowness of English identity and the complacency that can accompany it. Clough's '*straining* inquisitive critical mind', as Bagehot termed it, had an unsettled openness which especially appealed to Emerson and Charles Eliot Norton. Emerson remarked that his intellectuality 'seemed so little English', while Norton noted Clough's lack of 'insular narrowness' and 'hereditary prejudices'. There is an American as well as an antipodean theme in Clough's writing, which with his Europeanism contributes to its liberating freshness. He spent his early childhood in Charleston, South Carolina, and paid an extended visit to New England in the early 1850s with the intention of settling there. His Liverpool mercantile background and Welsh antecedents also helped to distance him from the ruling certainties that were embodied in Arnold's Rugby. Hearing Gaelic spoken in the Highlands, he comes to regard his own language as 'alien English' or 'awkward Saxon'. Yet Highland society is backward and hierarchical, a caricature of the feudal power-structure of English society which the Anti-Corn Law League and the Chartists were challenging in the 1840s. Emigration is Hewson's solution to the problem, and this is in keeping with the times – as the land utopias of the Chartists faded, foreign settlement took their place. Clough's poem follows that movement of the spirit with a high volatility which makes *The Bothie* such a compelling mix of intelligence and operatic joy.

Hewson is partly modelled on Clough's friend Thomas Arnold, who emigrated to New Zealand in 1847. Because Hewson is also a self-portrait, Clough is able through a combination of irony and collusive enjoyment to sketch his emotional immaturity and right-on values with a breathless, dashing brilliance.

After his brief flirtation with the Gaelic-speaking Katie, Philip falls in love with Elspie Mackaye, whose father approves of his radical views and is significantly described as dressed like a 'Saxon', not a Highlander. In a letter written from Scotland in 1845, Clough mentions a conversation with John Gibson Lockhart who spoke of 'the prevalence of infidelity even amongst the country folk of Scotland'. Lockhart said that all the small farmers in his neighbourhood were 'avowed unbelievers' and 'ascribed it greatly to Burns'. The 'natural tune' of Donald Mackaye's heart:

> Went to the noble words of that grand song of the Lowlands,
> *Rank is the guinea stamp, but the man's a man for a'that.*

Elspie and her father represent the spirit of Scottish radicalism, not Gaelic feudalism. By distinguishing them from the Highlanders, Clough makes them embodiments of secular, republican values.

Philip encounters Donald Mackaye after the clansmen's dinner in a barn:

> Four tables were in it;
> Two at the top and the bottom, a little upraised from the level,
> These for the chairman and Croupier, and gentry fit to be with them,
> Two lengthways in the midst for keeper and gillie and peasant.
> Here were clansmen many in kilt and bonnet assembled;
> Keepers a dozen at least; the Marquis's targeted gillies;
> Pipers five or six, among them the young one, the drunkard;

Many with silver brooches, and some with those brilliant crystals
Found amid granite-dust on the frosty scalp of the Cairn-Gorm;
But with snuff-boxes all, and all of them using the boxes.
Here too were Catholic Priest, and Established Minister standing.

Clough catches a type of time-warped tartan bogusness which belongs to this list of Philip's hates: 'Feudal tenures, mercantile lords, competition and bishops,/Liveries, armorial bearings, amongst other matters the Game-laws.' Philip is a radical poet who supports the Chartists and cherishes their 'dream of equality'. His egalitarianism naturally chimes with the tune in Donald Mackaye's heart and it also identifies him with Irish politics, for Chartism was seen by the English ruling class as 'a ramification of the Irish conspiracy'.

As the dream of equality spread through Europe that spring, *The Times* noted on 22 March that there was 'great commotion' in the Austrian Empire. The same issue carries a long report of a meeting of the Royal Highland Society at the Freemasons' Arms in London:

The CHISHOLM, in proposing the health of Her Majesty and the Prince Consort, said, that in conformity with good policy no less than good taste politics were excluded from the society; but, in the presence of such events as were at present agitating Europe to its very centre, he could not help congratulating the assembly upon the tranquillity which they enjoyed under the reign of their beloved Queen, whose limited monarchy he believed was the sure guarantee for the preservation of our well ordered civil and religious liberty.

There are toasts to the royal family, the army, the navy, the Indian army and the Church. Each toast is given in Gaelic by a 'gigantic Highlander' dressed in 'full Celtic garb'. The report is like a prose version of the dinner in *The Bothie* – both contrast forcibly with the electric current of revolutionary energy and communication that pulses through the poem. Clough revels in both the nostalgic, self-consciously heritage qualities of the status quo and Philip's equally self-conscious radicalism. Both the poem and the newspaper with its telegraphed reports are engaged in shrinking the world to a global village. Clough's muse is a super-communicator, a brilliant, Ariel-like reporter that girdles the earth more swiftly than 'magical missive electric'. It is this delight in the new technology as much as its republicanism that makes *The Bothie* such a unique expression of the spirit of 1848. Like a newspaper, it has a 'this very moment' speed and address.

For all its limiting contradictions, Clough's presentation of Elspie Mackaye is inspired by the egalitarian spirit of the age. His description of her simultaneous resistance and physical attraction to Philip are among the most brilliant passages in the poem. Elspie compares herself to the 'poor slender burnie' which the 'great salt tide' first forces its way into, then retreats from, leaving the burn 'brackish and tainted'. This is her assertion of autonomy against his dominating sexuality, but her mood changes as he becomes upset at what she has just said:

> Felt she in myriad springs, her sources, far in the mountains,
> Stirring, collecting, rising, upheaving, forth-outflowing,
> Taking and joining, right welcome, that delicate rill in the valley,
> Filling it, making it strong, and still descending, seeking,
> With a blind delicious forefeeling, the great still sea before it;
> There deep into it, far, to carry, and lose in its bosom,
> Waters that still from their sources exhaustless are fain to be added.

Elspie's passion for Philip, her stirred juices and heightened sensations, is also a symbol of the new democratic movement in Europe, its naturally organic creativity. But Elspie's assertiveness – she has boldly taken Philip's hand and kissed his fingers – is dissipated in the last two lines as she loses herself in the 'great still sea'.

Though this scene is unmatched in Victorian verse or prose, its beautifully coded expression of Elspie's sexual feelings eventually relapses upon a conventional picture of delicate female clinging to strong male. And Clough's apparently radical ambition is further distorted by the specific ethnic identity he gives Elspie. As Charles Kingsley noted in his enthusiastic review of *The Bothie*, Katie

> might pass for a type of the Celtic girl, such as you will meet in every village in Wales and Ireland, as well as the Highlands. And as a contrast, Elspie Mackaye, really a noble ideal of the true Scotchwoman, with all her rich

Norse character, her wild Dantesque imagination, her shrewd, 'canny' insight, her deep and strong affections, yet all crushed into order by that calm self-restraint which indicates, not coldness, but intense and victorious energy – we must say, that we know no recent fiction of a female character so genial, so original, and yet so natural.

The process of idealization is founded in a particular type of race consciousness that in the next century was to make Greta Garbo its symbol. Clough had a great admiration for the Swedish singer Jenny Lind, and Kingsley may be glancing at this in his reference to Elspie's 'rich Norse character'. In a letter to Clough, Thomas Arnold says that the 'mere sight' of Jenny Lind is enough 'to drive from one's mind forever all ideals but that of the pure guileless Northern maiden, in whom stormy passion is replaced by infinite supersensual Love, and intellectual power by direct contemplation of and communication with the Divine.' This ideal northern maiden is the British equivalent of an *aisling*, the visionary embodiment of national freedom in Irish Gaelic poetry.

Clough may appear to be moving out into another culture – Gaelic-speaking, Catholic – when actually he is seeking a north European, Protestant archetype of the female. His puritan radicalism is driven by a desire to find a primal purity outside the social structure of 1840s Britain, though it can also be viewed as a form of sexual tourism.

The Scottish Highlands were only beginning to be opened up to tourists in the 1840s – Queen Victoria and Prince Albert made their first trip north in 1842 and stayed for a more extended holiday in 1847. Soon the Highlands became an upper-class playground, a shaggy theme-park bleary with leisure and fake sentiment. One of Clough's major technical problems in *The Bothie* is how to avoid writing a form of tourist verse which turns the landscape into a consumable commodity inhabited by quaint life-sculptures. His solution is to demonstrate right from the start that the landscape is shaped by metropolitan power:

Hither from lodge and bothie in all the adjoining shootings
Members of Parliament many, forgetful of votes and blue-books,
Here, amid heathery hills, upon beast and bird of the forest

Venting the murderous spleen of the endless Railway Committee.

The landscape is a soiled, used thing, a leisure article with a price tag attached, a facetious bodge of clichés. Here, public men release their feral energies by rubbing out pheasants and deer.

By writing about that terrain and so turning it into a self-conscious object – a landscape – Clough knows that he, too, is implicated in the process of tourist consumption these lines ironize. In a letter, he speaks of visiting 'a strange solitary place called Loch Beoraik, where verily I think Saxon foot had never been before'. Like the bright young undergraduates in *The Bothie*, he is transforming the terrain into percepts that can often read like copywriters' routine phrases. The self-consciousness of the poem, its deliberate camp, is part of the imaginative risk he takes. Repeatedly the peaty burn is called an 'amber torrent', and this acts both as a ritual pseudo-Homeric phrase like 'wine-dark sea' and as an in-crowd reference. The private joke, the nickname, the esoteric slang word belong to the coterie language of male bonding:

Drumnadrochet was *seedy*, Glenmorison *adequate*, but at
Castleton, high in Braemar, were the *clippingest* places for bathing,
One by the bridge in the village, indecent, *the Town-Hall* christened.

The Gaelic and Scots place names are replaced by undergraduate slang as young men destined for careers in the law, journalism, parliament, appropriate one solitary place after another and label them 'stunners'. Smoking cigars, they consume the landscape and praise the stream water for being like champagne. Steamboats, railways and telegrams infiltrate Clough's language, giving it a glossy metropolitan urgency.

At moments, there are attempts to break through this insistently chic modernity so that the place's otherness can manifest itself beyond all the picturesque clichés:

There is a stream, I name not its name, let inquisitive tourist
Hunt it, and make it a lion, and get it at last into guide-books,
Springing far off from a loch unexplored in the folds of great mountains,

Falling two miles through rowan and stunted alder, enveloped
Then for four more in a forest of pine, where broad and ample
Spreads, to convey it, the glen with heathery slopes on both sides:
Broad and fair the stream, with occasional falls and narrows;
But, where the glen of its course approaches the vale of the river,
Met and blocked by a huge interposing mass of granite,
Scarce by a channel deep-cut, raging up, and raging onward,
Forces its flood through a passage so narrow a lady would step it.
There, across the great rocky wharves, a wooden bridge goes,
Carrying a path to the forest; below, three hundred yards, say,
Lower in level some twenty-five feet, through flats of shingle,
Stepping-stones and a cart-track cross in the open valley.

The opening lines repudiate the tourist's eye, but there is still the self-consciousness of a social percept in the 'wharves' of rock and narrow passage that a 'lady' – not a potato uprooter – could step across. The nautical and genteel language domesticates the prospect, while the three identical vowel sounds in 'for four more' give a rather blurred impression of sloppy haste in the writing. But then, in an enclosed basin below a waterfall, there opens out another strange, solitary place which holds the calmest expanse of pellucid water:

Beautiful there for the colour derived from green rocks under;
Beautiful, most of all, where beads of foam uprising
Mingle their clouds of white with the delicate hue of the stillness.
Cliff over cliff for its sides, with rowan and pendent birch boughs,
Here it lies, unthought of above at the bridge and pathway,
Still more enclosed from below by wood and rocky projection.
You are shut in, left alone with yourself and perfection of water,
Hid on all sides, left alone with yourself and the goddess of bathing.

This is almost the final vision; but Clough withholds, even imperils it, by appetitively insisting that the place has a 'picture-like beauty' with water like 'sparkling champagne'.

Hobbes – G. Warde Hunt, a future Chancellor of the Exchequer and First Lord of the Admiralty who was later to die of gout –

throws himself into the 'beaded sparklings', and the spot is then christened 'Hobbes's gutter'. The wilderness is tamed by this facetious discourse. Hobbes is a type of young Tory Leviathan whose presence has already the animal-like physicality and appetent drive of the successful politician.

The poem's shrill knowingness and undergraduate matiness – 'Arthur, the shapely, the brave, the unboasting, the glory of headers' – works against the 'eddying green waters' or puts the burn on the same level as those routine, cheery adjectives. Then, more than 400 lines later, Clough describes a series of bathes in the predictably amber torrent:

Duly there they bathed and daily, the twain or the trio,
Where in the morning was custom, where over a ledge of granite
Into a granite basin the amber torrent descended;
Beautiful, very, to gaze-in ere plunging; beautiful also,
Perfect as picture, as vision entrancing that comes to the sightless,
Through the great granite jambs the stream, the glen, and the mountain,
Beautiful, seen by snatches in intervals of dressing,
Morn after morn, unsought for, recurring; themselves too seeming
Not as spectators, accepted into it, immingled, as truly
Part of it as are the kine in the field lying there by the birches.

The students have ceased to be spectators; they are no longer consumers of the scene. Clough's aim has been to shed the brittle lightness of his high-spirited vocabulary and metre by switching from an operatic fulsomeness to a type of 'unsought for' but recurrent Wordsworthian vision whose classically simple integrity transcends a hectic commodity language.

But is there an innocent primal language? A language of transcendence? Isn't there always a whiff of cigar smoke among the pine trees? In a passage dropped from the 1848 version, Clough distinguished 'vernal emotion' from 'prurient talk', though he must have recognized that both phrases were equally dead. His problem lay in distinguishing the spirit which gives imaginative life from those routine letters that kill. It was a problem because the puritan imagination often mistakes the intention for the performance, and argues that a piece of bad writing is actually good because its author is deliberately ironizing its badness. This type of self-conscious irony is one aspect of camp, but it can exist only in operatic bursts, as Clough knew. Inauthenticity must be sporadic and intense, a cheap kinetic thrill carried on a wave of boldness and wit. It must never be prolonged.

With absolute confidence, Clough is able to move from northern wilderness to urban pastoral, skirting sentimentality, cliché, tourist or spectator enthusiasm and appropriation, in order to design this bravura moment where Philip exclaims in a letter to Adam:

As at return of tide the total weight of ocean,
Drawn by moon and sun from Labrador and Greenland,
Sets-in amain, in the open space betwixt Mull and Scarba,
Heaving, swelling, spreading, the might of the mighty Atlantic;
There into cranny and slit of the rocky, cavernous bottom
Settles down, and with dimples huge the smooth sea-surface
Eddies, coils, and whirls; by dangerous Corryvreckan:
So in my soul of souls through its cells and secret recesses,
Comes back, swelling and spreading, the old democratic fervour.

This is a revolutionary intellectual in the process of enacting rather than describing what 1848 feels like. The limber, gradually tumescent style has a democratic confidence and openness to nature that anticipates Whitman's populism.

Then the rackety, ever-expanding metropolis of Liverpool is shown through Hewson's restless consciousness:

But as the light of day enters some populous city,
Shaming away, ere it comes, by the chilly day-streak signal,
High and low, the misusers of night, shaming out the gas lamps –
All the great empty streets are flooded with broadening clearness,
Which, withal, by inscrutable simultaneous access
Permeates far and pierces to the very cellars lying in
Narrow high back-lane, and court, and alley of alleys: –
He that goes forth to his walk, while speeding to the suburb,

Sees sights only peaceful and pure; as labourers settling
Slowly to work, in their limbs the lingering sweetness of slumber;
Humble market-carts, coming-in, bringing-in, not only
Flower, fruit, farm-store, but sounds and sights of the country
Dwelling yet on the sense of the dreamy drivers; soon after
Half-awake servant-maids unfastening drowsy shutters
Up at the windows, or down, letting-in the air by the doorway.

In the rejected passage from 'Amours de Voyage' where Claude acknowledges the generous, organic creativity of political process, Clough wrote that 'now abideth – Politics, Art, and Love', but refused to say which was the greatest. His vision of dawn in Liverpool is an attempt to unite politics, love and art through the metaphoric identification of the early light, 'its broadening clearness', with a widening revolutionary consciousness that is shared by an individual – Philip Hewson – and by the stirring masses. Philip's stirred sexual feelings, like Elspie's in their earlier encounter, are identified with a democratic idea of the mass of the people. They redefine the traditional idea of the body politic.

In this momentarily idyllic urban setting, the city appears to be both organically and designedly beautiful:

School-boys, school-girls soon, with slate, portfolio, satchel,
Hampered as they haste, those running, these others maidenly tripping;
Early clerk anon turning out to stroll, or it may be
Meet his sweetheart – waiting behind the garden gate there;
Merchant on his grass-plat haply, bare-headed; and now by this time
Little child bringing breakfast to 'father' that sits on the timber
There by the scaffolding; see, she waits for the can beside him;
Meantime above purer air untarnished of new-lit fires:
So that the whole great wicked artificial civilized fabric –
All its unfinished houses, lots for sale, and railway outworks –
Seems reaccepted, resumed to Primal Nature and Beauty:–
– Such – in me, and to me, and on me the love of Elspie!

Where Emily Dickinson sees trade 'encroach upon a sacrament', Clough briefly identifies commerce and the sacral before introducing the final, bathetic, exclamatory crescendo. That last line doesn't mock or cancel what has gone before; instead, it is the impulsive riskiness of Philip's voice which infuses the dead printed signs – 'maidenly tripping/Early clerk anon' – with living spirit.

The revolutions of 1848 inaugurated the age of the masses, and these lines aim to texture Philip's feelings with the democratic spirit of the age. Although that year saw a revolution of the intellectuals everywhere except in Britain, Clough is trying to make a bridge between Philip, the radical intellectual, and the working class. In the previous year he had written a pamphlet attacking complacent attitudes to the Irish Famine, and he links Chartism with feminism and Franco-Irish republicanism in *The Bothie*. If his internationalist outlook has more than a trace of radical chic, the confident, impulsive hexameters which sing that internationalism rest on the Athenian ideal of free citizenship in a free state. They articulate his commitment to what Namier in his study of 1848 terms 'non-territorial ideology'.

Clough's poem was written, printed, revised and published within the space of two months. It reads as though it has been telegraphed into print from the front line of the *Zeitgeist*, like *Letter to Lord Byron* or *Autumn Journal*. It has the fluent urgency of Hazlitt's style of reportage. But Clough would appear to have been writing almost out of a kind of retrospective enthusiasm. The last great Chartist demonstration, bearing its petition to Parliament, dispersed in the London rain that April. By the end of May, the first wave of revolution in Europe had spent itself. Clough's wary scepticism would appear to have deepened in the months after publication, when he had the leisure to contemplate the consequences of his resignation from Oriel College. On 15 February 1849, he wrote from his mother's house in Liverpool to Thomas Arnold in New Zealand: 'I am not, my dear Tom, so clear as you are of the rottenness of the poor old ship here – Something I think we rash young men may learn from the failure and discomfiture of our friends in the new Republic.' He is referring to General Cavaignac's ruthless suppression of the Paris workers the previous June and to the election of Louis Napoleon as President of France in December. Even though the counter-revolution is triumphant, he still holds to the republicanism he shared with his friend. In a postscript written nine days later, he remarks:

Today, my dear brother republican, is the glorious anniversary of the great revolution of 48, whereof what shall we now say? Put not your trust in republics nor in any institution of man. God be praised for the downfall of Louis Philippe. This with a faint feeble echo of that loud last year's scream of *a bas Guizot* seems to be the sum total. Or are we to salute the rising sun with Vive l'Empereur and the green liveries?

The comradely enthusiasm is still there, though he is in effect sending Philip Hewson an elegy for 1848.

Turning to the situation in Italy, Clough exclaims: 'Meantime the Great Powers are to restore the Pope!' The Pope had fled from Rome in November 1848 because of the strength of republican feeling there. The Constituent Assembly meeting at Rome in February 1849 then declared that 'the form of government is a pure democracy, with the glorious title of the Roman Republic'. In order to prevent Austria from unilaterally reinstating Pius IX, Louis Napoleon sent an army to Italy in April. Under the leadership of Mazzini and Garibaldi, Rome decided to resist. The French were defeated initially, but in July Garibaldi was forced to flee, pursued by the armies of France, Spain, Austria and Naples. As Clough had predicted in his February letter to Thomas Arnold, the 'renascent' Roman republic was crushed by the Great Powers.

Despite his scepticism about the republic's chances of success, Clough could not resist another political tour. He travelled to Rome via France in April 1849, and again fired off a series of vivid letters to his family and friends. Writing to his sister, Anne, he reports in a rather affected manner: 'Perhaps it will amuse you hereafter to have a letter commenced while guns are firing and, I suppose, men falling, dead and wounded. Such is the case on the other side of the Tiber while I peacefully write in my distant chamber with only the sound in my ears.' The self-conscious insouciance of his Roman letters is analytically magnified in *Amours de Voyage* which he drafted that autumn. Here, the dawn-light enthusiasm of the earlier poem – that outdoor sense of enormous horizons – is replaced by a stringent scepticism and disabling self-regard which cannot admit the type of visionary synthesis Philip Hewson achieves in his description of city streets in the early morning.

Claude speaks with the confident, rather sterile superiority to bourgeois morality that was to become fashionable in literary circles later in the century. This type of coterie preening and cooing is the accent of the intelligentsia:

I do not like being moved: for the will is excited; and action
Is a most dangerous thing; I tremble for something factitious,
Some malpractice of heart and illegitimate process;
We are so prone to these things with our terrible notions of duty.

In its rejection of Victorian morality and its desire for the criminal and the factitious, this passage anticipates Wilde. So, too, does the fascination with the sexual underworld that inspired these lines on a Venetian prostitute:

Trips up a stair at last, and lands me;
Up with her petticoats, and hands me
Without one thought of hesitation
Much as one might a pot de chambre
The vessel that relieves le membre.

This cameo from an early draft of *Dipsychus* reads like a versified extract from *My Secret Life*, the anonymous sexual memoir Steven Marcus discusses in *The Other Victorians*. If *Dipsychus* is Clough's attack on Victorian priggishness and 'over-excitation of the religious sense', it was to be his last imaginative fling before his conventional marriage to Blanche Smith and the guilt-ridden doggerel of *Mari Magno*. In *Amours*, he wants to expose through dramatic speech the limitations of an apparently liberated temperament, and to show that for all his apparent freedom from conventional English values, Claude is really an insular snob.

Claude is a determinedly apolitical aesthete who has never predicted 'Parisian milleniums' and yet is able to sympathize with the Roman republic. The critical volatility of his voice is exciting:

Luther was foolish, – but, O great God! what call you Ignatius?
O my tolerant soul, be still! but you talk of barbarians,
Alaric, Attila, Genseric; – why, they came, they killed, they
Ravaged and went on their way; but these vile, tyrannous Spaniards,
These are here still, how long, O ye Heavens, in the country of Dante?
These, that fanaticized Europe, which now can forget them, release not
This, their choicest of prey, this Italy; here you see them –
Here, with emasculate pupils and gimcrack churches of Gesu,
Pseudo-learning and lies, confessional-boxes and postures, –
Here, with metallic beliefs and regimental devotions, –
Here, overcrusting with slime, perverting, defacing, debasing,
Michael Angelo's dome, that had hung the Parthenon in heaven,
Raphael's Joys and Graces, and thy clear stars, Galileo!

This sounds like the free spirit reacting against institutionalized religion, but the temper of Claude's spirit is essentially Protestant, and it is the pressure of that cultural legacy which constrains him. At times, he sounds like Lytton Strachey: 'Am I prepared to lay down my life for the British female?' But this type of camp wit gives him a boxed-in, sterile prissiness. Claude's intellect is neither free, nor radically subversive. His remarks are collusive, fearful, conservative and only brittly insouciant.

Claude's priggish irrelevance shows starkly if we contrast his letters with this proclamation which the triumvirs – Mazzini, Armellini, Saffi – published on 3 June:

Romans! – To the crime of attacking a friendly Republic with troops led on under a Republican banner, General Oudinot adds the infamy of treachery. He violates the written promise we have in our hands, not to attack before Monday. Arise, Romans! To the walls – to the gates – to the barricades! Let us prove to the enemy that Rome cannot be conquered even by treachery. Let the Eternal City rise to a man with the energy of one common thought! Let every man fight! let every man have faith in victory! let every man remember our ancestors, and be great! Let right triumph, and let eternal shame attend the ally of Austria! '*Viva la Republica!*'

Claude is able to distance himself from the struggle that produced this text. He notes 'a great white puff from behind Michael Angelo's dome', just as he observes with fastidious annoyance Mrs Trevelyn's 'slightly mercantile accent'. But for all his touristy detachment and cultivated posing, he is a shy wounded academic who groups people against a frozen series of backgrounds as though they were life-sculptures, not human beings. Clough's problem is to make Mary Trevelyn challenging and convincing, but he fails. Claude dominates the narrative, the Trevelyns are merely adjuncts to his personality.

Unable to find Mary, who has left on tour with her family, Claude wanders the streets of Florence. His love for Mary is agonized and self-conscious; then he finds a brief solace when he passes a barrel organ playing an English psalm-tune. This curiously Betjeman-like moment nearly reduces him to tears: 'Almost I could believe', he tells Eustace, 'I had gained a religious assurance.' But he rejects this temptation and tells Eustace in his final letter from Rome that he is probably going to travel eastward, then, 'with the coming of winter, to Egypt'.

This is Claude's last message, and the direction he is about to take is revealing: Egypt is the land of bondage, the territory of convention and orthodoxy that will stifle the spirit. Clough is implying that Claude will bandage his soul in mummy-cloth and become a devout Christian reactionary. Though Clough in the 1850s rejected his earlier radicalism, it would be wrong to follow his friends and view him as a promising intellectual who failed. It was his fate to be posthumously patronized in Arnold's third-rate elegy, but he left behind two long works which, with *Goblin Market* and *The Wreck of the Deutschland*, are the finest poetic achievements of the Victorian period.

Overthrowing the Fathers: Christina Rossetti

Sheepskin man
living in a caravan
when he gets out
everybody shout!

Kids in the deep middle of a journey, making up chants and kicking cadences around. Before the journey's over, their figures of spoken sound – Hopkins's phrase for poetry – will have melted away. Sometimes they take the most unpromising group of sounds, maybe a road number – B1258, say – and knock vocal sparks out of it. This is the now of utterance where an anarchic counter-culture is chucking harmless pebbles of pure sound at the moral walls of adult discourse. Those quartzy, triumphal cadences are the poetry of speech; for a stretched moment they make the world intimate and tribal again. Like a sand-painting, they can't last.

Rossetti and Hopkins drew on these chanting rhymes to form their vernacular poetic, but in terms of print, rather than oral culture, their revolutionary rejection of traditional metre can be traced back to Coleridge's 'Christabel'. In the preface to that poem, Coleridge describes this new rhythm, which emerges into print from oral tradition where it unites the speaking and the singing voice:

> I have only to add that the metre of Christabel is not, properly speaking, irregular, though it may seem so from its being founded on a new principle: namely, that of counting in each line the accents, not the syllables. Though the latter may vary from seven to twelve, yet in each line the accents will be found to be only four. Nevertheless, this occasional variation in number of syllables is not introduced wantonly, or for the mere ends of convenience, but in correspondence with some transition in the nature of the imagery or passion.

The preface is defensive because Coleridge knows that he is flouting his audience's expectations. Just as many of Clare's middle-class readers were angered by his use of local dialect words, so Coleridge fears his readers may spurn this speech-based metre:

> Is the night chilly and dark?
> The night is chilly, but not dark.
> The thin gray cloud is spread on high,
> It covers but not hides the sky.

The fourth, rather clumsy line, is a regular iambic tetrameter which is identical in structure to a subsequent line, 'The night is chill, the cloud is gray', an absolutely standard tetrameter with a tum-ti-tum ordinariness. Though dull, these lines are essential because they express the metrical norm which the other lines counterpoint. By varying syllable and stress (the first line begins with a reversed iambic foot and has only seven syllables), Coleridge overrides the predictability of normative metre. Letting these fluid, changing sound-patterns play in the inner ear, we glimpse the secret life of poetry, its subtle and intricate whale-song.

Ruskin was hostile to Coleridge's new metrical principle, blaming it for the many 'quaintnesses and offences' he detected in Christina Rossetti's verse. Dante Gabriel Rossetti agreed with Ruskin and objected to the 'metrical jolt' in 'The Prince's Progress'. A reviewer in the *Athenaeum* criticized the harsh 'discords' in Christina's poems, and another reviewer, in the *Catholic World,* dismissed her work as 'simply execrable'. Clearly, her metric challenged accepted ideas of poetic metre. In particular, her poems shook the cultural mausoleum that Tennyson had erected. As Edmund Gosse noted in his study of Swinburne, Rossetti's *Goblin Market* was hailed as a brilliant, innovatory volume when it was published in 1862. Gosse was writing in 1917, and in 1895 Alice Meynell paid tribute in the *New Review* to the 'very serious service' Rossetti had done to English versification by using 'afresh this voice of poetry – a voice that sings in musical time'. Meynell argued that this musical voice had been 'much neglected since Coleridge, and *he* used it so seldom! That is, he used redundant syllables freely, but a rest within the line most rarely.' Thus Coleridge's line, 'The night is chill, the cloud is gray', may be normative, but its use of the caesura is rare within the poem. Were it more common and were the lines often without redundant syllables, then the rhythm would be monotonous and conventional. Similarly, Rossetti varies her rhythms by following the fluent contours of the speaking voice and avoiding a choppy, caesural rhythm.

Hopkins was among the younger poets who admired *Goblin Market*'s radical new metric. He met Rossetti in 1864 and shortly afterwards wrote a letter to his friend A. W. M. Baillie in which he exclaims: 'Do you know, a horrible thing has happened to me. I have begun to *doubt* Tennyson.' His doubts were prompted by his reading of *Enoch Arden*, one of that season's new books, and they led him to formulate the term 'Parnassian' as a description of a certain kind of routine writing which lacks real inspiration. Such poetry is 'spoken *on and from the level* of a poet's mind'; it is a type of self-parody, a personal style which effortlessly reproduces itself without making any stylistic advances. It never breaks into 'poetry proper, the language of inspiration'. Eight years later, Hopkins preferred the 'pathos and pure beauty' of Christina's art to Dante Gabriel's verse, remarking that the 'simple beauty' of her work 'cannot be matched'. Although that adjective 'simple' may appear patronizing, her work was crucial to his discovery of 'sprung rhythm', the vernacular aesthetic he describes in his letters and in the preface he wrote for his poems.

In particular, Hopkins was influenced by Rossetti's 'The Convent Threshold', which begins:

> There's blood between us, love, my love,
> There's father's blood, there's brother's blood;
> And blood's a bar I cannot pass:
> I choose the stairs that mount above,
> Stair after golden skyward stair,
> To city and to sea of glass.

What attracted Hopkins in these lines was their vocal movement, the utterly unforced naturalness of an individual speaking voice that refuses the predictable rhythmic contours of these lines from *Enoch Arden* which he quotes in his letter to Baillie:

The mountain wooded to the peak, the lawns
And winding glades high up like ways to Heaven,
The slender coco's drooping crown of plumes,
The lightning flash of insect and of bird,
The lustre of the long convolvuluses
That coil'd around the stately stems, and ran
Ev'n to the limit of the land, the glows
And glories of the broad belt of the world,
All these he saw.

Tennyson's furry vowels never allow the speaking voice to disturb their bland sonorities. This is public, official discourse, which can be recited aloud, though only in a waffling, melodious monotone.

The speaking voice is spontaneous and improvisatory, like these lines from 'The Lowest Room': 'But just suppose the horse,/ Suppose the rider fell?' Or the famous rejection in ' "No, Thank You, John" ':

Here's friendship for you if you like; but love, –
No, thank you, John.

Both these examples are much more sophisticated vocal gestures than the rather forced abruptness of 'Racked, roasted, crushed, wrenched limb from limb', and 'Kneel, wrestle, knock, do violence, pray' from 'The Convent Threshold'. But Hopkins's ear was caught by the earlier poem's vocal presence and packed heavy stresses.

His apprentice poem 'A Voice from the World' was a reply to 'The Convent Threshold':

This ice, this lead, this steel, this stone,
This heart is warm to you alone.

These lines aim for *haecceitas,* literally for thisness, and they allow us to glimpse Hopkins calling on Rossetti for aid in defining a metric he was eventually to term 'sprung rhythm'. *This* ice, *this* lead, *this* steel – this is the warm, living human voice, here and now. It is a dramatic and eruptive voice whose spontaneity challenges Tennyson's sculpted lines.

Both Rossetti and Hopkins looked for inspiration to nursery rhymes, weather saws, street chants and the instant rhymes children invent. Hopkins cites 'Ding dong bell/Pussy's in the well' as an example of sprung rhythm, arguing that if each line has three stresses 'or three feet it follows that some of the feet are of one syllable only'. In *Sing-Song: A Nursery Rhyme Book,* Rossetti designs her own anthology of apparently anonymous rhymes which appear to come out of oral tradition. By inventing these little cat's paws of pure rhythm, she playfully demonstrates the enormous distance which separates her intimate vernacular from Tennyson's institutional Parnassian.

Rossetti's verses are remarkable for their delight in those rhythmic patterns children love:

> 'Kookoorookoo! kookoorookoo!'
>   Early birds begin their singing;
> 'Kikirikee! kikirikee!
>   The day, the day, the day is springing.

This is the scrake of dawn, where poetry begins as a precious series of unique cadences that triumph over death and change:

> Dead in the cold, a song-singing thrush,
> Dead at the foot of a snowberry bush, –
> Weave him a coffin of rush,
> Dig him a grave where the soft mosses grow,
> Raise him a tombstone of snow.

Each line has its own metrical pattern which builds not a verse mausoleum but a transitory oral monument that exists only in the chanted words.

The intimacy of these varying tones contrasts – and is intended to contrast – with that 'rowdy, or bullying, element' that William Morris identified in Tennyson's work. In his life of Swinburne, Gosse describes Tennyson as a 'upas tree' beneath whose branches 'true imagination withered away'. Swinburne hailed Rossetti as the Jael who led the Pre-Raphaelites to victory – she had driven a nail through the Laureate's temples.

That there is a polemical intention behind Rossetti's writing is true, but hers is a peaceable style which absolutely refuses the aggressiveness Swinburne attributes to it. Rather, it is Tennyson's heavy metal style which bangs out the imperial certainties of Victorian Britain:

> Let your reforms for a moment go!
> Look to your butts, and take good aims!
> Better a rotten borough or so
> Than a rotten fleet and a city in flames!
> Storm, Storm, Riflemen form!
> Ready, be ready against the storm!
> Riflemen, Riflemen, Riflemen form!

The over-exclamatory demotic of 'Riflemen Form!' speaks for the reactionary patriotism many of Tennyson's readers held to. Their attitudes can be felt in that kitsch lustre that glints throughout his verse.

But Rossetti's indirect – indirect because unstated – objection to Tennyson's style is aimed at that peculiar conjunction of military, industrial and masculine sexual values which, like some early railway terminus, is located in the clanging lines of 'Locksley Hall'. Tennyson's poem was published in 1842 and its trochaic octameters are intended to thunder along like a fast steam train down those 'ringing grooves' Tennyson mistook for flanged railway lines. The rapidity of the metre gives each cliché – 'lustrous woodland', 'dusky race' – the pointed heaviness of a steam shuttle, so that the lines have a curiously mass-produced texture, as if we're listening to a tune being beaten out on a series of cheap tin trays. As Christopher Ricks notes in his exemplary edition of Tennyson, there is an allusion to Keats's 'The Eve of St Agnes' in these lines:

> Love took up the glass of Time, and turned it in his glowing hands;
> Every moment, lightly shaken, ran itself in golden sands.

In Keats's poem, Porphyro sets out an erotic feast:

These delicates he heaped with glowing hand
On golden dishes and in baskets bright
Of wreathèd silver; sumptuous they stand
In the retired quiet of the night.

Keats's poem exemplifies, in a cynically uncritical manner, the commodification of sexual desire. He offers it to his readers as a luxurious item for their consumption:

And still she slept an azure-lidded sleep,
In blanchèd linen, smooth and lavendered,
While he from forth the closet brought a heap
Of candied apple, quince, and plum, and gourd,
With jellies soother than the creamy curd,
And lucent syrops, tinct with cinnamon;
Manna and dates, in argosy transferred
From Fez; and spicèd dainties, every one,
From silken Samarcand to cedared Lebanon.

This stanza is immediately followed by the lines beginning 'These delicates he heaped with glowing hand', which Tennyson echoes in 'Locksley Hall'. Like images in some Condé Nast publication, these 'sumptuous' candied fruits are commodities that have travelled along exotic trade routes. Luxury items, fetishized objects only private wealth can acquire, their existence ratified by British naval power, they are also symbols of the poetic imagination which echo the lists of eastern place names in *Paradise Lost*.

Keats's poetry was extravagantly admired by the Pre-Raphaelites: William Morris said 'La Belle Dame Sans Merci' was 'the germ' from which all the poetry of the group sprang. Dante Gabriel did a drawing inspired by the poem and Holman Hunt's picture based on 'The Eve of St Agnes' was exhibited at the Academy in 1848. Christina read an abridged version of 'The Eve of St Agnes' in a popular miscellany when she was nine years old. When she later read the full text of the poem, she can hardly have failed to notice its voyeurism and insistently sexual frissons. In Keats's intensely masculinist fantasy, Madeline is told by 'old dames':

how, upon St Agnes' Eve,
Young virgins might have visions of delight,
And soft adorings from their loves receive
Upon the honeyed middle of the night.

Later, Madeline undresses in an unconsciously teasing manner: she loosens 'her fragrant bodice; by degrees/Her rich attire creeps rustling to her knees'. This is an erotic cliché which underwrites, and is produced by, male power. The watching Porphyro is in control.

When Porphyro plays Madeline an old song called 'La belle dame sans mercy', Keats describes how:

Beyond a mortal man impassioned far
At these voluptuous accents, he arose,
Ethereal, flushed, and like a throbbing star
Seen mid the sapphire heaven's deep repose;
Into her dream he melted, as the rose
Blendeth its odour with the violet,
Solution sweet – meantime the frost wind blows
Like Love's alarum pattering the sharp sleet
Against the window-panes; St Agnes' moon hath set.

This is a parody of the moment in *Paradise Lost* when Ithuriel finds Satan squatting at the ear of the sleeping Eve and touches him lightly with his spear. The allusion is keyed by the pun Ethereal/Ithuriel, and to the knowing reader for whom Keats is collusively writing it is Porphyro's erect penis or 'throbbing star' that is the witty equivalent of Ithuriel's spear.

The sexual suggestiveness of this passage alarmed Keats's friend Richard Woodhouse, who acted as an adviser to John Taylor. Woodhouse told Keats's publisher that he feared it would 'render the poem unfit for ladies', saying he had told Keats this. Keats had replied that 'he does not want ladies to read his poetry: that he writes for men'. Originally, he had written a shorter and much less sexually explicit passage whose reticence he now regretted. Defending the new version, Keats said 'that he should despise a man who would be such an eunuch in sentiment as to leave a maid, with that Character about her, in such a situation: and should despise himself to write about it'.

Woodhouse and Taylor held to a Christian moral prudishness which conflicts with Keats's aggressive libertinism and macho values. To a devout Christian such as Christina Rossetti, the passage must almost certainly have been offensive. Where 'The Eve of St Agnes' is a type of soft porn which enforces those dominant masculine values Rossetti challenges in her poems, *Goblin Market* is an expression of the dialogic imagination, a type of reply-poem or anti-poem which sets itself the task of subverting and challenging an established predecessor.

Keats's imagery of fruit and moonlight is picked up in the lines where Lizzie reminds her sister, Laura, of how Jeanie met the goblin men 'in the moonlight,/Took their gifts both choice and many,/Ate their fruits and wore their flowers'. Laura rejects Lizzie's warning and says that she 'ate and ate my fill', yet her mouth 'waters still':

> Have done with sorrow;
> I'll bring you plums tomorrow
> Fresh on their mother twigs,
> Cherries worth getting;
> You cannot think what figs
> My teeth have met in,
> What melons icy-cold
> Piled on a dish of gold
> Too huge for me to hold,
> What peaches with a velvet nap,
> Pellucid grapes without one seed.

Laura's speech is Keatsian and dangerously tempting – that gold dish of fruit is a critical allusion to both 'The Eve of St Agnes' and 'Locksley Hall'. It develops the 'iterated jingle' – the commercial jingle, 'Come buy, come buy' – that Laura in her state of desperate sexual arousal can no longer hear. 'Must she no more such succous pasture find,/Gone deaf and blind?' Rossetti asks, then describes Laura trudging home, 'her pitcher dripping all the way'. At night, she wakes and gnashes her teeth 'for baulked desire'.

The phrase 'succus pasture' states her erotic feeling plainly (the noun 'succus' means 'juice, fluid secretion of a gland, expressed juice'), though the term's rareness conceals its sexual reference. But the image of the dripping pitcher, the poem's insistent juiciness, codes a type of sexual sensation which is Rossetti's version of that imaginative masturbation Byron criticized in Keats's verse.

Goblin Market's revolutionary vernacular challenges Keats and Tennyson's self-consciously literary language, as well as polemicizing a long tradition of amatory verse:

Laura stretched her gleaming neck
Like a rush-imbedded swan,
Like a lily from the beck,
Like a moonlit poplar branch,
Like a vessel at the launch
When its last restraint is gone.

The images are listed with an ironic perfunctoriness which underlines the fact that they are routine erotic phrases. Dealt out like a hand of cards, these inert images are answered later in the poem:

White and golden Lizzie stood,
Like a lily in a flood, –
Like a rock of blue-veined stone
Lashed by tides obstreperously, –
Like a beacon left alone
In a hoary roaring sea,
Sending up a golden fire, –
Like a fruit-crowned orange-tree
White with blossoms honey-sweet
Sore beset by wasp and bee, –
Like a royal virgin town
Topped with gilded dome and spire
Close beleaguered by a fleet
Mad to tug her standard down,

That *double entendre* in the last line fuses violence with male randiness: this is the secular evil Lizzie's steadfast spirituality resists.

The blue-veined stone is Marian, perhaps an allusion to 'The Bishop Orders His Tomb at St Praxed's Church', where Browning's dying lecher imagines *lapis lazuli* 'Blue as a vein o'er the Madonna's breast'. Rossetti is reclaiming the image from the bishop's blasphemously violent and acquisitive sexuality.

The orange tree alludes to this stanza from George Herbert's 'Employment':

> Oh that I were an Orenge-tree,
> That busie plant!
> Then I should ever laden be,
> And never want
> Some fruit for him that dressed me.

Herbert was one of Rossetti's favourite poets, and by invoking him she implies that Lizzie is the rock of the Anglican Church (the Victorian, and therefore post-Williamite, orange tree is an even more emphatically Protestant symbol here than it is in Herbert's poem). The Marian blue and the Protestant orange balance each other to produce a subtle, unusually steadfast symbol of Anglicanism resisting the combined forces of secularization and commercialized sexuality.

This image of resistant rock is reworked in 'Enrica', where the 'liberal glow' of the Italian woman, her full-blown ampleness and warmth, is contrasted with:

> We Englishwomen, trim, correct,
> All minted in the selfsame mould,
> Warm-hearted but of semblance cold,
> All courteous out of self-respect.

Writing partly from inside the Italian immigrant community, Rossetti appears to criticize English reserve; then, at the very last moment, she offers that sea-rock image as a symbol of the British national character:

> But if she found us like our sea,
> Of aspect colourless and chill,

Rock-girt; like it she found us still
Deep at our deepest, strong and free.

The idea of a free Protestant nation is asserted against Italy's Catholicism and political subjection. There is a similar, though less complex, patriotism in 'In The Round Tower at Jhansi, June 8, 1857', which is set during the Indian Mutiny and lacks the double vision of 'Enrica' or '"Italia, Io Ti Saluto"'.

Rossetti's Protestant British identity is modified in a neglected long poem which is one of her finest achievements. In '"The Iniquity of the Fathers Upon the Children"', Margaret's alienated perspective and desire for full personal autonomy contrast with the numbing traditionalism of her village society:

Our neighbouring gentry reared
The good old-fashioned crops,
And made old-fashioned boasts
Of what John Bull would do
If Frenchman Frog appeared,
And drank old-fashioned toasts
And made old-fashioned bows
To my Lady at the Hall.

The rhythmic monotony and perfunctory listing enforces the dreariness of this society, its agrarian conservatism and fixed social and gender roles. Against its dullness, Margaret's voice takes on a unique poignancy – 'But my Mother, Mother, Mother,/Oh, I know her from all other.' The lady at the hall is Margaret's mother and guardian: Margaret is illegitimate and her mother never acknowledges their real relationship. Dante Gabriel was perturbed by the poem's criticism of Victorian morality and advised his sister not to include it in her 1866 volume, *The Prince's Progress*. Christina didn't take his advice, though she dropped 'Under the Rose' from the title in the British edition of the volume.

The biblical title is anti-patriarchal, though to readers nowadays the resigned Christian piety which closes the poem seems deeply conventional. Rossetti is much less radical than Emily Dickinson in her subversion of the institutions that oppressed women in the nineteenth century. She admired Dickinson's 'wonderfully Blakean gift', but was critical of the 'startling recklessness' of her technique. Rossetti's carefully modulated vernacular differs from Dickinson's eruptive speech-pulses, though the poetic they share is the expression of an ambition to achieve absolute female autonomy. That 'polar privacy', as Dickinson terms it, is won through the challenge that a poetic based on the patterns of human speech offers to Keats and Tennyson's commodity language. Orality – the vernacular imagination – can be a means of resisting the dominance of the nation state, though this is not always so. Robert Frost brings many beautiful sentence-sounds to the service of the state, while Rossetti and Dickinson seek a private lyric space where the soul is 'admitted to itself'. By occupying that self-defining solitude, they challenge the 'argent' heraldic language that belongs with the state's hardware, its myths and slogans and lies.

Hopkins on the Rampage

In May 1884 Coventry Patmore told Robert Bridges that Hopkins's poetry had 'the effect of veins of pure gold imbedded in masses of unpracticable quartz'. Patmore's criticism is based on an idea of literary decorum that rests on a belief in the class system: the gold of a pure poetic English must be permanently cordoned off from the quartzy masses grunting their rough and worthless dialects. Yet it was from various regional and working-class vernaculars that Hopkins drew his essential melodic inspiration:

> Lancashire – 'of all the wind instruments big drŏŏm fots me best'. – Old Wells directing someone how to set a wedge in a tree told him that if he would put it so and so he would 'fot it agate a riving'. – The omission of *the* is I think an extension of the way in which we say 'Father', 'government' etc: they use it when there is a relative/in order to define. – They sae *frae* and *aboon*.

Hopkins's fascination with regional speech shows frequently in the journals and it was this loving egalitarian curiosity which led him to become a contributor to Joseph Wright's *English Dialect Dictionary*.

'Felix Randal' is shaped out of his attentive listening to Lancashire speech, and the gruff line 'Ah well, God rest him all road ever he offended' is pitched out from the talk of mill-towns and Pennine villages. Anyone who enjoys the extremes of impulsive affection and vitality in regional speech is bound to notice that Hopkins's inner ear is awash with an infinite and exquisite sense of unique vocal patterns.

The reception history of Hopkins's verse shows that while some critics followed Patmore and objected to its 'cumulative cacophony', others such as Leavis argued that Hopkins worked always in the spirit of 'the living English language'. Leavis insisted on Hopkins's central Englishness and although this accords with the poet's feisty patriotism ('a great work by an Englishman is like a great battle won by England', he remarked canonically to Bridges), it distorts the accepted notion of centrality. We do not expect Matthew Arnold to address us in a Lancashire accent, because the needs of a centralized state with expanding imperial markets dictate a single monolithic ruling voice and a language drained of natural stress patterns. And for all its displays of patriotic muscle, Hopkins's language issues from the ranks, not from the officer class. That language rips out of slums, back streets, building sites, workshops and the 'sheer plod' of rural drudgery.

Hopkins listened intently to demotic speech in Liverpool, Glasgow, Lancashire mill-towns, Wales, Dublin, and by converting to Catholicism he made himself marginal to the power structure in Britain and merged his imagination with the proletariat's experience. This identification with the people's suffering did not follow necessarily from his conversion (like a later convert, Evelyn Waugh, he could have identified with the recusant aristocracy), but it is crucial to recognize the sense of solidarity with popular experience that Hopkins gained by his rejection of his 'national old Egyptian reed', Anglicanism. By refusing the self-defining solitudes of Protestant individualism, he came to sympathize with the deprivations of powerless working people:

> My Liverpool and Glasgow experience laid upon my mind a conviction, a truly crushing conviction, of the misery of town life to the poor and more than to the poor, of the misery of the poor in general, of the degradation even of our race, of the hollowness of this century's civilisation: it made even life a burden to me to have daily thrust upon me the things I saw.

This conviction of immiserated poverty and the wild push of a popular revolutionary energy straining against the hegemony of Victorian English give Hopkins's poems their pouring, pelting, 'all in a rush' quality of hectic movement.

Despite his many reactionary outbursts, Hopkins cannot simply be classed as a conservative writer – like Dostoevsky he is forever plunging his imagination into the destructive currents within the social moment. His imagination is drenched in the 'rash smart sloggering brine' – his image for history in that great counter-reformation poem *The Wreck of the Deutschland*, where he draws on atavistic memories of the Thirty Years War in order to imagine a future Catholic victory over Protestantism. Thus Death's jocose drum-speech which opens the second part of the poem builds an image that resembles a seventeenth-century German woodcut, and this military imagery is superimposed on a vision of the 'wrecking' process which Hopkins, like Conrad, saw as being central to nineteenth-century 'civilization' – Bismarck's Germany and Victorian England especially. The link is made in Hopkins's remark to Bridges that English civilization 'is in great measure founded on wrecking'. His poem is a vision of imminent social catastrophe and in his famous Red letter to Bridges he justifies the working class's wish to 'wreck and burn' a civilization founded on wrecking: 'I am afraid some great revolution is not far off', he tells Bridges: 'Horrible to say, in a manner I am a Communist.'

If we accept that there is a link between the analytic political anxiety of the letters and Hopkins's poetry, then we can detect a revolutionary intoxication, an expressionist whap of pure energy, in the opening lines of 'That Nature is a Heraclitean Fire and of the comfort of the Resurrection':

Cloud-puffball, torn tufts, tossed pillows | flaunt forth, then chevy on an air-
Built thoroughfare: heaven-roysterers, in gay-gangs | they throng; they glitter in marches.
Down roughcast, down dazzling whitewash, | wherever an elm arches,
Shivelights and shadowtackle in long | lashes lace, lance, and pair.
Delightfully the bright wind boisterous | ropes, wrestles, beats earth bare
Of yestertempest's creases; in pool and rutpeel parches
Squandering ooze to squeezed | dough, crust, dust; stanches, starches
Squadroned masks and manmarks | treadmire toil there
Footfretted in it. Million-fuelèd, | nature's bonfire burns on.

Hopkins wrote these lines in late July 1888 in Co. Dublin, and rather like a painting by Jack Yeats they enact the rainfresh swim of wind-driven Irish light (significantly, the elmy shivelights play a Nash-like English light against the vernacular Irish whitewash). The crowded sense of consciousness expanding and some Miltonic echoes of the civil war in heaven – those gangs of roysterers are drunk like the sons of Belial – give a social edge and pressure to what is ostensibly a nature poem that modulates suddenly into an apocalyptic vision.

This rushed texture may have been prompted by the fact that Hopkins was writing in the aftermath of a particularly stressful moment in Anglo-Irish relations – the crisis of 1886–7, to which he responded with passionate sensitivity in his letters to Bridges. The tearing light and airy cavalry battalions in the poem enact the pressures of political crisis. No wonder, then, that the next poem Hopkins wrote was the rigidly metrical and sternly patriotic marching-song 'What Shall I Do for the Land that Bred Me'. His discomfiting exposure to Irish nationalism understandably provoked him to express his deep-felt English nationalism.

Hopkins's acute political observation shows in these remarks which he made to Bridges in February 1887, more than a year before he wrote both poems:

> Yesterday Archbishop Walsh had a letter in the *Freeman* enclosing a subscription to the defence of Dillon and the other traversers on trial for preaching the Plan of Campaign and saying that the jury was packed and a fair trial impossible. The latter was his contribution to the cause of concord and civil order. Today Archbp. Croke has one proposing to pay no taxes. One archbishop backs robbery, the other rebellion; the people in good faith believe and will follow them. You will see, it is the beginning of the end: Home Rule or separation is near.

Hopkins is living the social crisis of impending Home Rule or separation in 'That Nature is a Heraclitean Fire', though in suggesting this I am conscious that such a reading flies in the face of the apolitical consensus his critics share.

Four months later, in July 1887, Hopkins implored Bridges to influence people in England in order to bring them 'to a just mind and a proper resolution about Ireland'. His letter anticipates the stormy hurrying light of 'That Nature is a Heraclitean Fire' and we need to read the poem with this passage vividly in mind:

> recognise with me that with an unwavering will, or at least a flood of passion, on one, the Irish, side and a wavering one or indifference on the other, the English, and the Grand Old Mischiefmaker loose, like the Devil, for a little while and meddling and marring all the fiercer for his hurry, Home Rule is in fact likely to come and even, in spite of the crime, slander, and folly with which its advance is attended, may perhaps in itself be a measure of a sort of equity and, considering that worse might be, of a kind of prudence.

The Grand Old Mischiefmaker is Gladstone, and the imagery of heavenly havoc in the poem echoes Hopkins's view of him as a devilish and impetuous Home Ruler, all wind and wild light. Both the poem and the letter rework Milton's parliament of fallen angels with its 'sound of blustering winds', and this enables Hopkins to give a new shimmer to the idea of political flux. The Heraclitean fire is a metaphor for intense social crisis, and it is unfortunate that an obsessive critical attention to Hopkins's aesthetic theories has dulled the cutting political edge of his imagination. Like Milton, the poet he most strongly identified with, Hopkins is the victim of an ahistorical literary criticism.

Although he detested Gladstone, Hopkins's imagination responds enthusiastically to those mass emotions which made Gladstone the great popular leader of the age. At times his response shows in a type of democratic or populist eroticism which has close affinities with Whitman's gay imagination, as he acknowledged when he told Bridges, 'I always knew in my heart Walt Whitman's mind to be more like my own than any other man's living.' He praised the 'savagery' of Whitman's art and said his rhythm resembled his own verse in its 'last ruggedness and decomposition into common prose'. Like Whitman, he was devoted to raw, common speech, and such devotion necessarily expresses a wide social viewpoint which regards unpracticable quartz as being real gold, mined and minted by the people. This love of what Hopkins termed 'tykishness' shows in an exchange of letters with Patmore where Hopkins corrects Patmore's misunderstanding of a remark he once made to the effect that Patmore the poet had less of the 'tyke' in him than any man he knew:

> As there is something of the 'old Adam' in all but the holiest men and in them at least enough to make them understand it in others, so there is an old Adam of barbarism, boyishness, wildness, rawness, rankness, the disreputable, the unrefined in the refined and educated. It is that that I meant by tykishness (a tyke is a stray sly unowned dog) and said you have none of; and I did also think that you were without all sympathy for it and must survey it when you met with it wholly from without. Ancient Pistol is the typical tyke, he and all his crew are tykes, and the tykish element undergoing dilution in Falstaff and Prince Hall appears to vanish, but of course really exists, in Henry V as king.

Tactfully Hopkins remarks: 'I thought it was well to have ever so little of it', and he concludes by praising Patmore's unrefined habit of smoking heavily because 'to know one yields to a vice must help to humanise and make tolerant'.

Hopkins's analysis of 'tykishness' is a justification of his own poetic – according to the *OED* a 'tyke' is also a low-bred boor, and for all its sophisticated discipline Hopkins's verse aims often at a blurting boorishness and lack of refinement. We can detect in his fascinated definition of the word a revealing delight in a particular kind of yobbo populism and muscular brutality, as well as a violent British nationalism which is enforced by his linking of tykishness with Henry V. It is as if deep down he wishes he were out on the rampage. His imagination pushes towards that condition of absolute war which Clausewitz defined as the blind explosion of force untrammelled by ideas.

If Hopkins resembles Kipling in his love of military muscle, he may also be seen as the English equivalent of Hugh MacDiarmid – both are provocative, unsettling poets whose synthetic demotic beats against a normative language of social control. Yet for all their polemical urgency they share a deep imaginative totalitarianism – MacDiarmid's praise of Lenin, Hopkins's creation of that hero of labour Harry Ploughman, reveal a self-abasing admiration for rigid order. Their imaginations share a risky, over-the-top extremism and a studied rejection of conventional notions of poetic taste.

Among the critics who pioneered appreciation of Hopkins this century, only Elsie Duncan-Jones was disturbed by his sometimes brutal eroticism – an aggressive attitude which helps produce those moments of deliberate bad taste in the verse. There are precedents in baroque art that might be cited in justification of the orgasmic stanza (28) in *The Wreck of the Deutschland*, where Hopkins makes the tall nun's death resemble a combination of sexual intercourse and a cavalry charge: 'Let him ride, her pride, in his triumph, despatch and have done with his doom there.' Perhaps future critics will pay more attention to the element of camp baroque in Hopkins's art?

Future readers, though, will have problems with Catherine Phillips's edition of the poems: it is a fussy and distracting text which ought not to replace Gardner and MacKenzie's fourth edition.* Phillips's stated editorial practice is to adopt for text 'the version which I believe to be that last written'. As a result, many of the poems are pestered with metrical marks, most of which Gardner and MacKenzie wisely relegated to the excellent and much fuller notes in their edition. Implying that she would have preferred to print the whole agonized gamut of curlicues, ties, outrides and double stresses, Phillips vulnerably remarks that 'cost and editorial opinion' at Oxford University Press have restricted metrical marks in the text to simple stresses. Clearly there was some disagreement, and the result is a botched compromise between minimal stress marks and the full range of markings. For the reader who is familiar with Gardner and MacKenzie's texts Phillips's over-marked replacements can grate on the aural vision. Also, the editorial technique of signalling note references with a balloon-like degree sign is distracting and unnecessary. The poems appear to be set in a field of pikes and soap bubbles.

*Hopkins's readers must be grateful to Phillips for printing the poems in chronological order and for including a good selection from the journals. However, her selection from the letters is inadequate – the 'Red' letter is missing and so too is the crucially important letter to A. W. M. Baillie in which Hopkins doubts Tennyson and discovers Parnassian. The ferocious and exacting imagination of the Jesuit poet deserves a more sensitive editor.

Phillips's decision to choose the latest manuscript versions forces her to reject the A[1] text of 'The Handsome Heart':

> 'But tell me, child, your choice; what shall I buy
> You?' – 'Father, what you buy me I like best.'
> With the sweetest air that said, still plied and pressed,
> He swung to his first poised purport of reply.
>
> What the heart is! which, like carriers let fly –
> Doff darkness, homing nature knows the rest –
> To its own fine function, wild and self-instressed,
> Falls light as ten years long taught how to and why.
>
> Mannerly-hearted! more than handsome face –
> Beauty's bearing or muse of mounting vein,
> All, in this case, bathed in high hallowing grace . . .
>
> Of heaven what boon to buy you, boy, or gain
> Not granted? - Only . . . O on that path you pace
> Run all your race, O brace sterner that strain!

This was the version chosen by Bridges, and Phillips rightly calls it 'more lively'; however, she shunts it into the notes at the back of her edition and instead prints the B version:

> 'But tell me, child, your choice,|your fancy; what to buy
> You?' – 'Father, what you buy me|I shall like the best'.
> With the sweetest earnest air|his purport, once expressed,
> Ever he swung to, push|what plea I might and ply°
>
> Him. Áh, whát the heart is!|Like carriers let fly – °
> Doff darkness: homing nature,|nature knows the rest – °
> Heart to its own fine function,|wild and self-instressed,°
> Falls as light as, life-long,|schooled to what and why.
>
> Heárt mánnerly|is more than handsome face,°
> Beauty's bearing or|muse of mounting vein;
> And whát when, as ín this cáse,|bathed in high hallowing grace? –

Of heaven then now what boon | to buy you, boy, or gain°
Not granted? None but this, | all your road your race°
To match and more than match | its sweet forestalling strain.

Phillips justifies her decision to print this stammering, inchoate wreck of a fine sonnet by arguing that in 1883–4 Hopkins cancelled Bridges's composite of the earlier versions. Bridges felt that B had none of the 'charm and freshness' of A^1, but his tender editorial care is spurned in the new edition.

Although minimal stress markings do create a more accessible text, Hopkins's interventionist scansion sometimes helps the ear receive the unique and exact sound he wishes to deliver to his readers. For example, I have been fascinated for the last twenty years by these lines:

I wake and feel the fell of dark, not day.
What hours, O what black hoürs we have spent
This night! what sights you, heart, saw; ways you went!

A lot hangs on that umlaut in the second line – 'black hoürs' – and to my ear the result is a cavernous protracted Shakespearean guttural that still survives in Ulster speech. (Hopkins comments on Ulster pronunciation in a letter to Dixon.) He wrote this tragic sonnet in Ireland and he seems to be rubbing his nose in that dark *ur*-sound like a demented hellfire preacher terrifying his congregation at the thought of eternity and damnation. Phillips annoyingly drops the umlaut and prints: 'What hours, O what black hours we have spent'. Stripped of that terrible ululation the line becomes a bland nine-syllabled nothing – like one of the Binsey poplars, its perfect inscape has been silenced.

Writing beyond Writing: Emily Dickinson

In a recipe for turnip soup the cookery writer Ambrose Heath asserts that turnips have 'an entirely masculine flavour, peppery and very definite'. For several centuries male writers have been saying much the same thing about poems: from Dryden to Hopkins and beyond, adjectives like 'masculine', 'virile', 'manly' were used freely as value-judgements in critical discourse. As Helen McNeil points out in her centenary study, Emily Dickinson entered the twentieth century as the writer of a series of 'over-sensitive, coy, rather ill-disciplined poems'. Feminist critics have challenged this sexist view of her writing, arguing that she radically undermines traditional masculine values. In another centenary study, however, John Robinson insists that she is a timeless lyric poet whose work is not 'centrally representative of women'. Robinson's refusal to consider Dickinson's polemical and subversive imagination is disappointing, but it can be argued that certain writers identify with various generic categories – national, sexual, political – while others identify against them. I would no more want to publish a book of essays entitled *We Men* than I would want to identify with one called *We Irish*. Dickinson ironically addresses a lover as 'Burglar! Banker – Father!' and in many of her poems she identifies herself against the dominant masculine values of nineteenth-century American culture. She searched for role models among famous women writers of her day – George Eliot, the Brontës, Elizabeth Barrett Browning. Yet as Christanne Miller points out, Dickinson didn't actively support the political campaign for women's rights 'or, apparently, sympathise with women generally'. It is in the radical new language of the poems themselves that the battle against the father is fought.

Dickinson's eruptive, intense vernacular challenges the way in which men use language as a means of achieving and consolidating power:

He fumbles at your Soul
As Players at the Keys
Before they drop full Music on –
He stuns you by degrees –
Prepares your brittle Nature
For the Ethereal Blow
By fainter Hammers – further heard –
Then nearer – Then so slow
Your Breath has time to straighten –
Your Brain – to bubble Cool –
Deals – One – imperial – Thunderbolt –
That scalps your naked Soul –

When Winds take Forests in their Paws –
The Universe – is still –

The initial image is of a pianist idly running his fingers along the keys before beginning to play, an apparently unstudied, even clumsy action which is actually deft, professional, contrived, a sly way of getting the audience on his side. The concrete action for which the multiple pianists are mirror analogies is that of a preacher who adopts the strategy of saying something disarmingly casual to an audience (maybe he makes some routine announcements) in order to lull them and get their attention before beginning to speak. Such premeditated casualness, with all the sympathy that sudden intimacy or unexpected clumsiness can enlist, sometimes has the effect of completely mesmerizing an audience. Then – *wham!* – all the rhetorical stops come out and the congregation are squeezed in the palm of the preacher's hand.

Placed next to 'your soul', that verb 'fumbles' is so concrete and intrusive that we see either a seducer trying to undo a bodice button or the preliminary to spiritual murder. There is a curiously similar moment in *Washington Square* when Catherine Sloper fears that her tyrannical father is trying to destroy her, body and soul, as they argue in a cold Alpine valley: 'There was a kind of still intensity about her father which made him dangerous, but Catherine hardly went so far as to say to herself that it might be part of his plan to fasten his hand – the neat, fine, supple hand of a distinguished physician – in her throat.' Here the free female spirit struggles with a murderous patriarch. The New England puritanism which formed Dickinson's imagination, as it formed James's, asserts the primacy of the individual conscience over all controlling authorities. In Dickinson's poem, authority enforces itself through a gradual stunning process that is both soothing and playful. This sinister seduction combines the concert/sermon figure with the idea of entering an abattoir, a blacksmith's forge or a church where a marriage service will take place. You are the bride being prepared for the 'Ethereal Blow'. He is butcher/blacksmith/bridegroom, a preacher who plays cat and mouse with his audience. Dickinson's metaphors almost tear the poem apart, but the last two lines return us to the image of a lulled, still audience just before the beginning of a performance by a cunning, windy rhetorician who is every bit as feral and violent as Samuel Richardson's Lovelace.

Like Richardson, Dickinson writes to the moment, polemicizing a masculinist language:

Our lives are Swiss –
So still – so Cool –
Till some odd afternoon
The Alps neglect their Curtains
And we look farther on!

Italy stands the other side!
While like a guard between –
The solemn Alps –
The siren Alps
Forever intervene!

Switzerland typifies Protestant patriarchy, and even now we can see how those values are expressed and enforced in a section of the Swiss Civil Code entitled 'General Effects of Marriage':

160. The husband is the head of the conjugal union. He chooses the place of abode and duly provides for the maintenance of wife and children.
161. The wife acquires the husband's surname and citizenship. She must to

the extent of her ability assist him by word and deed in his effort to maintain the home. She has the management of the household affairs.
162. The husband represents the conjugal union. He is also personally liable for his own acts whatever may be the system under which the matrimonial property is held.

For Dickinson, our lives are Swiss, like watches or legal codes. Everything is staked out for us in the high-precision language of legal draughtsmanship and cultural engineering. According to Article 166 of the Code, a wife can exercise 'more extensive powers' only with the express or tacit consent of her husband. It is for those more extensive powers that 'we' – i.e. women – look beyond the Alps. The poem is addressed to a specifically female experience: a supposedly more 'universal' reading of the poem as articulating any experience of being trapped in a routine boredom has the effect of denying its polemical pitch. Such a reading would fail to notice that Dickinson is inverting the traditional image of woman as 'siren', and is applying it to the male solemnity and custodial presence of the Alps.

At roughly the same time (probably in 1859), Dickinson wrote another poem which plays with conventional gender imagery by first giving the 'immortal' Alps bonnets and sandals, and then inquiring:

Meek at whose everlasting feet
A Myriad Daisy play –
Which, Sir, are you and which am I
Upon an August day?

By posing this provocative question in such a flippant manner, Dickinson unsettles the Rock of Ages and questions Calvinist assumptions about social roles. And the confident, challenging address of the poem, its intent dashes, novel use of the indefinite article in the second line, and explosive freedom from standard punctuation, substitute an oral style for the Swiss precision of printed text. Dickinson's poems are poised between existing as a series of unique speech-moments and a gathering of familiar letters. Miller points out that Dickinson's habit of leaving variant word choices marked in the margins of bound manuscript copies of her poems serves to multiply meaning, and she aligns this habit with Julia Kristeva's argument that multiple meaning and fragmentation of formal syntax challenge the 'phallic' posture of mastery and control in language, and so allow for the creation 'of new and unprivileged meanings'.

Only seven of Dickinson's poems were published during her lifetime; it is probable that her dislike of seeing them become printed texts was partly caused by a wish never to see them subordinated to male editorial control. As a puritan she is hostile to the formal tyranny of print: it arrests the intense process of letter-writing and speech. Although Dickinson shares a vernacular aesthetic with Robert Frost – a consuming worship of speech-sounds – she appears to have viewed letter-writing as superior to speech because of the spoken word's debt to 'attitude and accent'. A letter 'always feels to me like immortality because it is the mind alone without corporeal friend'. One could argue, however, that Dickinson is searching in her poems for a type of gestural or body language which combines accent, attitude and physical gesture:

> The only Ghost I ever saw
> Was dressed in Mechlin – so –
> He wore no sandal on his foot –
> And stepped like flakes of snow –

The use of ' – so – ' incorporates a hand gesture which gives the poem an extraordinary presence, as if Dickinson's actual, living voice is addressing us as we read. This is one extreme of puritan authenticity, and its origin may be traced to that codifier of male dominance in marriage, St Paul.

In order to perceive Paul's influence on Dickinson's imagination we need to postulate a hectic series of texts that aspire to exist only as speech-moments. The idea of a writing beyond writing is impossible, a contradiction. Written or printed signs last; speech doesn't. Yet clear-cut and decisive as the argument may seem, the puritan imagination persists in opposing it. Writing to the Corinthians, Paul rhetorically questions the need for epistles of commendation 'to you, or letters of commendation from you' (2 Corinthians, 3). And he asserts: 'Ye are our epistle written in our hearts, known and read of all men. Forasmuch as ye are manifestly declared to be the epistle of Christ ministered by us, written not with ink, but with the Spirit of the living God; not in tables of stone, but in fleshy tables of the heart.' This is an antinomian, born-again attitude which asserts that 'our sufficiency' derives from God: 'Who also hath made us able ministers of the new testament; not of the letter, but of the spirit: for the letter killeth, but the spirit giveth life.' Paul contrasts this new spiritual text, a sort of original writing degree zero, with the Mosaic Law or 'ministration of death, written and engraven in stones'. Death is a material text, spirit is life, voice, feeling, righteousness. A written or incised text is like the 'vail' which Moses put over his shining face when he came down from Mount Sinai with the renewed tables of stone. That Mosaic Law or 'ministration of condemnation' is now abolished, 'for until this day remaineth the same vail untaken away in the reading of the old testament; which vail is done away in Christ'. The new Christian ethic is identified with the 'great plainness of speech' that we believers profess. This isn't a veiled language but a series of direct, sincere, glorious utterances.

Such a concept of immortal speech is deeply rooted in Dickinson's imagination:

A word is dead
When it is said,
Some say.

I say it just
Begins to live
That day.

The spoken word is infinite and eternal because in not being a series of signs it does not submit to the deadly bondage of the letter. The writer must therefore aim to go beyond writing into a kind of speech continuum. Reading Dickinson, we engage with the illusion of melting through the mortal legalism of a printed text into a new libertarian speech: 'Now the Lord is that Spirit: and where the Spirit of the Lord is, there is liberty.' That plain speech is evident in the flowing airy script – the spirit's *écriture* – in the Belknap edition of Dickinson's manuscripts.

Although Dickinson refused to be saved, her imagination gongs with a Calvinist sense of the terrors of consciousness and a Pauline affirmation of glorious living speech. The convinced idealism of her language rejects both rigid masculine legalism and the 'Dimity convictions' mocked in the poem which begins:

What Soft – Cherubic Creatures –
These Gentlewomen are.

As Miller shows, the language of traditionally 'feminine' gentleness was recommended in a series of nineteenth-century American advice books to women which gave frequent instructions on language use, tonal inflexion and manner of speaking. In Mrs Gilman's *Recollections of a Southern Matron*, women were told that the 'three golden threads' which wove domestic happiness (every 'true woman's' goal) are to repress a harsh answer, confess to a fault, 'and to stop (right or wrong) in the midst of self-defence, in gentle submission'. The advice of *The Mother's Assistant and Young Lady's Friend* was 'Always conciliate', and *The Lady's Amaranth* stated that a woman governs by persuasion: 'The empire of woman is an empire of softness . . . her commands are caresses.' Domestic life is seen as a still, cool empire of caressing speech. This is the cultural status quo from which Dickinson's exclamatory, interrogative, often wildly erotic language perpetually liberates itself. For such an imagination, conventional sentence structure is imprisoning and claustrophobic. Dickinson must break free from its formal prosiness:

They shut me up in Prose –
As when a little Girl
They put me in the Closet –
Because they liked me 'still'.

Stillness is oppression, fixity, the enemy of the free spirit. Only a restless language can resist or stay ahead of its institutional orthodoxies.

In a related poem, Dickinson asserts her freedom from formal structures by stating, 'I dwell in Possibility –/A fairer House than Prose.' She is a hypothesis rather than a dweller on solid earth. This means that her imagination exists in a condition of profound ontological insecurity and unfinished knowing, where the *Angst* of consciousness is often imaged as oppression, threat, terror – that 'certain Slant of light' which oppresses like the 'Heft' of cathedral tunes. Consciousness very painfully perceives the ontic character of the world; only by trying to ride the surge of its own processes can it hope to elude a dread closure. Desperate to avoid that Mosaic bondage, these poems are impatient with rational control and unambiguous meaning. They push language to its limits and disrupt standard grammar, syntax and typography (Dickinson's early editors, like John Clare's, imposed normative patterns on the poems). For Dickinson, as for the poets of post-war Eastern Europe, the act of writing is a process of deconstruction which witnesses against inherited institutions. Those poets write always out of a consciousness of the pervasive power of the state, and though Dickinson's consciousness is directed at the means by which her culture enforces gender roles and circumscribes her freedom, deep down this attitude is reinforced by a scepticism about the nature of the American republic.

In a now classic letter to Susan Gilbert, the close friend who was to marry her brother Austin, Dickinson expresses her critical vision of the institution of marriage, that empire of subordinate softness she dedicated her life to refusing:

I have always hoped to know if you had no dear fancy, illumining all your life, no one of whom you murmured in the faithful ear of night – and at whose side in fancy, you walked the livelong day; and when you come home, Susie, we must speak of these things. How dull our lives must seem to the bride, and the plighted maiden, whose days are fed with gold, and who gathers pearls every evening; but to the *wife*, Susie, sometimes the *wife forgotten*, our lives perhaps seem dearer than all others in the world; you have seen flowers at morning, *satisfied* with the dew, and those same sweet flowers at noon with their heads bowed in anguish before the mighty sun;

think you these thirsty blossoms will *now* need naught but – *dew*? No, they will cry for sunlight, and pine for the burning noon, tho' it scorches them, scathes them; they have got through with peace – they know that the man of noon, is *mightier* than the morning and their life is henceforth to him. Oh, Susie, it is dangerous, and it is all too dear, these simple trusting spirits, and the spirits mightier, which we cannot resist! It does so rend me, Susie, the thought of it when it comes, that I tremble lest at sometime I, too, am yielded up. Susie, you will forgive me my amatory strain – it has been a very long one, and if this saucy page did not here bind and fetter me, I might have had no end.

This is a visionary analysis of marriage as a sacrifice to patriarchy in which millions of women's lives are absorbed into the dominating 'man of noon'. These dependent lives, lives without autonomy (i.e. 'peace'), are implied in Dickinson's frequent images of sun and wind scorching or pummelling grass, flowers, trees. In the poem 'He fumbles at your Soul' the preacher's evangelical discourse 'scalps your naked Soul' and is symbolized as a feline wind taking the forest of the congregation in its paws. This type of male power is intent on destroying personal autonomy and is essentially a *social* force, a culturally created, conditioned and conditioning system of values.

Dickinson therefore abolishes the distinction between nature and culture which conservative apologists make, and writes them as one:

> I suppose the time will come
> Hinder it a little
> When the Corn in Silk will dress
> And in Chintz the Apple.

The silky corn and chintzy apple figure as images in a commercial for bridal costumes, and Dickinson's laid-back irony fuses this with the brilliantly ambiguous image of the snow-covered earth:

> I believe the Day will be
> When the Jay will giggle
> At his new white House the Earth
> That, too, halt a little –

A house for newly-weds, a new grave, an institution like the white mansion on Pennsylvania Avenue, a snowy whiteness everywhere –

the jay is giggling at the deadly soppiness of marriage here. Dickinson's last line, with its packed stresses and wry combination of dentals and labials, is a perfectly crafted speech-moment, one of her wittiest evasions of closure. All her writing expresses a desire to be unfettered, and in this last line that desire is voiced through a change of cadence.

One of her most beautiful rhythmic effects occurs after the insistent trochaics of:

Under the Light, yet under,
Under the Grass and the Dirt,
Under the Beetle's Cellar
Under the Clover's Root,

where the pounding chthonic rhythm is subtly slowed in the next quatrain:

Further than Arm could stretch
Were it Giant long,
Further than Sunshine could
Were the Day Year long.

Of the four stresses in the last line, three are consecutive, so that the rhythm seems to still into a gigantic, stretched spondee. This change, this unique arresting cadence, is a moment of voiced immortality where the spirit speaks clearly and completely. Crucially, it depends upon a departure from a closeting, rhythmic norm.

For Dickinson, this world is 'not Conclusion' but a site of unrelenting spiritual process, where tempests 'mash' the air and imaginary creatures 'chuckle' on the roofs. Her Calvinist nightmare contains an alert awareness of evil and a psychologically analytic idea of the individual soul. Its pressure can be felt in this passage from a letter to a friend, Abiah Root, whom Dickinson was to drop after Root's marriage to the Reverend Samuel Strong:

When I am not at work in the kitchen, I sit by the side of mother, provide for her little wants – and try to cheer, and encourage her. I ought to be glad, and grateful that I *can* do anything now, but I do feel so very lonely, and so anxious to have her cured. I hav'nt repined but *once*, and you shall know all the why. While I washed the dishes at noon in that little 'sink-room' of our's, I heard a well-known rap, and a friend I love *so* dearly came and asked me to ride in the woods, the sweet-still woods, and I wanted to exceedingly – I told him I could not go, and he said he was disappointed – he wanted me very much – then the tears came into my eyes, tho' I tried to choke them back, and he said I *could*, and *should* go, and it seemed to me unjust. Oh I struggled with great temptation, and it cost me much of denial, but I think in the end I conquered, not a glorious victory Abiah, where you hear the rolling drum, but a kind of a helpless victory, where triumph would come of itself, faintest music, weary soldiers, nor a waving flag, nor a long-loud shout. I had read of Christ's temptations, and how they were like our own, only he did'nt sin; I wondered if *one* was like mine, and whether it made him angry – I could'nt make up my mind; do you think he ever did?

The eager puritan address of Dickinson's rapid prose surrounds domesticity with ideas of temptation, Christ, sin, then relaxes for a moment in that lovely phrase, 'the sweet-still woods', which points towards the infinite possibilities of erotic desire in the verse. It is a highly dramatic passage which inflates the quotidian with such momentousness that it almost bursts in the writing.

The temptation here is sexual, but the conjunction of male visitor and noon carries with it the fear of submitting to the 'man of noon' and believing the sun can shine out of a man's eyes. Dickinson scorns such dependence:

She rose to His Requirement – dropt
The Playthings of Her Life
To take the honorable Work
Of Woman, and of Wife –

Her rejection of marriage is plainly stated here, but less obviously she uses certain words and images to challenge some of the assumptions of her native culture. Many of her poems read like the work of an obsessive and dedicated monarchist who is forever dreaming of crowns, courtiers, gems, diadems, coronations, queens, earls. The reason for this, I would guess, is that she found many of the institutions created by the American Enlightenment sterile and restrictive and wholly masculine. The masonic virtues of the state could find no place for the queen of the night, so Dickinson mocked her culture's egalitarianism and social atomization with fruity Bourbon, often Catholic, images. She aimed for the 'polar privacy' of complete personal autonomy, paradoxically employing aristocratic imagery as a means to that end.

Her autonomy is triumphantly asserted in:

I'm ceded – I've stopped being Theirs –
The name They dropped upon my face
With water, in the country church
Is finished using, now,
And They can put it with my Dolls.
My childhood, and the string of spools,
I've finished threading – too –

'They' are the social forces which sought to shape and control her consciousness – all those men of noon whose sermons and edicts scalped her soul. Throwing off their domination, she concludes by imagining herself as fully empowered and sovereign, self-crowned like a female Napoleon:

My second Rank – too small the first –
Crowned – Crowing – on my Father's breast –
A half unconscious Queen –
But this time – Adequate – Erect,
With Will to choose, or to reject,
And I choose, just a Crown –

The language is insistently royalist, and this is Dickinson's polemical method of extending and subverting American English as Noah Webster had defined it in his smugly aggressive Calvinist manner.

Dickinson's family owned a copy of *An American Dictionary of the English Language*, where she would have read Webster's preface, in which he remarks that the principal differences between 'the people of this country and all others' arise from different forms of government, law, institutions and customs: 'Thus the practice of hawking and hunting, the institution of heraldry and the feudal system of England originated terms which now form a necessary part of the language of that country; but, in the United States, many of these terms are no part of our present language – and they cannot be, for the things which they express do not exist in this country. They can be known to us only as obsolete or as foreign words.' Despite its pulsing modernity, Dickinson's language is stuffed with what Webster would dismiss as obsolete or foreign words, like 'Aragon' or 'escutcheon'. Queens supplied her with role models that did not exist in a republican culture and language dominated by men. She refused to accept Webster's literally chauvinist delimitation of language, nor could she share his chiselling confidence in 'new and peculiar' institutions and 'new terms'. And though it would be quite wrong to align her with Eliot's royalist élitism, her writing is a critique of mercantile values. Addressing a rare type of March light, she says, it 'passes and we stay':

> A quality of loss
> Affecting our Content
> As Trade had suddenly encroached
> Upon a Sacrament.

Like Clarissa Harlowe, Dickinson sets her epistolary poems against all that is meant by 'encroachment'. She discovers and asserts her sovereign sense of self against those institutions which would deny it.

The Great Horn-Handled Jack-Knife: *Great Expectations* as Epic Poem

Charles Dickens is firmly bedded in British cultural mythology. When he died the London *Times* spoke for the nation in an editorial which affirmed that: 'Statesmen, men of science, philanthropists, the acknowledged benefactors of their race, might pass away, and yet not leave the void which will be caused by the death of Dickens.' *The Times* demanded that Dickens should be buried in the 'sacred dust' of Westminster Abbey, and on 14 June 1870 the dead writer received what was in effect a state funeral. An elegy in *Punch* stated:

> He sleeps as he should sleep – among the great
>   In the old Abbey: sleeps amid the few
> Of England's famous thousands whose high state
>   Is to lie with her monarchs – monarchs too.

Dickens was a bourgeois republican with strong popular sympathies, but in England there is only an underground republic of letters, and so writers are never given a civic crown of bay leaves. Instead, they are allowed to ascend posthumously into the royal family.

This identification of the writer with the national state and the monarchy is a type of social cement which a polemical criticism has recently begun to question. Cultural mythology speaks a dead language, yet it depends on literary texts which surprise their readers by voicing a living language. Dickens knew this very well and he loved to parody the junk language of bureaucrats, lawyers and hack journalists:

> Our readers will learn, not altogether without interest, in reference to the recent romantic rise in fortune of a young artificer in iron of this neighbourhood (what a theme, by the way, for the magic pen of our as yet not universally acknowledged townsman TOOBY, the poet of our columns!) that the youth's earliest patron, companion, and friend, was a highly-

respected individual not entirely unconnected with the corn and seed trade, and whose eminently convenient and commodious business premises are situate within a hundred miles of the High-street. It is not wholly irrespective of our personal feelings that we record HIM as the Mentor of our young Telemachus, for it is good to know that our town produced the founder of the latter's fortunes. Does the thought-contracted brow of the local Sage or the lustrous eye of local Beauty inquire whose fortunes? We believe that Quintin Matsys was the BLACKSMITH of Antwerp. VERB. SAP.

Dickens wrote *Great Expections* during Palmerston's second administration, and his excerpt from the local paper echoes a remark which Palmerston made in the previous decade:

We have shown the example of a nation, in which every class of society accepts with cheerfulness the lot which Providence has assigned to it; while at the same time every individual of each class is constantly striving to raise himself in the social scale – not by injustice and wrong, not by violence and illegality, but by preserving good conduct, and by the steady and energetic execution of the moral and intellectual faculties with which his creator has endowed him.

Palmerston's supreme chauvinism easily reconciles individual social mobility with the existing class structure. His complacent confidence in British values is reflected in an editorial in *The Times* on the day Dickens began to write *Great Expectations* (4 October 1860). There the leader-writer congratulated 'the friends of liberty' on the step which had been taken 'in the direction of Italian liberty'. By listening to his generals' advice, it would appear that Garibaldi was acting like a sensible British liberal.

Dickens's novel is a parable of upward mobility launched at a highly self-satisfied society. It is a text which employs a type of symbolic code to make its audience of family readers doubt the very print in which they read and confirm their social existence. But how could a writer aim to unsettle certain illusions when he was frantically producing a serial fiction in order to boost his magazine's declining sales? (Charles Lever's dull serial, *A Day's Ride*, had caused many readers to desert *All the Year Round*.) The answer – or part of the answer – depends on an intuition, explored in the story, that the alternative to official mythic printed language is fluidly rooted in the eddies, the surprises, the spontaneous lunges of common speech. Before print, was the human voice – the unofficial voice of poetry powerless against the state and the status quo. It is that insistent, brooding, unillusioned, coolly sensitive voice which narrates *Great Expectations* and which plays against all that is signified by the moribund cliché VERB. SAP. at the end of the unctuous paragraph in that dirty old copy of the local paper which Pip reads in the Blue Boar.

Right from the beginning of the story, print or fixed signs have an alienating effect: they are identified with death and unhappiness. So Pip's mother exists through his creative misprision as '*Also Georgiana*', a sign on a tombstone. She is an appendage of her husband, Philip Pirrip, but to the young reader her first name is 'Also', and so she seems to float independently of him. Pip's education begins with these graveyard texts: he spells out the incised letters and imagines the family he never knew. Starting early on his rise to the status of literate gentleman, he scratches a letter to Joe on his slate:

> mI deEr JO i opE U r krWitE wEll i opE i shAl soN B haBelL 4 2 teeDge U JO aN theN wE shOrl b sO glOdd aN wEn i M preNgtD 2 u JO woT larX an blEvE ME inF xn PiP.

The spoken tenderness of this is poignant, for the affectionate message contains the threat of future alienation: the illiterate Joe, a kind blacksmith who happily reads his prayer-book upside down, will one day be educated – or at least judged by educated values. Now, in the moment of the hearth's warmth, he doesn't understand that Pip will write himself out of their Edenic oral world. The hearth is covered with all the letters of the alphabet: death's signs have infiltrated the house. And even though it is a statement of his bond of love with Joe, Pip's slate symbolizes the decomposition of paradisal speech, the beginnings of the Fall.

Children learning to write progress from words composed of single, autonomous letters to what is termed 'joined writing'. Dickens, I believe, associates joined writing with one of the major symbolic images in the story – chains. Pip notes that the great front entrance of Satis House has two chains across it, and this is an image of a society locked or deadlocked by bogus aristocratic tradition –

the daughter of a successful brewer, Miss Havisham is a fake Virgin Queen, a dusty Gloriana. She is a supremely sterile image of Palmerston's smug reconciliation of upward mobility and a fixed social hierarchy.

Writing, social mobility and power are fused when Joe tells Pip that the king upon his throne 'with his crown upon his 'ed, can't sit and write his acts of Parliament in print, without having begun, when he were a unpromoted Prince, with the alphabet'. Power expresses itself in print and print is a form of violence – this is imaged in the large old English þ which Pip first supposes to be a design for a buckle. This uncomfortable sign anticipates the 'character that looked like a curious T' which Pip's brain-damaged sister chalks upon her slate. The T-like sign may signify a hammer, but really it signifies Orlick, who has felled Mrs Gargery with the leg-iron which clamped Magwitch's ankle. And so the letter 'T', a hammer and the leg-iron are identified – the chalked sign becomes a 'character' in the story.

Pip has complex feelings of guilt about his part in helping Magwitch, and symbolically this conjunction of guilt, escaped convict, leg-iron, stolen file, hammer-like T points to Dickens's terror at his own imagination, an imagination which had for years been setting signs on paper, then watching printed sheets shoot out of steam presses. But in order to reach his present position of immense scriptorial power the young Dickens had to devote his enormous energy to mastering shorthand so that he could report parliamentary debates. He first learnt the shorthand alphabet and then proceeded to 'a procession of new horrors, called arbitrary characters; the most despotic characters I have ever known'. The signs needed to encode the speeches of powerful men are described in *David Copperfield,* where Dickens uses the terminology of dictatorship – horrors, arbitrary, despotic – and where he intends David's surname to carry in its suggestion of 'copperplate' both a metallic, even Murdstonian, quality and the idea of formal, written characters. In *Great Expectations* the signs become symbolic of social violence, but Dickens also internalizes that violence – as a young man the shorthand characters troubled his sleep; now a hammer-like T points to his demonic imagination. That imagination is symbolized as a psychopathic blacksmith, a type of Kentish Ripper, who hits a woman on the back of the head with a hard metal instrument. Pip is symbolically linked to Orlick by the leg-iron and they are both linked to Dickens, the producer of the printed text.

But Dickens knows and believes that his imagination isn't simply murderous, direct, powerful – it is also innocent and capable of a redeeming love. So Pip is Handel, the Harmonious Blacksmith, the boy who loved Joe the tender Blacksmith. Both Pip and Joe are anarchists who whisper seditious words to each other as they follow the military search party across the marshes: 'I treasonably whispered to Joe, "I hope, Joe, we shan't find them." And Joe whispered to me, "I'd give a shilling if they had cut and run, Pip." ' Those powerless whispers articulate that primal oral lovingkindness which Dickens wants to believe precedes a jagged social reality where tyrannical legal blacksmiths behave like Stalin in Mandelstam's epigram:

> He forges decrees in a line like horseshoes,
> One for the groin, one the forehead, temple, eye.
>
> He rolls the executions on his tongue like berries.
> He wishes he could hug them like big friends from home.
>
> (trans. W. S. Merwin and Clarence Brown)

Seditious whispers were punished by death in Stalin's state, and the novel's narrative voice is never more tenderly intent - never more Dantesque in its exacting gravity – than in the descriptions of prisoners about to be hanged. Dickens hated capital punishment, and his image of the condemned coiner as a 'dead plant' (Wemmick walks among the prisoners 'as a gardener might walk among his plants') expresses his antipathy to legal murder. As Dickens writes the coiner into existence, the eyes of the condemned pigeon-fancier seem to be trying to avoid the fixity of cold print:

a portly upright man (whom I can see now, as I write) in a well-worn olive-coloured frock-coat, with a peculiar pallor over-spreading the red in his complexion, and eyes that went wandering about when he tried to fix them, came up to a corner of the bars, and put his hand to his hat – which had a greasy and fatty surface like cold broth – with a half-serious and half-jocose military salute.

The unfixed yet exact description respects the suffering uniqueness of the man - its realism is neither photographic nor voyeuristic, and the tender empathy of Dickens's visual writing vouchsafes the man as an absolute human value. The fatty surface of his hat isn't presented as repulsive, but more in the manner of Joseph Beuys as an elemental life object.

Because Dickens's imagination returns obsessively to the idea of punishment, there is a distinctive knot in his narrative voice – a short, hard lump of a word – which sticks out like a kind of code-sign that concentrates the punitive theme of the story. The word is 'jack': it appears to be lodged in Dickens's imagination like one of those epiphanic sounds and words which help shape Stephen Dedalus's imagination.

The word first occurs when Joe advises Pip to hide from Mrs Joe's rampaging: 'Get behind the door, old chap, and have the jack-towel betwixt you.' (A jack-towel will later figure in Jaggers's daily passage from the legalized violence of the public world into his personal privacy.) When Mrs Joe pours tarwater down Pip's throat, she holds his head under her arm 'as a boot would be held in a boot-jack'. This is perhaps the first hint that Mrs Joe is in rebellion against her gender role and is punishing the nearest males for the subservient role society has forced on her. Like a version of Emily Dickinson's 'My Life had Stood a Loaded Gun', she blasts away at Joe and Pip. Joe offers this interpretation when he tells Pip 'very serous' that he'd seen so much of his poor mother 'drudging and slaving and breaking her honest hart and never getting no peace in her mortal days' that he finds himself quite unable to fulfil a traditional male role. This gives us an unexpected insight into Mrs Joe's reasons for rampaging, but it is an insight which coexists with the more obvious symbolic presentation of Pip's sister as an embodiment of driven, demonic energy, like Orlick, Jaggers and Estella's mother. She is 'given to government' and is associated with the Lords of the Admiralty and Treasury. She is also a 'master-mind', but an unknown village master-mind. Unknown precisely because she is female and working-class.

In his famous elegy, Gray celebrates the wasted potential of common labourers, and it is Pip's use of the term 'Jacks' instead of 'knaves' which causes Estella to exclaim 'what coarse hands he has! And what thick boots!' She calls Pip 'a common labouring-boy', and their apparent class difference is concentrated in the term 'Jacks'. But at a deeper level – a level deep as Australia – they are both linked indissolubly to an escaped convict with a most common object: a jack-knife.

The word next appears in the professional context of Jaggers's law-office. He has a closet inside his room which smells of scented soap, and inside the door of the closet there is an 'unusually large jack-towel on a roller'. Jaggers washes his hands whenever he returns from a police-court or has just dismissed a client. The act of washing is clearly a version of Lady Macbeth's guilt, and this implies that Jaggers is a murderous criminal. The implication isn't direct because it is mediated through the existence of a female murderer, Estella's mother, whom Jaggers employs as a domestic servant. The act of washing and then drying his hands on a jack-towel is an attempt to acquire a bogus innocence. Jaggers is a professional legal machine and so he cannot know that powerless suffering which Dickens allows his readers to intuit through a series of plant images: the plant-like felons in Wemmick's conservatory, the smell of the blackcurrant leaf which Biddy rubs to shreds in her hand as Pip complains priggishly about Joe's backward learning and manners, and the description of the prisoners condemned along with Magwitch.

Dickens draws a contemptuous contrast between the sheriffs with 'their great chains and nosegays, other civic gewgaws and monsters, criers, ushers, a great gallery of people' and the prisoners who are 'all formally doomed': 'and some of them were supported out, and some of them sauntered out with a haggard look of bravery, and a few nodded to the gallery, and two or three shook hands, and others went out chewing the fragments of herb they had taken from the sweet herbs lying about'. Dickens had observed public executions and his vision of social barbarism resembles Elizabeth Bishop's fable 'The Hanging of the Mouse':

> With the help of some pushes and pinches from the beetles, the executioner got the mouse into position. The rope was tied exquisitely behind one of his little round ears. The mouse raised a hand and wiped his nose with it, and most of the crowd interpreted this gesture as a farewell wave and spoke of it for weeks afterwards. The hangman's young son, at a signal from his father, sprang the trap.
>
> 'Squee-eek! Squee-eek!' went the mouse.
>
> His whiskers rowed hopelessly round and round in the air a few times and his feet flew up and curled into little balls like young fern-plants.

Like Dickens, Bishop employs an organic image to suggest the unfathomably precious fragility of the individual life: the mouse and the condemned prisoners are identified with the primal reality of fern-plants and sweet herbs.

This vision of organic innocence is similar to that of Gauguin or Douanier Rousseau and is not to be confused with the superficially innocent domestic private life which Wemmick enjoys at Walworth, where the Union Jack flies over his gothicky wooden castle. The term 'union jack' refers to a 'jack flag', which is a small-sized union flag. Since 1707 this union flag has been inserted in the upper canton of the ensign (in British nautical usage an ensign is a flag with a white, blue or red field). The term 'union jack' is often applied to a full-sized union flag. In recent years, the Union Jack has become a familiar image identifying British-made goods. Diesel trucks, packets of fish fingers, fan heaters, paper sacks of 'patriot potatoes' are all likely to have a Union Jack stamped on them.

Flags express and are part of the imagination of a nation – for those whose first love is the Irish tricolour the Union Jack is 'a butcher's apron', but for those who espouse a British rather than an Irish nationalism, the red-white-and-blue flag can have a highly positive significance. For the fundamentalist group known as the

British Israelites the Union Jack symbolizes the historic destiny of Anglo-Saxon Protestantism.*

Wemmick's castle-home is a subtle embodiment of Victorian manifest destiny; its flag unites two worlds which are only superficially opposed: bourgeois domesticity and the public reality of the law courts. Wemmick is Crusoe in suburbia, while the term 'union jack' which Dickens employs in this context introduces a specifically maritime dimension that links the London suburbs and the London legal world to the idea of the sea and imperial dominance. The drab, derogatory, obvious instrumentality of the word 'jack' insists on its sinister metallic punitiveness. From 'boot-jack' to a word which does not appear in the text – 'jackboot' – is no great leap of the imagination.

And yet Wemmick's private life appears so very attractive. How many generations of patriot readers have bathed in a soppy illusion as Wemmick takes the red-hot poker from the Aged and repairs to the battery – *bang!* goes the Stinger and shakes 'the crazy little box of a cottage as if it must fall to pieces'. But it never does, and the reader is relieved – the fictional world is intact. Yet Dickens has designed the rebarbative quaintness of this scene with great subtlety – Wemmick's cannon is a softened version of the cannons that sound on the marshes when a convict has escaped. Wemmick's wooden castle – wooden as the hulks are wooden – is another

*In a revealing booklet, 'The Symbolism of the Union Jack', A. J. Ferris offers this pseudohistorical account of how the Union Jack was formed:

In A. D. 1194, Richard I of England introduced the Cross of St. George as the Standard of England, and this remained the national flag until the Union with Scotland. In 1603, King James VI of Scotland became James I of England, as a result of which the first Union Jack was formed in 1606 by the addition of the Cross of St. Andrew which formed the background of the new flag. The name 'Union Jack' came from King James, whose name is 'Jacobus' in Latin, and 'Jacob' in Hebrew. Then in 1801, there was formed the more familiar Union Jack by the addition of the Cross of St. Patrick, sandwiched in between the flags of Scotland and England. Thus the formation of the Union Jack came about as the result of the progressive merging of the inhabitants of the British Isles under one throne, the throne of David. The complete Union Jack thus symbolises the RE-UNION OF JACOB.

prison, even though for him it is a refuge from the office in Little Britain. Dickens's narrative voice in this novel often has the sober definition of Wordsworth's in *The Prelude*. It may be that Dickens is remembering this passage:

> When the proud fleet that bears the red-cross flag
> In that unworthy service was prepared
> To mingle, I beheld the vessels lie,
> A brood of gallant creatures, on the deep
> I saw them in their rest, a sojourner
> Through a whole month of calm and glassy days
> In that delightful island which protects
> Their place of convocation – there I heard,
> Each evening, pacing by the still seashore,
> A monitory sound that never failed, –
> The sunset cannon. While the orb went down
> In the tranquillity of Nature, came
> That voice, ill requiem! seldom heard by me
> Without a spirit overcast by dark
> Imaginations, sense of woes to come,
> Sorrow for human kind, and pain of heart.

Wemmick's wooden domestic fortress and the British counter-revolutionary fleet are seen in calm sunshine, but the ground of Dickens's vision is a black Hulk lit by the flare of torches as Magwitch disappears inside:

> The boat had returned, and his guard were ready, so we followed him to the landing-place made of rough stakes and stones, and saw him put into the boat, which was rowed by a crew of convicts like himself. No one seemed surprised to see him, or interested in seeing him, or glad to see him, or sorry to see him, or spoke a word, except that somebody in the boat growled as if to dogs, 'Give way, you!' which was the signal for the dip of the oars. By the light of the torches, we saw the black Hulk lying out a little way from the mud of the shore, like a wicked Noah's ark. Cribbed and barred and moored by massive rusty chains, the prison-ship seemed in my young eyes to be ironed like the prisoners. We saw the boat go alongside, and we saw him taken up the side and disappear. Then, the ends of the torches were flung hissing into the water, and went out, as if it were all over with him.

Again, this is like a moment out of Dante, and that word 'cribbed', with its echo of Macbeth's 'cabin'd, cribb'd, confin'd', carries a powerful sense of hereditary guilt.

The word recurs later in the story when Magwitch takes out his jack-knife in his lodgings and sits down to a meal. The opened knife seems to release a popular unrefined language as his thieves' cant plays against the standard language:

> He was full of plans 'for his gentleman's coming out strong, and like a gentleman,' and urged me to begin speedily upon the pocket-book, which he had left in my possession. He considered the chambers and his own lodging as temporary residences, and advised me to look out at once for a 'fashionable crib' near Hyde Park, in which he could have 'a shake-down'.

Having outlined his plans for Pip's final ascent into the heaven of fashionable gentility, Magwitch finishes his breakfast and wipes his knife on his leg – a leg that had once been chained. To rise in social station is the equivalent of escaping from a prison hulk or returning from Australia – except that you never shake off that 'curious flavour of bread-poultice, baize, rope-yarn, and hearthstone, which attends the convict presence'. Upward mobility depends on the existence of thousands of anonymous convicts who dwell inside that institutional smell.

This is the point of the sly joke about Jaggers's professional reserve being as deep 'as Australia'. Great and Little Britain are built over a deep, hidden shaft that bottoms out in the colonies. And Dickens collapses the implications of this into a radioactive pun which is Wemmick's response to Pip's next remark: 'I said I supposed he had a fine business, and Wemmick said, "Ca-pi-tal!"' On the civil surface of their conversation, 'capital' means 'excellent', but its emphatic syncopated delivery hints at other meanings beneath that surface – capital punishment, capitalist, capital ship. Dickens stresses certain words in order to concentrate significance – the marshes become 'meshes', and this suggests the nets of language and class and nation.

Just before we learn, in the third paragraph of chapter 20, that Jaggers's address is Little Britain, this remark prepares us for the emphasis we should place on the name of his business location:

We Britons had at that time particularly settled that it was treasonable to doubt our having and our being the best of everything: otherwise, while I was scared by the immensity of London, I think I might have had some faint doubts whether it was not rather ugly, crooked, narrow, and dirty.

Those last four adjectives are more than literal descriptions of Pip's first observations of London streets. They link in with Wemmick's method of explaining Jaggers's artfulness and 'natural depth' by instancing the cutlery in his house. The cutlery is made of 'Britannia metal', an alloy of tin and copper which looks like silver if it's polished hard. As to the absence of plate, Wemmick explains 'that's only his natural depth, you know. A river's its natural depth, and he's his natural depth.' The link between Wemmick's fake silver cutlery and the natural depth of his reserve makes the symbolic conjunction Little Britain/Britannia metal/river (the Thames). Dickens is analysing the British national character as a naturalized type of controlled legal violence – hard polished metal, deep river sending ships out to the Empire, death masks of hanged criminals, a hangman's drop. These are the prime ingredients of that character.

Jaggers's official cutlery is set against another piece of cutlery – Magwitch's 'great horn-handled jack-knife'. To Pip, it is a banal and ugly object, like one of those grisly secondhand gadgets advertised in *Exchange & Mart*, but for Dickens it assumes a sacral, totemistic power: 'he had a barrack way with him of hanging about one spot, in one unsettled manner, and going through one round of observances with his pipe and his negro-head and his jack-knife, and his pack of cards, and what not, as if it were all put down for him on a slate . . .' Pipe, negro-head tobacco, cards, jack-knife, slate – many of these objects are greasy with use, like the condemned coiner's hat, but they assume the mythic status of those quotidian artefacts that are often invested with a fetishistic magic in naïve or vernacular painting. Dickens mocked the 'salt-spoon' school of painting in *Nicholas Nickleby*, but in this late novel he turns to what is now termed 'primitive painting' in order to ground his social vision in the powerless depths of the popular imagination. Such art is associated with the lower ranks of the army and navy (hence Magwitch's 'barrack way'), with the sideshows of touring fairs and with inn parlours.

Anyone looking at examples of naïve art cannot help noticing that it communicates – especially the keepsakes for soldiers' and sailors' families – strangely contradictory, even queasy, feelings. Like Woolwich, Malta and Quebec Bagnett in *Bleak House*, the often regimented figures convey a sense of personal powerlessness combined with national pride. Their trapped optimism and tender stoicism exist on the interface between domesticity and military service. Animals in such paintings often abolish history and perspective to resemble the cave-paintings at Lascaux, and so appear innocent of a particular cultural or national style. Objects are either part of the seamless, tapestry-like flow of the painting, or they possess a banal specificity which insists on their uniqueness (primitive still-lifes often include spoons, knives, forks, corkscrews and cheese cradles). Such objects are identical with non-genteel words – 'crib' or 'jack', for example – and they signal the perception of deep spiritual value in the language and minimal possessions of working people.

Dickens's imagination was especially drawn to those proletarians who were conscripted by the social structure. The grandson of domestic servants (his grandmother was Lord Crewe's housekeeper), the son of a clerk in the Navy Pay Office, he lived as a small child in Ordnance Terrace, Chatham, at the dockyard heart of the empire. As a child he saw a convict hulk on the Thames, watched convict labourers carrying planks in the dockyards and saw a squad of soldiers blow up a row of houses so that a prison could be built in their place. Dickens had no illusions about squaddies or jack tars, but his reiterated descriptions of Magwitch's reflex mannerisms and his few personal possessions point to his compassionate sense of their unpropertied, anonymous, regimented lives. Magwitch, however, comes out of an even less individualized social level, and he represents a type of revolutionary force gathering in the social depths. His experience of exploitation and punishment is concentrated in his few worn possessions, simple objects which have a living presence in the story. Magwitch has neither a mace, a great seal, nor a crozier – instead he wields that great horn-handled jack-knife, symbol of anonymous communal suffering and fierce integrity.

There is a similar moment in *The Prelude*, where Wordsworth celebrates the 'plain and seemly countenance' of the 'lowly' cottages he knew as a child:

> Eager and never weary we pursued
> Our home-amusements by the warm peat-fire
> At evening, when with pencil, and smooth slate
> In square divisions parcelled out and all
> With crosses and with cyphers scribbled o'er,
> We schemed and puzzled, head opposed to head
> In strife too humble to be named in verse:
> Or round the naked table, snow-white deal,
> Cherry or maple, sate in close array,
> And to the combat, Loo or Whist, led on
> A thick-ribbed army; not, as in the world,
> Neglected and ungratefully thrown by
> Even for the very service they had wrought,
> But husbanded through many a long campaign.
> Uncouth assemblage was it, where no few
> Had changed their functions; some, plebeian cards
> Which Fate, beyond the promise of their birth,
> Had dignified, and called to represent
> The persons of departed potentates.
> Oh, with what echoes on the board they fell!
> Ironic diamonds, – clubs, hearts, diamonds, spades,
> A congregation piteously akin!
> Chief matter offered they to boyish wit,
> Those sooty knaves, precipitated down
> With scoffs and taunts, like Vulcan out of heaven:
> The paramount ace, a moon in her eclipse,
> Queens gleaming through their splendour's last decay,
> And monarchs surly at the wrongs sustained
> By royal visages. Meanwhile abroad

Incessant rain was falling, or the frost
Raged bitterly, with keen and silent tooth;
And, interrupting oft that eager game,
From under Esthwaite's splitting fields of ice
The pent-up air, struggling to free itself,
Gave out to meadow grounds and hills a loud
Protracted yelling, like the noise of wolves
Howling in troops along the Bothnic Main.

Wordsworth makes the 'homely' and domestic carry prophetic images of revolution: they embody the idea of equality just as surely as the wind brings the message of European war and terror in the last decade of the century. Departed potentates, thick-ribbed armies, decaying queens, surly monarchs and pent-up 'air' struggling to free itself like a people in revolt – this is a future politics made momentarily cosy and mock-heroic. The interior and the worn playing-cards belong to popular culture and are from the point of view of the vernacular imagination natural images of the good. Elevated though it is, Wordsworth's language aims to design a naïve painting in these lines: like Dickens he perceives a profound value in ordinary, used objects.

The theatrical equivalent of vernacular painting is melodrama, so when Wopsle appears in a nautical melodrama Dickens isn't simply mocking the audience and the cast's illusion of popular power: 'This led to Mr Wopsle's (who had never been heard of before) coming in with a star and garter on, as a plenipotentiary of great power direct from the Admiralty, to say that the Swabs were all to go to prison on the spot, and that he had brought the boatswains down the Union Jack, as a slight acknowledgment of his public services.' The Swabs are the ship's officers and the scene shows a touching populist belief that somehow corrupt members of the ruling class can be swept away while the power structure and its insignia (star and garter Union Jack) remain intact. With tender mockery, Dickens is here honouring a dramatic form which fascinated him all his life – he often acted in melodrama and would have known that in the 1820 the Adelphi staged melodramas with elaborate nautical sceni effects. The fact that Wopsle sees Compeyson in the audience is one of Dickens's means of signalling that Wopsle and his ludicrous dramatic vehicles are not simply ludicrous – they embody the communal experience of the people and can assist Pip in spite of his snobbery.

It is appropriate, then, that the next appearance of the obsessive word 'jack' should be in the dirty public house – the 'Ship' – by the Thames. Pip, Magwitch, Herbert Pocket and Startop are staying there on the night before they attempt to get Magwitch out of the country: 'No other company was in the house than the landlord, his wife, and a grizzled male creature, the "Jack" of the little causeway, who was as slimy and smeary as if he had been low-water mark too.' The Jack – here the word means odd-job man – wears a bloated pair of shoes which he exhibits as Pip and the others are eating their eggs and bacon. Those bloated shoes – swollen like a drowned body – are described as 'interesting relics that he had taken a few days ago from the feet of a drowned seaman washed ashore'. Dickens is rubbing his readers' noses in something muddy, smelly and uniquely revolting.

Out of this moment he produces a dialogue which hammers the word 'jack' to death, rather as Shakespeare does in Falstaff's famous plea to that paragon of upward mobility, Prince Hal. The Jack asks the company if they have seen a four-oared galley going up with the tide:

> When I told him No, he said she must have gone down then, and yet she 'took up too', when she left there.
>
> 'They must ha' thought better on't for some reason or another,' said the Jack, 'and gone down.'
>
> 'A four-oared galley, did you say?' said I.
>
> 'A four,' said the Jack, 'and two sitters.'
>
> 'Did they come ashore here?'
>
> 'They put in with a stone two-gallon jar, for some beer. I'd ha' been glad to pison the beer myself,' said the Jack, 'or put some rattling physic in it.'
>
> 'Why?'
>
> '*I* know why,' said the Jack. He spoke in a slushy voice, as if much mud had washed into his throat.
>
> 'He thinks,' said the landlord: a weakly meditative man with a pale eye, who seemed to rely greatly on his Jack: 'he thinks they was, what they wasn't.'

'*I* knows what I thinks,' observed the Jack.

'*You* thinks Custum 'Us, Jack?' said the landlord.

'I do,' said the Jack.

'Then you're wrong, Jack.'

'AM I!'

In the infinite meaning of his reply and his boundless confidence in his views, the Jack took one of his bloated shoes off, looked into it, knocked a few stones out of it on the kitchen floor, and put it on again. He did this with the air of a Jack who was so right that he could afford to do anything.

'Why, what do you make out that they done with their buttons then, Jack?' asked the landlord, vacillating weakly.

'Done with their buttons?' returned the Jack. 'Chucked 'em overboard. Swallered 'em. Sowed 'em, to come up small salad. Done with their buttons!'

'Don't be cheeky, Jack,' remonstrated the landlord, in a melancholy and pathetic way.

'A Custum 'Us officer knows what to do with his Buttons,' said the Jack, repeating the obnoxious word with the greatest contempt, 'when they comes betwixt him and his own light. A Four and two sitters don't go hanging and hovering, up with one tide and down with another, and both with and against another, without there being Custum 'Us at the bottom of it.'

The dialogue makes everyone uneasy, but we can see that it is more than a signal that Magwitch is being pursued. The Jack is an anarchist, a smuggler, a kind of otter swimming in the unofficial economy – he imagines customs officers swallering their buttons and the buttons coming up 'small salad' – mustard and cress. The Jack wants to humiliate the official reality which the Swabs represent and turn its metal insignia into something innocent and organic. Magwitch, like Dickens himself, also wanted to humiliate the power structure. In the Jack's dialogue with the landlord Dickens is celebrating the primitive, lawless, innocent energy of the common people – men and women forced into menial jobs, cribbed in uniforms, their souls crushed like Pip's head in the boot-jack of his sister's arm.

It is therefore ironically appropriate that the Jack is last seen being instructed to recover Compeyson's drowned body, because although he may appear to be a marginal free spirit, a *bricoleur* on a mudbank, he is also a scavenger and a parasite, a version of Jaggers and Wemmick, who extract portable property from bodies that are about to become corpses. The Jack's bloated shoes and Miss Skiffins's brooch have much in common.

A short paragraph later, Pip takes his place at the side of the recaptured Magwitch: 'my repugnance to him had all melted away, and in the hunted wounded shackled creature who held my hand in his, I only saw a man who had meant to be my benefactor, and who had felt affectionately, gratefully, and generously, towards me with great constancy through a series of years. I only saw in him a much better man than I had been to Joe.' This is a humanist moment, a movement of Pip's spirit, but its significance becomes starkly clear if we set it next to some lines by another great primitivist visionary. Hopkins uses the term 'jack' in 'My Own Heart Let Me More Have Pity On', where it modulates into the surprise of God's grace:

> Soul, self; come, poor Jackself, I do advise
> You, jaded, let be; call of thoughts awhile
> Elsewhere; leave comfort root-room; let joy size
>
> At God knows when to God knows what; whose smile
> 's not wrung, see you; unforeseen times rather – as skies
> Betweenpie mountains – lights a lovely mile.

And in 'That Nature is a Heraclitean Fire', he identifies that scrunchy, shackled monosyllable 'Jack' with immortality:

> In a flash, at a trumpet crash,
> I am all at once what Christ is, | since he was what I am, and
> This Jack, joke, poor potsherd, | patch, matchwood, immortal diamond,
> Is immortal diamond.

The word fascinated Hopkins, and his neologism 'Jackself' is glossed by Laura Riding and Robert Graves, who list the other uses of 'jack' in combination: jack-screw, jackass, jack-knife, Jack Tar, Jack Frost, Jack of all trades, boot-jack, steeple-jack, lumber-jack, jack-towel, jack-plane, roasting-jack. From these combinations of the term Riding and Graves derive its central meaning: 'a person or thing that is honest, patient, cheerful, hard-working, undistinguished – but the fellow that makes things happen, that does things that nobody else would or could do'. Hopkins's Jackself is therefore this workaday self which he advises 'to knock off work for awhile'.

It is an acute reading, but it leaves out the instrumental, iron quality of the word, its associations with knavishness and sin. Hopkins implies that a jack's smiles – a menial's smiles – are 'wrung', or forced, or extorted from him. They are not spontaneous or unforeseen, like God's smile. The melting of Pip's repugnance towards Magwitch – an aging, used man with a furrowed bald head and iron grey hair at the sides – is the equivalent of the immortal divine grace that Hopkins draws out of his use of the word 'Jack'. Pip is now enabled to love Magwitch, and as Pip is recovering from his illness we witness an image of innocent writing when Joe, the blacksmith and man of the people, first speaks to Pip in his 'dear old home-voice' and then proceeds to 'indite a note to Biddy, with my love in it':

> Evidently, Biddy had taught Joe to write. As I lay in bed looking at him, it made me, in my weak state, cry again with pleasure to see the pride with which he set about his letter. My bedstead, divested of its curtains, had been removed, with me upon it, into the sitting-room, as the airiest and largest, and the carpet had been taken away, and the room kept always fresh and wholesome night and day. At my own writing-table, pushed into a corner and cumbered with little bottles, Joe now sat down to his great work, first choosing a pen from the pen-tray as if it were a chest of large tools, and tucking up his sleeves as if he were going to wield a crowbar or sledgehammer. It was necessary for Joe to hold on heavily to the table with his left elbow, and to get his right leg well out behind him, before he could begin, and when he did begin, he made every down-stroke so slowly that it might have been six feet long, while at every up-stroke I could hear his pen spluttering extensively. He had a curious idea that the inkstand was on the side of him where it was not, and constantly dipped his pen into space, and seemed quite satisfied with the result. Occasionally, he was tripped up by some orthographical stumbling-block, but on the whole he got on very well indeed, and when he had signed his name, and had removed a finishing blot from the paper to the crown of his head with his two forefingers, he got up and hovered about the table, trying the effect of his performance from various points of view as it lay there, with unbounded satisfaction.

This is a perfect vernacular moment – the pen-tray is like a chest of large tools, it is no more superior to them than the word 'knave' is superior to the word 'jack'. But this is a utopian image – as if writing and publication can resemble innocent labour, or a labourer can write and that seem natural. This is impossible, because if a labourer's writing were to be published it would exist in the professional public world of Jaggers's law office with its scrivener, printed documents and death masks.

Curiously, *Great Expectations* was dedicated to a friend of Dickens's, Chauncey Hare Townsend, who also befriended an agricultural labourer whose oral writings became part of British print culture – John Clare. Clare called Townsend 'a valued friend & brother bard' and Townsend wrote a sonnet to Clare in April 1820. Thirty years later Townsend published a sonnet to Dickens:

> Thy vigorous hand
> Smites but to heal, and turns with master-ease
> The mighty engine of the popular mind
> To indignation, which shall purge the land
> Of sanctioned sins.

Townsend was fascinated by the 'popular mind,' and we can see a poignant, tongue-tied meeting across the ironclad class-barriers of the 1820s (the period in which *Great Expectations* is set) in Clare's account of his first meeting with Townsend:

> Chauncy Hare Townsend came to see me it was one evening in summer and asked me if John Clare lived there I told him I was he and he seemed supprised and askd agen to be satisfied for I was shabby and dirty he was dissapointed I dare say at finding I had little or nothing to say for I had always had a natural depression of spirits in the presence of strangers that took from me all power of freedom or familarity and made me dull and silent for [if] I attempted to say any thing I coud not reccolect it and made so many hums and hahs in the story that I was obliged to leave it unfinished at last I often tryd to master this confusion by trying to talk over reasonings and arguments as I went about in my rambles which I thought I did pretty well but as soon as I got before any body I was as much to seek as ever – C.H.T. was a little affecting with dandyism and he mimicked a lisp in his speech which he owd to affectation rather then habit otherwise he was a feeling and sensible young man he talkd about Poets and poetry and the

fine scenery of the lakes and other matters for a good while and when he left me he put a folded paper in my hand which I found after he was gone was a sonnet and a pound bill he promised and sent me Beatties Minstrel some letters passd between us and I sent him a present of my Village Minstrel when I never heard of him afterwards he has since published a Volume of Poems

There are several accounts of how interpreters used to become incapable of speech in the presence of Stalin, and Clare's speechlessness when faced with even a sympathetic member of a powerful social class is a form of inviolable voice. Joe Gargery is such a voice; his reunion with Pip symbolizes Dickens's bourgeois dream of uniting the world of speech, love, kinship bonds, physical labour, with the world of office work, decent economic prosperity, print. Deep down he knew this was impossible, but another part of his mind refused that knowledge. This does not mean, though, that Dickens sympathized with Clare. In 1865 he read Frederick Martin's *The Life of John Clare* and in a letter dismissed the biography as the 'preposterous exaggeration of small claims'. He called Clare 'Incompetent'. Nevertheless, I want to believe that Clare's experience is one of the marshy imaginative roots of the novel, and that the novel is dedicated to Townsend because he told Dickens about Clare.

Essentially Joe is an oral poet, like Clare, and his unwritten couplet on his father:

Whatsume'er the failings on his part,
Remember reader he were that good in his hart

is a pure speech-moment hijacked into print. Joe tells Pip that he made it 'my own self. I made it in a moment. It was like striking out a horseshoe complete, in a single blow.' This is another utopian image which unites poetry, physical labour, tools, but it is a totally powerless moment. *Bang, bang, bang* go Stinger and the steam presses and the cannon on the marshes. Their noise easily drowns the buzz of voices, the sounds of Joe Gargery or Felix Randal fettling a bright and battering sandal.

Yeats's Hunger-Strike Poem

Texts – literary texts, pieces of published writing – can grow tired. Or is it that their interpreters – individual readers, teachers, scholars, critics – grow tired and the texts then seem to wither into *écriture*? In certain social climates the idea of 'literariness' dies away and the institution of literature becomes visible, like a target. Because many critics have used the quality of 'literariness', the thisness of individual literary texts, to support an often unspoken ideological position, other critics have sought to deconstruct both texts and criticism and to deny the existence of that quality.

In a famous consideration of Greek art, Marx asked why 'the social childhood of mankind' should not exert 'an eternal charm as an age that will never return'. Despite Marx's belief in the 'eternal charm' of great art, a belief in art's timeless universality now seems to be the exclusive property of conservative critics and of anxious liberal humanists. In *The Meaning of Conservatism* Roger Scruton speaks admiringly of the 'social conservatism expressed and advocated by James, Conrad, Yeats, Pound, Eliot, Joyce, Waugh and Lawrence – to name only the greatest of those who created our modern literature'. And George Steiner has argued that most serious political poetry and fiction belongs to the conservative camp:

> If so much of classic writing is 'élitist' in its technical resources and appeal, this is very obviously because literature of a more concentrated, self-conscious sort will always draw on more complex and richly referential levels of discourse and understanding. Motions of spirit which aim at perfection are, as Spinoza reminds us, difficult.

Steiner's statement, with its gauche reference to Spinoza, has to be seen in the context of the argument about critical practice which has been developing in Britain for some years now. It is a statement that Steiner has not been able to defend, and it issues from a critical attitude which is conservative and aristocratic in outlook. From this point of view, the transcendental or universal properties of the literary text become analogous to those of the monarchy. In his revealing analysis of conservatism Scruton argues that the legitimacy of monarchical rule 'arises "transcendentally", in the manner of the duties and obligations of family life'. And if we substitute 'literature' for 'monarch' and 'Crown' in this hilarious paragraph of Scrutonese, it is possible to observe the function of literary texts in British society:

> Consider the Englishman's allegiance to the Crown, as he envisages and enacts it. Monarchy is an institution, with a complex constitutional background, that elevates the person of the monarch above the realm of individual character and endows him or her with the dignity and, so to speak, the objectivity of office. It is not the personal qualities of the Queen that draw the Englishman to her nor is it any considered knowledge of the function and history of the Crown. It is rather a sense of the monarch as a symbol of nationhood, as an incarnation of the historical entity of which he is a part. His loyalty to the monarch requires ceremonial enactment, customary usage, an established code of deference: for this is the style of all symbolic gestures in which society and individual are merged.

Yeats would probably have endorsed this statement, but it is not my intention to discuss the royalism of the national poet. Instead, I want to begin by noting that Yeats's writings are taught and discussed as part of what Roger Scruton terms 'our literature' – i.e. English literature – and are therefore subject to the same stresses which have forced a reassessment of the literary canon.

Yeats's 'Easter 1916' is generally acknowledged to be a very 'great' poem, but it is also an extremely tired text – a text whose printed characters seem baked and gummed over with the attentions of several critical generations. Yeats put Pater's sentences about the *Mona Lisa* at the beginning of his *Oxford Book of Modern Verse*, and like that perspex-shielded painting Yeats's 'Easter 1916' stands like a tired aesthetic monument behind the riot shields of the critics. Is it really possible, I wonder, to say anything new about this poem? Can anyone face listening to it ever again?

The last critical account of the poem which I heard was during an interview with a member of a local Unionist Association somewhere in Co. Armagh. Sitting outside a tin meeting-hall among the apple orchards, the Unionist spoke of his reactions to the Anglo-Irish Agreement and referred to a headline about the agreement in the *Irish Times*. The headline said 'ALL IS CHANGED' and the Armagh Unionist formulated his opposition to the agreement by saying that the headline had been taken from a poem by Yeats and that this poem was pro-Sinn Fein. Three pieces of paper – agreement, newspaper story, poem – were placed together to form an argument. And three other pieces of paper were inevitably part of the argument – the Ulster Covenant of 1912, Pearse's Declaration of the Irish Republic in 1916, the Anglo-Irish Treaty of 1921. If I insist on identifying all six bits of *écriture* as *écriture*, this is because we've been used for a long time now to the idea that 'Easter 1916' and other great poems like 'On a Grecian Urn' and 'Michael' are more like pieces of marble. These well-wrought *objets d'art* are so universal, so effortlessly and charmingly eternal, that they have nothing to do with the social world, the now of journalism and current events which is so productive of printed paper.

In Britain this idea of the magical, transcendent properties of the literary artefact has been a powerful form of social cement – it has helped to express and create the idea of consensus. As Chris Baldick notes in his study *The Social Mission of English Criticism*, the new academic subject called English Literature was partly designed to meet 'the specific needs of the British empire expressed in the regulations for admission to the Indian Civil Service'. At home in England the subject served a different purpose, as is shown by an 1880 handbook called *How to Teach English Literature*. This handbook states bluntly that the subject helps to 'promote sympathy and fellow feeling among all classes'. For many years now Yeats's poetry has been part of that subject and has therefore performed a function for which it was never intended – the creation of a social consensus within Britain. It would appear that Yeats's writings have sent certain people out to vote for his publisher.

The alignment of Yeats with consensus politics can be seen clearly in a letter which the Leavisite critic Geoffrey Thurley wrote to the *New Statesman* protesting that a centenary article on Joyce's politics implicitly encouraged 'just that fanaticism which Joyce, like Yeats, detested so much'. It is curious to see Yeats – one of the most fanatical and opinionated of modern writers – surviving as a posthumous moderate. But it is undoubtedly true that printed texts – set texts for examinations – by Yeats and Joyce have formed part of an agreed cultural fabric which is now crumbling in Britain. The Yeats text explicated in Britain is very different from the Yeats text explicated in Co. Armagh. The Ulster critic reads a poem which pins itself unreservedly to an ideological position, while the English critic discovers a text which is full of Anglican balances, wetness, fudge. In the *Critical Survey* (autumn 1962) we can watch a critic describing 'Easter 1916' as 'a very ambivalent poem, as we should expect'. This critic adds that Yeats's lines about water-and-cloud-movement offer us 'the very feel of life'. This is a humanist statement and one which confuses art with experience by using the word 'life' as a critical term.

A further distortion of the text is apparent in this statement: 'Here, then, is the world of change and delight; and it is the stone in the centre that strikes chill. The opposition between casual comedy and meaningful heroism is balanced now by this very different opposition, between lilting beauty and the motionless dark.' Later in the 1960s, the source of this quotation – the *Critical Survey* – was to help produce a series of Black Papers on education through its companion journal, the *Critical Quarterly*. In retrospect we can see how the liberal humanism of 1962, the 'motionless dark' of conservative reaction and the new entrepreneurial conservatism need to become the targets of a polemical criticism. Such a criticism must be alive to the unexamined cultural assumptions which inform, for example, the use of that word 'balanced' in the account of Yeats I've just cited. Through the use of that word Yeats, or rather his text is confirmed into the Church of England. Like the BBC, he gives balanced coverage.

One of the key sources of this idea is the dedicatory preface to the Authorized Version of the Bible. There, the translators point out that 'things of this quality have ever been subject to the censures of illmeaning and discontented persons', but that the monarch' acceptance of their text 'shall more honour and encourage us, than all the calumniations and hard interpretations of other men shall dismay us':

> So that if, on the one side, we shall be traduced by Popish Persons at home or abroad, who therefore will malign us, because we are poor instruments to make God's holy Truth to be yet more and more known unto the people, whom they desire still to keep in ignorance and darkness; or if, on the other side, we shall be maligned by selfconceited Brethren, who run their own ways, and give liking unto nothing, but what is framed by themselves, and hammered on their anvil . . .

On the one hand ignorance and darkness, on the other self-conceit and subjectivity. The scriptural translation aims to steer a middle course between them and it aims also to identify itself as text with God and with King James. Everything makes, if not sense, at least common sense.

Or used to make common sense. It is not possible now for critics to uphold what Roland Barthes terms 'the old obscurantist myth according to which ideas are noxious if they are not controlled by "common sense" and "feeling"'. Therefore a series of subjective value judgements – judgements hammered out on the anvil of this lectern – will not be worth listening to. Traditional literary criticism is dead. The particular pressures of these times demand a criticism which, as Walter Benjamin argues in 'The Author as Producer', has 'absolutely no use for such rigid isolated things as work, novel, book'. Such a criticism has to 'insert them into the living social context'. Thus, if we locate 'Easter 1916' in its moment of production – that 'moment of socialization' as Jerome McGann terms it – the static, monumental nature of the text begins to shift and shimmer. This involves arguing that a literary text is like a play, because just as a play's significance is partly that of its first audience's reception, so the meaning of a poem – in so far as a poem has a meaning or any single meaning – can be located in the society of immediate responses to it. This makes the poem look less like an urn in a national museum and more like a pamphlet or a piece of journalism. And so the hard, discontented interpretations hammered out on the critical anvil of Armagh Unionism insist that poems have social meanings, meanings tied to particular political moments in particular societies.

As everyone knows, Yeats composed the poem entitled 'Easter 1916' between early May and 25 September 1916. Looking at the *Collected Poems*, we might tend to assume that the poem was published in late 1916, though it appears in the volume *Michael Robartes and the Dancer*, which was published in 1921 by the Cuala Press. Yeats had published his previous volume, *The Wild Swans at Coole*, in 1919, and its title poem is dated October 1916 in the periodical in which it first appeared, the *Little Review*. Thus Yeats had finished 'Easter 1916' a month before 'The Wild Swans at Coole' and could therefore have published it in the 1919 volume. He chose not to.

Instead he arranged for Clement Shorter to print 'Easter 1916' in an edition of twenty-five copies for distribution among his friends. This publication is generally believed to have been in late autumn 1916*. The poem came into being as a kind of underground, dissident or *samizdat* text, and had it been published other than privately in 1916 must have provoked enormous controversy. Yeats would also have suffered in various ways by such publication. Although Shorter's pamphlet gives 1916 as the date of publication, it is my view that it was published in the following year but given the more topical date, 1916, as the date of publication. This serves to identify the political event with the act of writing and the act of publication, and so create a sense of intense presence as history and text fuse.

That the poem was in fact published in 1917 may be deduced from a letter which Yeats wrote to Clement Shorter, in which he says: 'I have now copied out the Rebellion poem and enclose it . . . Please be very careful with the Rebellion poem: Lady Gregory asked me not to send it you until we had finished our dispute with the authorities about the Lane pictures. She was afraid of it getting about and damaging us and she is not timid.' In the summer of 1916

*Joseph Hone says 'Easter 1916' was written within a few weeks of the executions and printed 'almost at once' by Clement Shorter.

Yeats was suspected of being pro-German and the British authorities took private soundings in order to discover his opinions. Yeats thought he might lose his Civil List pension and he wrote to Lady Gregory that the Rising put them all under suspicion. As further evidence of the poem's date of publication being 1917 I would cite an inscription on one of the twenty-five copies – 'to Henry Maggs, April 1917'. This suggests that the manuscript was received in late March and printed and distributed the following month.

The poem remained a secret or underground text for four years. It finally surfaced into public light on Saturday 23 October 1920. The date is exact because the poem appeared in the *New Statesman* of that date. It stands there, shorn of the date 'September 25, 1916' which appears in all subsequent printings, among various articles, reviews, letters and transitory opinions which have been long forgotten. Out of all this dead paper only the poem survives, but it is in that fertilizing ash that it is bedded and grows. The lead article attacks the government's conduct of the Anglo-Irish War, the same issue contains another article, 'The History of Reprisals' and there are numerous other references to the war. If Yeats was worried in March 1917 about the poem coming to public notice, he was also worried in January 1920, as we can see from a letter he wrote to J. C. Squire, the editor of the *London Mercury*, in reply to a letter rejecting some of his poems. John Kelly suggests that Squire rejected those poems on the grounds of their obscurity, and Yeats responded by saying he would try to send something else:

> but if I do not the reason will be that the only alternative is a group of poems which I want published together & which get their weight & fire from a little group of verses, suggested by the Irish Rebellion. I doubt if you would care to risk these in the present disturbed state of Ireland; I haven't made up my own mind as to whether I ought to risk them. While Irish youth is in its inflammable state I may end by publishing them only in one of my sisters' expensive little books where they can do no harm. I dont feel at the present moment that I should separate the other poems from them.

The 'group of poems' which Yeats wanted published together are presumably the ten poems published in the *Dial* in November 1920. A sub-group within that series – 'Sixteen Dead Men', 'The Rose

Tree', 'On a Political Prisoner' and 'Easter 1916' – are presumably the 'little group of verses, suggested by the Irish Rebellion'.

In 'Passion and Cunning: An Essay on the Politics of W. B. Yeats' Conor Cruise O'Brien has praised Yeats's decision to publish 'Easter 1916' and 'The Rose Tree' in 1920 as 'probably the boldest of Yeats's career', and he has also noted the characteristic prudence that informed the decision. O'Brien states: 'By publishing the 1916 poem in 1920 he placed himself openly "on Ireland's side" in the fight with England but he closed no doors in terms of contemporary politics. For it was known, in 1920, that Ireland was going to get some form of self-government.' The publication of 'Easter 1916' is so rooted in the arguments which were to lead to the establishment of the southern theocracy and the northern statelet that those arguments and events are necessarily part of the poem's significance.

Yeats was in the United States from mid-January to the end of May 1920, and it was during that period that certain events took place which were to lead to the poem's publication in the *New Statesman* on 23 October 1920.

On 20 March 1920 Tomás MacCurtáin, the Lord Mayor of Cork, was shot dead in his home by a gang of masked raiders who would appear to have been members of the RIC. Mac Curtáin was also Commandant of the Cork Brigade of the IRA. His civic post of Lord Mayor was immediately filled by Terence MacSwiney. MacSwiney was arrested on 12 August 1920, and at once went on hunger-strike. He was court-martialled four days later on a charge of being in possession of treasonable documents and was found guilty of having a copy of a police cipher under his control and of being in possession of two police documents. He was sentenced to two years' imprisonment and the following morning was put on board a British naval sloop. On 18 August he was handed over to the Governor of Brixton Jail.

MacSwiney's long hunger-strike – it lasted for seventy-four days – attracted world-wide attention, and according to Richard Ellmann was the only incident in the entire Anglo-Irish War which stirred James Joyce's imagination. On 27 August, nine days after MacSwiney's transfer to Brixton Jail, Joyce sent a postcard from Paris to his brother, Stanislaus, in Trieste. As Ellmann points out, Joyce associated 'MacSwiney's battle with his own against English officialdom in Zurich'. He sent Stanislaus a poem entitled 'The Right Heart in the Wrong Place':

Of spinach and gammon
Bull's full to the crupper,
White lice and black famine
Are the mayor of Cork's supper
But the pride of old Ireland
Must be damnably humbled
If a Joyce is found cleaning
The boots of a Rumbold.
S.O.S.

Rumbold – the hangman barber in *Ulysses* – was the British Minister to Switzerland in 1918, and in the poem Joyce relates his personal grievance against Rumbold to MacSwiney's hunger-strike. MacSwiney was possibly a distant relation of Joyce's, so the personal and the historical fuse in the atavistic reflex of that reference to 'black famine' – to the Great Hunger. It is scarcely necessary to remind anyone in Ireland that hunger-strikes trigger profound emotions in people who do not necessarily share the ideology of militant republicanism. They give visible force to the idea of the soul, as Joyce's ironic distress call indicates.

The effect on Joyce – an instinctive tribal reflex – can be gauged from that postcard to Stanislaus, a postcard which lets us glimpse the bedrock of Joyce's imagination. The effect on Yeats – a writer who was not nurtured in the Irish Catholic tradition – may be surmised through a consideration of some of MacSwiney's public statements and certain remarks Yeats made in correspondence. We need to remember that Yeats is guarded in private letters because there was censorship in 1920 and some of his letters were tampered with.

Terence MacSwiney was a poet and playwright, and his first play, *The Last Warriors of Coole*, was produced in 1907. His poems – 'In a Mist', for example – have that dreamy astringency familiar to any student of Yeats:

> Something there is of sympathy around;
> A mist is on the world, and unknown powers
> Seem to shake dimly and mysteriously
> On the deserted land and thro' the air
> And in the turbulent sea, as if, there met,
> They did unite their strength and, all combined,
> Hurled in fierce restlessness upon the shore.
> And I do feel with them in sympathy,
> For I too am in mist, and I do hurl
> The waves of my emotion on the strand
> Of Life's great mystery.

MacSwiney also delivered a famous speech when he was nominated as Lord Mayor of Cork after MacCurtáin's murder. He was nominated in Irish by Alderman Liam de Roiste, seconded by Alderman Barry, and was supported by Sir John Scott, the leader of the local Unionists. He was unanimously elected, and having spoken in Irish he then delivered his speech in English. In that speech he referred both to MacCurtáin's murder and to the events of Easter Week, 1916. Recalling the first council meeting after MacCurtáin's election as Lord Mayor, he said:

> I realised that most of you in the minority here would be loyal to us, if doing so did not threaten your lives; but that you lacked the spirit and the hope to join with us to complete the work of liberation so well begun. I allude to it here again, because I wish to point out again the secret of our strength and the assurance of our final victory. This contest of ours is not on our side a rivalry of vengeance, but one of endurance – it is not they who can inflict most, but they who can suffer most, will conquer – though we do not abrogate our function to demand and see that evil-doers and murderers are punished for their crimes.

That phrase – 'it is not they who can inflict most, but they who can suffer most, will conquer' – stuck, and it was frequently cited during the 1981 hunger-strikes in the North of Ireland. MacSwiney's imagery of Calvary and martyrdom, as well as the Fenian élitism of a trope he uses elsewhere in his speech – 'to prove us worthy of a noble line, to prepare us for a great and noble destiny' – read like the public enactment of poetic images by a civic leader. The language of the printed text is functional, though it would have had more immediacy for a newspaper reader in 1920. To a listener present on the occasion of the speech there would have been the *hwyll* in MacSwiney's voice and the power of the occasion itself to charge the inert text with dangerous currents.

At certain moments in a nation's life public official language and poetic inspiration fuse – at this critical point a certain type of poet is integrated into society. Such poets are not pure, and there is a price to pay for the risks they take in allowing their imaginations to become burdened by the living moment. When this happens something molten issues into the public light and we observe the powerlessness of institutional reality to control the imagination.

Two days before Joyce sent his postcard, three British cabinet ministers – Churchill, Balfour and Edward Shortt – met at 10 Downing Street to discuss MacSwiney's case. The British Labour Party was urging his release on the grounds that he was a political prisoner, and notes of the meeting recorded that considerable discussion took place 'with regard to the effect on the country of the apparent climb down of the Government if he were to be released'. It was finally decided to ask General Macready's opinion as to the effect in Ireland: the general advised against releasing MacSwiney. On 11 September, when MacSwiney had been on hunger-strike for thirty days, Lloyd George and Bonar Law summoned Sir George Newman (the Chief Medical Officer at the Board of Education and Ministry of Health) and begged him to use every effort to keep him alive. According to Thomas Jones's *Whitehall Diary*, Newman 'kept him alive for another forty-two!' The solid calibration of days and dates reminds us that this is how the events which will later be termed 'history' actually feel inside the unstable pull of the social moment.

In late August 1920 there were serious disturbances in Lisburn and in Belfast, where there were some thirty deaths between 21 and 23 August, followed by the imposition of a curfew. On 20

September the Black and Tans sacked Balbriggan, and it was at roughly this point that Yeats began to consider revising *The King's Threshold*, his 1903 play about an ancient Irish hunger-striker. On 26 September he wrote to Lennox Robinson: 'If I can make a few hour's leisure I will examine "The King's Threshold" which I think of partly rewriting. The Mayor of Cork may make it tragically appropriate.' The next day he wrote to Lady Gregory telling her that he is going to 'examine *The King's Threshold*. If I feel I can do it I shall give it the tragic end it has always needed and make some other changes. Events this Autumn may make it very appropriate. If I can come down we would talk over the chance of good performance.' Two days later he wrote again to Lennox Robinson and discussed a future production of MacSwiney's play *The Revolutionist*. Clearly Yeats felt moved by MacSwiney's hunger-strike to make or plan certain public responses.

In *The King's Threshold* Seanchan resolves to 'starve or get again the ancient right of poets'. That right is to be a member of the great council of the state, a council whose other members – bishops, soldiers, 'Makers of the Law' – believe it against 'their dignity / For a mere man of words to sit amongst them'. Yeats's sense of affinity with MacSwiney could not have been naturally tribal, as Joyce's was, but it rested on a shared nationalism and that usually invisible and unspoken fellow feeling which writers have. MacDonagh and Pearse were poets – now another poet was setting his life and his imagination on the line. The publication of 'Easter 1916' in the last stages of MacSwiney's hunger-strike, or shortly after his death, would serve to place MacSwiney as next in the tradition of dead martyrs for Ireland and would also be a shot in the propaganda war. An example of the way in which the war was waged is this report in the London *Times*, the day after MacSwiney's death:

SECRET POLICE CIPHER

Iron Cases for Bombs

A statement issued by the Irish Office says that a letter, of which the following is a copy, was found in the City Hall at Cork at the time of Alderman McSwiney's arrest:–

The letter begins:

G.H.Q. Dublin, 30/6/20
To O.C. Cork No 1, – Will you kindly report as soon as possible if there are any facilities in your area for the manufacture of grenades.

The letter is signed 'T. Mc., Director of Munitions', and the statement adds: 'It will be remembered that McSwiney was O.C. Cork No 1.'

The Times, in an editorial in the same issue, condemned the release of this letter and implied that it was a forgery. The newspaper was sympathetic to self-government for Ireland and had in June 1919 engaged a young Irish barrister, R. J. H. Shaw, as its adviser on Ireland.

On 5 October 1920 *The Times* published a letter from Asquith which proposed a radical policy – that Ireland be granted the status of an autonomous Dominion. Yeats went to Ireland in October 1920 and saw *Michael Robartes and the Dancer* through his sisters' press. In a letter to Lady Gregory (30 October 1920) he mentions that before he left he wrote to Asquith 'whom I heard was often in Oxford and asked if I might call on him as I had a suggestion to make':

To my surprise he came to see me – this was some days before he wrote to the *Times* – and stayed some time talking of Ireland to George and myself. As I do not know where this letter will go I will not say what was said. He said of my suggestion, 'I will bear it in mind, Mr Yeats', but I don't suppose he will act on it now. I don't want my interview with Asquith talked of for it was of no importance, except that his coming at all shows that he has Ireland much in his mind.

And at the end of the letter Yeats adds that he is thinking of 'putting *King's Threshold* into prose for Abbey'.

On 9 October Lloyd George delivered a speech in Carnarvon in which he stated that there would be no Dominion Home Rule for Ireland and that the IRA 'murder gang' would be broken up. The following day, 10 October, a huge 'Hands Off Ireland' demonstration took place in Trafalgar Square. On 12 October *The Times* reported that eleven prisoners on hunger-strike in Cork Jail had entered their sixty-second day of starvation, and on 16 October a half-day general strike took place in Cork City for the release of MacSwiney.

These reports from the London *Times* are part of the ticker-tape of events in October 1920:

> 12/10/20
> The Lord Mayor of Cork
>
> It was stated by the friends of the Lord Mayor of Cork yesterday afternoon that there was practically no change in his condition.
>
> The Lord Mayor Alderman McSwiney, who has been on strike in Brixton Prison for 60 days, is serving a sentence of two years' imprisonment for being in possession of a secret police cypher and other documents.

> 19/10/20
> Parliament Today
> Coal Debate First
> The Shadow of Ireland

On 21 October, Sir Haman Greenwood is reported as having told the House of Commons that:

> He had made up his mind that it was essential to search Ireland for arms, including Ulster. (Labour cheers.)
>
> An Ulster preacher had accused him of being a Sinn Feiner with a Papist wife. (Laughter.) His splendid wife – without whom he could not go on with the government of Ireland – and himself were very quiet members of the Church of England.

The same issue of *The Times* reports:

> The Press Association states that the Lord Mayor of Cork had a serious turn yesterday following an attack of delirium. Last night his condition wa reported as serious. Yesterday was the 69th day of his hunger strike.

The Times for Saturday 23 October, the day on which 'Easter 1916 was published in the *New Statesman*, contains a report on th finances of the Irish Bill under the headline 'HOME RULE WITH FULL PURSE/CASE FOR GENEROUS TERMS', an advertisement for hotel called the British Empire Hotel, a report on an ambush o soldiers in Co. Cork, a report on the new special constabulary, and parliamentary report headlined 'HOME RULE BILL'. This Bill was

> for the better government of Ireland within the United Kingdom. It was nc a bill for the separation of Ireland from England. (Cheers.)

The mood of the House of Commons may be gauged from a letter that Asquith wrote on 20 October in which he mentions that he had agreed a form of motion about Irish reprisals with Labour:

Pringle has returned from his mission to Ireland and has this morning been providing me with some powder and shot. You could see from the temper which was displayed at question time yesterday, that this House of Commons is breast-high in favour of reprisals. They make one almost sick of politics.

On 25 October *The Times* reported:

The Lord Mayor of Cork still lies in a critical state, but there has been no change since Saturday either for the better or the worse. He had some sleep yesterday morning, and was not delirious. He has now been on hunger strike for 73 days.

The following day, 26 October, *The Times* reported MacSwiney's death 'at 5.40 yesterday morning on the 74th day of his hunger strike', and among the many reports of reactions to MacSwiney's death it carries a story dated 'Dublin Oct. 25':

The news of the Lord Mayor of Cork's death has been received with genuine regret in Dublin and throughout the country. His political opponents, while supporting the Government's action in the matter, are willing to do full justice to Mr McSwiney's courage and idealism. He will now take a high place in Sinn Fein's roll of 'martyrs', and there will be much passionate denunciation of the Government in Nationalist newspapers.

Mr McSwiney's death is, indeed, a lamentable incident in the long and too often lamentable history of the relations between Great Britain and Ireland. The Republican 'heroes' of 1916 have become already landmarks in Nationalist Ireland's struggle for freedom. The country is told day after day that acceptance of anything less than the full Republican demand would be a betrayal of their memory. Mr McSwiney's death will intensify this feeling, and will increase the difficulties which now cause moderate Irishmen of all parties almost to despair of a constitutional settlement.

Below this report from Dublin there is a report from Belfast which mentions that a Sinn Fein flag was hoisted in memory of MacSwiney:

This led to the display of Union Jacks, and eventually to two crowds stoning each other.

In the riot that followed, Joseph McLeod of Church Street East in Belfast was shot through the head.

These news reports and events were part of Yeats's consciousness in the autumn of 1920 and they belong to the production history of 'Easter 1916'. So, too, does *The Times* editorial on MacSwiney:

> His sincerity and his courage are now, at all events, vindicated beyond all question. He was arrested on August 12, and was tried by Court-martial four days afterwards. He was found guilty of having under his control a copy of a police cipher, and of being in possession of two seditious documents. For these offences he was sentenced to two years' imprisonment, and with them only can he justly be charged. We therefore condemn, as grossly unjust, official suggestions that he was, in reality, guilty of other crimes. Particularly odious is the production, on the day of his death, by the Irish office, of a letter from Dublin, alleged to have been found in the Cork City Hall at the time of the Lord Mayor's arrest, but upon which, apparently, no count in the indictment was based. Action of this kind can but intensify the feelings which his death will inflame among Irishmen the world over. When first we realized that he was indeed likely to persist in refusing to take food, we urged upon Ministers the folly of permitting him to die, and counselled his release as an act of grace. Had he been clearly convicted of participation in any crime of violence, we should not have done so; but we considered that the offences proved against him were not sufficiently grave to warrant the Government in carrying the law to its strictly logical conclusion. We have never regretted, and do not now regret, the advice which we then tendered. We felt that, in some circumstances, logic is a poor thing, a thing, moreover, out of keeping with our national political temperament. It is apt to be the solace of arid minds, a mere line, 'length without breadth', drawn on the outside of things, like the tenuous wake of a small craft upon the surface of the deep while the great tides roll and surge below.

This editorial statement is probably the work of R. J. H. Shaw, the Irish adviser to *The Times*. The use of the definite article in 'the Cork City Hall' is characteristic of Irish English, as is the word-order of 'When first we realized' (in standard English it would be 'When we first realized'). The entire editorial reads like an eloquent speech for the defence in a court case. This suggests that behind the anonymous editorial pronouncement there is an *émigré* Irishman ventriloquizing for the English national imagination, rather like Burke's half-ironic praise of the 'great cattle, reposed beneath the shadow of the British oak' in *Reflections on the Revolution in France*. For Irish nationalists, John Bull and the sea are friends, and the leader-writer's invocation of the mighty deep is an appeal to that idea of intuitive wisdom and national power which believes itself superior to the mere logic of the small boat or to the importunate Jacobin grasshoppers which disturb Burke's placid pastures.

Three days after *The Times* editorial appeared, Yeats wrote to Lennox Robinson and discussed the production of MacSwiney's play *The Revolutionist*; it was produced four months later at the Abbey, and was a spectacular success. Although Yeats's interest in MacSwiney is clear, there are no letters extant relating to the publication of 'Easter 1916' in the *New Statesman* (the editorial correspondence was destroyed during the London Blitz). What seems clear is that Yeats's poem cannot be isolated from the public events of the summer and autumn of 1920 and that we need to consider the poem in relation to those events *and* to its first audience. Poems, like plays, are inspired by and for audiences, and here it is helpful to consider Sir William Rothenstein's memories of Yeats's conversations during the Easter period, 1916:

> He spoke of the leaders as innocent and patriotic theorists, carried away by their belief that they must put their theories into practice. They would fail and pay the penalty for their rashness . . . He obviously felt some discomfort at being safe in England when his friends were risking their lives in Dublin, and fretted somewhat that he had not been consulted, had been left in ignorance of what was afoot.

That Yeats felt isolated and guilty is apparent, and according to MacSwiney's sister her brother had similar feelings: 'But that Terry, who had hoped, and prayed and planned for a soldier's post in the front line of battle, should have had to watch, helpless, while the men of Easter week fought and fell, was so intense a pain that only those who knew him down the years could ever understand.' The memory of Easter Week ran through MacSwiney's farewell notes in Brixton, and in his last note to Cathal Brugha he wrote 'the pain of Easter Week is properly dead at last'.

MacSwiney's long fast against the state concentrated memories of Easter 1916, so that for Yeats October 1920 was exactly the right moment to publish his poem. Here, another remark which Rothenstein recorded is pertinent: 'Speaking of painting he quoted his brother Jack as saying that he painted to please himself. "This", he said, "is not my attitude to poetry. You must remember your audience; it is always there. You cannot write without it." ' As the verse of 'In a Mist' shows, Terence MacSwiney was part of Yeats's audience, and so too was the British Labour Party, some of whose most influential members read the *New Statesman*. That party had established a commission to inquire into the Anglo-Irish War in the autumn of 1920, and Yeats's poem might be regarded as a piece of evidence submitted to the commission.

The production history of Yeats's text is complex, and it seems certain that the poem is as much 'about' the events of the summer and autumn of 1920 as it is about the events of Easter 1916. It is not a poem with a fixed and descriptive historical reference, but one which embodies certain particular and eternal dangers as well as those 'eternal charms' about which I have been unable to speak.

Salid Oil and Alexandrines: Yeats's Letters

Towards the end of his inaugural lecture at the Collège de France, Roland Barthes observed that 'the myth of the great French writer, the sacred depositary of all higher values, has crumbled since the Liberation'. In Ireland lately there has developed a liberating impulse to desacralize a national institution called Yeats, and in a seminal pamphlet, *Heroic Styles: The Tradition of an Idea*, the country's most significant and influential critic, Seamus Deane, has criticized the way in which an acceptance of 'the mystique of Irishness' can involve readers in the 'spiritual heroics' of a Yeats or a Pearse. The result is a belief in 'the incarnation of the nation in the individual'.

Deane's essay is crucially important because its criticism of romantic nationalism issues not from that weary, zero-conservative outlook popularized by the revisionist historians, but from a stringent and essentially hopeful analysis of the present political crisis. Deane insists that we must demystify Yeats's heroic nationalism and states that: 'Everything, including our politics and our literature, has to be rewritten – i.e. re-read. That will enable new writing, new politics, unblemished by Irishness, but securely Irish.'

Opening John Kelly and Eric Domville's scrupulous and magnificent edition of Yeats's letters, I readied myself to take a sling-shot at the great Cuchulain – the impulse dissolved in helpless love, chortles, pure delight. The old monster, I realized, has managed here his last and finest trick, for he appears in these pages not as the superb glittering imago but as pupil and pupa, an earnest, eager, driven young man who is often shy and unsure of himself, short of money, screwed by publishers, and in a desperate rush. Only Yeats could make a dense stack of business letters read with all the blossomy excitement of a *Bildungsroman*. This is a typical example of his epistolary style:

58 Eardley Crescent | South Kensington
22 March

Dear Miss Tynan

I send you the only forms I can find.

Mr O Leary told Seeley Bryers & Walker to send on 50 to me, but they never came. I dare say you could get some from Mr O Leary. I will write to him about it tonight. I cannot write much now to you – as I am writing in Horne's office (Horne of the 'Hobbey Horse'). He may be hear any time – I have been busy these last two days making up material in the British Museum reading room for a story about Father John O Hart.

Horne has just come in and tells me that your poem will be in next 'Hobby Horse' –

I was at the Southwick Literary Club last night – Crilly lectured on Miss Fanny Parnell.

I must finish now as I want to talk to Horne.

Your Friend
W B Yeats

I got £2 from 'United Ireland' as soon as I get it changed I will send your father the 5/– I borrowed.

This brief letter to the writer Katharine Tynan is a complete fusion of politics, publishing, writing and economics. The vivid and detailed editorial notes illuminate the text so that John O'Leary (revolutionary), Daniel Crilly (Irish Party Member for North Mayo), and Fanny Parnell (patriotic poet and sister of Charles Stuart) take on an almost fictive existence, like characters in a novel. Herbert Horne and Yeats's view of him, Yeats's 'hushed, musical, eerie' manner of speaking on that night in Southwark, as well as Crilly's recent trial on a political charge, all become intensely present, so that a hasty scrawl in a London editor's office is transformed into a fragment of pure *Geist*. Yeats has the very engaging gift of being a bad speller (like an Irish Tidd he is saying, 'Sir, I Ham a very Bad Hand at Righting'), and the effect of his lovely, rushed distortions – 'woemen', 'immagination', 'gorgious', 'idia' – is to make these letters seem to issue, not from the institution of writing, but from the native oral tradition. This is speech ('He may be hear any time') which has just happened into writing with the minimum of formality, and as a result you feel the tug of those strong kinship bonds which are so much part of oral culture. The Classical scholar Eric Havelock has evoked the oral culture of Ancient Greece as a 'mnemonic world of imitation, aggregative, redundant, copious, traditionalist, warmly human, participatory', and Yeats's letters offer glimpses of that world. They seem to be outside that 'chirographic control' whose dominance Walter Ong questions in his stimulating polemic *Orality and Literacy*. Yeats's carelessness is compulsive and attractive – he apologizes for not rewriting a page which he's just let 'get into some salid oil', he is busy reading a poem 'in long unrhyming lines – alexindrines I think you call them'. These are snatches of unselfconscious talk, and they have all the warm intense presence of urgent speech. It is this oral distinctness which prevents these letters from acquiring or serving a canonical or institutional reality – unlike Pope, Yeats is not writing with one eye on future publication.

Even so, it is easy to sentimentalize orality, especially when the expatriate is nostalgic for the 'trembling light' of Ireland and for the sheer communal crack and pizzazz of the spoken word there. But Yeats knows that power resides in the printed word, and so most of these letters deal with publishing matters, literary politics, tactics aimed at making 'sure of a good review', and nudging reminders like '*Freeman* (have a friend who does the books on it)'. Yeats's essential belief that literary publication is what is nowadays termed 'cultural production' shows when he complains of being 'hard up for Banshee and Pooka stories', a phrase which identifies natural magic with printed texts and paper currency. The Irish *punt*, the coinage of *Sáorstat Éireann*, whose design Senator Yeats would help to choose, wait in the future, but they were brought into existence partly by Yeats's consuming desire to bring oral folk tradition on to the printed page.

Yeats knew that in many respects orality is synonymous with powerlessness and failure (Tidd, the Cato Street Conspirator, was executed, as were untold thousands of Irish rebels), and in *Autobiographies* he remembers how Oscar Wilde once remarked to him 'we are a nation of brilliant failures, but we are the greatest talkers since the Greeks'. In one of his open letters to *United Ireland* he warns that a nation can become 'thoroughly stupefied by oratory', and here Yeats the nationalist cultural impresario attempts to refine and sophisticate those vehement, polarizing simplicities which still to this day bang out from the Irish tradition of public speaking.

The Yeats we hear talking in these letters is a young nation-builder, and it is his relentless dedication to that task which prevents him from appearing to be simply a young man in a hurry, a careerist dipping and dodging through literary London. There are very few revealing personal moments, though occasionally an expatriate wonder breaks through and England is made strange: 'I wonder any body does any thing at Oxford but dream and remember the place is so beautiful. One almost expects the people to sing instead of speaking. It is all – the colleges I meen – like an Opera.' Yeats's saddened alienation gives way the following year to a more confident analysis of the foreignness of England:

This is a most beautiful country, about here – I walked sixteen miles on Sunday – going to the places in Matthew Arnolds poems – the ford in 'the Scholour Gipsey' being furthest away & most interesting. How very unlike Ireland the whole place is – like a foreign land (as it is). One underſtands (a long S, I notice, has got in here out of the book I am copying) English poetry more from seeing a place like this. I only felt at home once – when I came to a steep lane with a ſtream in the middle. The rest one noticed with a foreign eye, picking out the strange and not as in ones own country the familiar things for interest – the fault by the way of all poetry about countries not the writers own. The people, I notice, do not give you 'a fine day' or answer yours, as in Ireland.

It would seem that the expatriate experience is one of being enclosed in a private imaginative ghetto, cut off from manners, landscape, the textures and surfaces of English life – this quietly lacerating sense of isolation is present throughout these letters and must partly account for their restless urgency, their utterly unlaidback style.

Yeats was badly treated by various publishers, and after being messed about by Kegan Paul he wrote to Katharine Tynan:

I am not very hopeful about the book. Somewhat inarticulate have I been I fear. Some thing I had to say. Dont know that I have said it. All seems confused incoherent inarticulate. Yet this I know I am no idle poetaster. My

> life has been in my poems. To make them I have broken my life in a morter as it were. I have brayed in it youth and fellowship peace and worldly hopes. I have seen others enjoying while I stood alone with myself – commenting, commenting – a mere dead mirror on which things reflect themselves. I have buried my youth and raised over it a cairn – of clouds. Some day I shall be articulate perhaps. But this book I have no great hopes of – it is all sluggish incoherent. It may make a few friends perhaps among people of my own sort – that is the most. Do what you can for it.

This is an uncharacteristically personal passage which seems on the one hand dramatically self-conscious, and on the other to be an attempt to answer the Kantian question 'What am I for?' Yeats is describing the revolutionary's sense of being a dead man on leave, of having no personal life, but in doing so he is also engaging in a piece of literary realpolitik – 'Do what you can for it', he concludes. This is the poet as literary strategist and manipulator, issuing a nudging order to a poet whose work he has also promoted.

Early in their friendship, Yeats advised Tynan to 'remember by being as Irish as you can you will be the more origonol and true to your self and in the long run more interesting even to English readers'. This is another version of the expatriate contradiction – inhabiting two places at the one time – and it demands that the Irish writer should help create a national literature by promoting 'that wild Celtic blood, the most un-English of all things under heaven'. The products of all that wildness and blood-magic are then consumed by large numbers of English readers. In a further twist of the contradiction, Yeats reveals now and then that he actually hates the English. He is the archetypal chthonic nationalist, as we can see in his account of a House of Commons debate where Tim Healy, the nationalist MP for Longford, attacked the London *Times* for its publication of forged letters in the notorious 'Parnellism and Crime' series.

Healy, Yeats tells Tynan, 'made a rugged passionate speech the most human thing I heard, I missed Dillon however. Altogather I was delighted with Healey the others on both sides were sophisticated and cultivated in him there was good earth power . . . I hear that Burne Johnes is a furious Home Ruler says he would be a

Dynamiter if an Irishman.' It is a short leap of the tongue from earth power to Home Rule to dynamite, and the editors note that two years before Yeats wrote this letter the Fenians had attempted to blow up the Houses of Parliament. It makes me wonder what Yeats and Burne Jones would have said had they seen Norman Tebbit under the ruins of the Grand Hotel.

For Yeats, 'good earth power' is the force which inspires what he terms 'sound national doctrine'. That doctrinal force is to be felt in political speeches and is to be inculcated by printed texts (notably by a history of Fenianism in a publishing series he wanted to promote). Yeats is concerned to produce and propagate a culture, and his correspondence bulges with accounts of publishing battles and subterfuges. Though he admires what is of the earth, natural, 'Irish', he knows that culture is neither organic nor natural – it is synthetic and artificial, rooted in economics, power, ideology. Yeats's nationalist ideology is sometimes feverish and emotional – as when he is introduced to William Sharp and hates 'his red British face of flaccid contentment' – though he is capable of tolerantly describing his Oxford landlady as 'a good woman with a pale ungenial English face'. As his devoted editors point out, Yeats identified with the radical nationalist tradition – Tone, Emmet, Mitchel – and drew back from the constitutional nationalism of O'Connell. For all the youthful trepidation these letters manifest ('I am afraid I have bothered you . . . I fear you are busy and these questions are a trouble'), the tight core of separatist pride reveals itself when he breaks off from a discussion of publishing business to tell Ellen O'Leary, his mentor John O'Leary's sister:

> I was at a big 'Home Rule' party at a Mrs Hancoks Saturday. Mrs Gladstone was there and made a speach, a very short one, likewise Stransfield, Justin Macarthy, & Lord Aberdeen made speeches long or short. All these good English Home Rule people how they do patronise Ireland and the Irish. As if we were some sort of deserving poor for whom bazars and such like should be got up. Yet they are really in earnest on this Home Rule question I find.

John O'Leary was President of the Supreme Council of the Irish Republican Brotherhood, the radical republican organization to which Yeats belonged and which was to lead the 1916 uprising, nine years after O'Leary's death. As the editors note, O'Leary exerted 'one of the most powerful influences' on the young Yeats because of his role in the struggle for Irish independence (O'Leary was sentenced to hard labour for conspiracy in 1865).

Although many critics have presented Yeats as an agonized liberal humanist, his remoteness from that softer ideology is evidenced by his reaction to the murder in 1889 of Dr P. H. Cronin, an alleged British spy: 'He seems to have been a great rascal. It was really a very becoming thing to remove him – if he be dead and the man found at Chicago be not some one else. A spy has no rights.' This deliberate and pitiless statement, made in a letter to Katharine Tynan, is immediately followed by a characteristic disclaimer: 'There! you will be angry with me for all these dreadful sentiments. I may think the other way to morrow.' And though Yeats placed his imagination on the line, writing always under intense pressure in a great opinionated melt like a uranium rod in a reactor, there is no evidence that he ever moved from visceral nationalism to a pacific gentleness. His public tolerance was strategic and his ideological rejection of Irish Unionism did not lead him to reject Unionists as people or to scorn their traditions (he had after all first discovered 'the pleasure of rhyme' by reading Orange songs in his grandfather's hayloft). He tried to awaken Dublin Unionists to new Irish books, and lectured the Sligo Orangemen on fairy lore: 'I found that the comic tales delighted them but that the poetry of fairy lore was quite lost on them. They held it Catholic superstition I suppose.'

Much of Unionist culture is hostile to art and the underground life of the imagination, but by distinguishing between the politics of the partisan (i.e. an exclusion of Unionists by terming them 'West Britons') and the politics of the patriot, Yeats was able to argue for an inclusive idea of Irish nationhood. In an open letter to *United Ireland* (14 May 1892), he remarked: 'Ireland is between the upper and the nether millstone – between the influence of America and the influence of England, and which of the two is denationalising us most rapidly it is hard to say. Whether we have still to face a long period of struggle, or have come to the land of promise at last, we need all our central fire, all our nationality.' Reading these sentences, I wrap the New Ireland Forum Report round me once again and feel coul. If it's now impossible to be warmed by the central fire of inspired nationalism, what other form of heating is there?

Hibiscus and Salvia Flowers: D. H. Lawrence

Lawrence wrote 'Hibiscus and Salvia Flowers' on 31 January 1921. He was then staying at Fontana Vecchia, in Taormina, Sicily, a popular winter resort under Mount Etna. His poem may be regarded as a distinctively puritan response to the political situation in Italy – it is written to the moment and represents a volatile, complex engagement with Italian socialism. If we regard Lawrence as belonging to the libertarian, essentially right-wing strand within English nonconformism – as embodying an ethic of puritan individualism whose economic philosophy we now term 'monetarism' – it may be possible to argue that 'Hibiscus and Salvia Flowers' represents a movement of sympathy towards an ideological position hostile both to Lawrence's late-Romantic heroism and to individualism.

From 1918 to 1920, there was a growing conviction on the part of the Italian working class that a socialist revolution was inevitable. This conviction was shared by the mass of workers and socialists. However, in March 1919 Mussolini launched his Fascist movement and in the autumn of 1920 his Fascist squads began their punitive expeditions. When the Italian Communist Party was founded in January 1921 (the same month in which Lawrence wrote his poem), the revolutionary wave was on the ebb; the workers had been defeated and had lost their confidence in the possibility of revolution. In Britain, the July unemployment figures showed that 22.4 per cent of all insured workers were unemployed, and it is likely that Lawrence's poem depends on an interplay between his sense of the condition of Britain and the developing political situation in Italy.

Lawrence's political statements are many and confusing, and his essay 'Democracy' can be seen as issuing from an essentially *laissez-faire* philosophy – that doctrine of 'doing as one likes' which Matthew Arnold criticizes in *Culture and Anarchy* and which is hostile to his idea of the state. As a nonconformist and member of a faith and culture which Arnold despised, Lawrence detests the state – it is mechanical, not organic, and it reduces individual human beings to a statistical aggregate: 'What a loathsome little beast he is, this Average, this Unit, this Homunculus. Yet he has his purposes. His is useful to measure by. That's the purpose of all averages.' For Lawrence, the law of averages 'holds good for the stomach', but in 'the free, spontaneous self, one man's meat is truly another man's poison', and it is therefore impossible to 'draw' any average. This brisk distinction between individual spiritual needs and average material necessities enables Lawrence to state confidently:

> Now we will settle for ever the Equality of Man, and the Rights of Man. Society means people living together. People *must* live together. And to live together, they must have some Standard, some *Material* Standard. This is where the Average comes in. And this is where Socialism and Modern Democracy come in. For Democracy and Socialism rest upon the Equality of Man, which is the Average. And this is sound enough, so long as the Average represents the real basic material needs of mankind: basic material needs: we insist and insist again. For Society, or Democracy, or any Political State or Community exists not for the sake of the individual, nor should ever exist for the sake of the individual, but simply to establish the Average, in order to make living together possible: that is, to make proper facilities for every man's clothing, feeding, housing himself, working, sleeping, mating, playing, according to his necessity as a common unit, an average. Everything beyond that common necessity depends on himself alone.

Lawrence argues that the state exists merely for the 'proper adjustment of material means of existence' and for nothing else. The state, he argues, is a 'dead ideal' and nation, democracy and socialism are similarly dead ideals: 'They are just vast hotels, or hostels, where every guest does some scrap of the business of the day's routine – if it's only lounging gracefully to give the appearance of ease – and for this contribution gets his suitable accommodation.'

Lawrence's essay on democracy is part of his argument with Whitman, and when he states that 'the Whitman One Identity, the *En Masse*, is a horrible nullification of true identity and being' Lawrence's puritanism, a puritanism that is necessarily based on the doctrine of the supremacy of the free individual conscience, reject

Whitman's concept of democracy as at best 'servile, serving the free soul', and at worst 'sheer self-destruction'. And like a preacher he rises to this declamatory conclusion:

Let us put them in their place. Let us get over our rage of social activity, public being, universal self-estimation, republicanism, bolshevism, socialism, empire – all these mad manifestations of *En Masse* and One Identity. They are all self-betrayed. Let our Democracy be in the singleness of the clear, clean self, and let our *En Masse* be no more than an arrangement for the liberty of this self. Let us drop looking after our neighbour. It only robs him of his chance of looking after himself. Which is robbing him of his freedom, with a vengeance.

This is in fact a spiritual version of self-help, an ideology which expresses a peculiarly American – and therefore unBritish – hostility to social welfare, to the idea of community, compassion, the need to be responsible for and to other people. It is a naked monetarist ethic which is opposed nowadays by patrician conservatives, socialists, liberals and Marxists. Yet Lawrence belongs also to the opposition because of his hostility to private property, and in the conclusion to 'Democracy' he states: 'If we are to keep our backs unbroken, we must deposit all property on the ground, and learn to walk without it. We must stand aside. And when many men stand aside, they stand in a new world; a new world of man has come to pass. This is the Democracy: the new order.'

Lawrence's letters for the period 1916–21 sometimes support the arguments of 'Democracy' and sometimes run counter to them. Writing to Lady Cynthia Asquith (11 December 1916), he reacts to the news of Asquith's resignation and replacement by Lloyd George:

I too expect a national disaster before very long . . . It is no use adhering to that old 'advanced' crowd – Cambridge, Lowes Dickinson, Bertie Russell, young reformers, Fabians – they are our disease, not our hope. We want a clean sweep, and a new start. And we will have it. Wait only a little longer. Fusty, fuzzy peace-cranks and lovers of humanity are the devil. We must get on a new track altogether. Damn humanity, let us have a bit of inhuman, or non-human truth, that our fuzzy human emotions can't alter.

This is a characteristic rejection of the middle ground, of compassion and of liberal humanism – it glints with that distinctive modernist cruelty and resembles an ideological, committed cast of mind.

Here, as so often in his work, Lawrence appears to occupy a position on the extreme right, and in March 1920 he writes to Samuel Koteliansky: 'What remaining belief I had in Socialism dies out of me more and more as the time goes by.' Nine months later, again writing from Sicily, Lawrence tells Eleanor Farjeon: 'If I knew how to, I'd really join myself to the revolutionary socialists now. I think the time has come for a real struggle. That's the only thing I care for: the death struggle. I don't care for politics. But I know there *must* and *should* be a deadly revolution very soon, and I would take part in it if I knew how.' Ten days later Lawrence wrote 'Hibiscus and Salvia Flowers', a poem that dramatizes, like a personal letter or a quick, urgent piece of journalism, his feelings about revolutionary socialism.

The poem begins with a noisy refrain based on the traditional children's song 'Hark hark/the dogs do bark/the beggars are coming to town', which is also echoed in Ariel's first song in *The Tempest*. So the socialists are beggars who disturb the peace, intruders like the mariners who land on Shakespeare's mediterranean island. Dressed in the 'same unremarkable Sunday suit', the Sicilian socialists are young and loutish and stare with the 'gang-stare' and 'a half-threatening envy'. 'They' look at 'us', and by 'us' Lawrence means 'every *forestière*,/Every lordly tuppenny foreigner from the hotels, fattening on the exchange'. It is clear from a letter Lawrence wrote two weeks earlier that he was uneasy at being identified with the rich foreigners in the hotels. Writing to Dr Anton Kippenberg, he gives detailed information about the differing prices of hotel rooms and adds: 'My wife and I are poor people. We live here and keep house for ourselves. So we know well enough what it is to be scared of hôtel prices.'

The initial voice of the poem, however, is elegantly and confidently hostile towards the socialists, who are 'Sans any distinction at all except loutish commonness'. They are '-Ists! -Ists!', hissing ideologists:

Bolshevists,
Leninists,
Communists,
Socialists.

But in answer to the question which immediately precedes this litany – 'How do we know then, that they are they?' – Lawrence says, 'Alas, salvia and hibiscus flowers', and he lovingly repeats the phrase, a phrase which both smooths out and preserves something of that hissing, spitting exclamation: '-Ists! -Ists!' There is a lovely combination of broad open vowels with a sticky fricative in the phrase 'Salvia and hibiscus flowers', and it is hard to avoid hearing a pun on saliva.

It is at this point that we can begin to discern the form of Lawrence's poem: it is based on the technique of personal witness familiar to anyone who has listened to street preachers or attended evangelical church services. In a reprise of the opening refrain – and a reprise is one of the necessary techniques of extempore witness – Lawrence cries: 'Hark! Hark! / The dogs do bark! Salvia and hibiscus flowers.' He then introduces a standard puritan allusion to the Book of Exodus, asking 'Who smeared their doors with blood?' The socialists are like the Israelites in Egypt – the red flowers they wear are reminiscent of the Israelites' blood-smeared door-posts: 'And the blood shall be to you for a token upon the houses where ye are: and when I see the blood, I will pass over you, and the plague shall not be upon you to destroy you, when I smite the land of Egypt.'

Lawrence's allusion to this verse from Exodus isn't simply personal – it springs naturally from his nonconformist, puritan inheritance. The Book of Exodus was central to the English puritan imagination and we may compare Lawrence's use of it with Richardson's in *Pamela*: 'I think I was loth to leave the house. Can you believe it? – what could be the matter with me, I wonder? . . . Surely I cannot be like the old murmuring Israelites, to long after the onions and garlic of Egypt, when they had suffered there such heavy bondage?' We may compare this with a statement by the contemporary puritan preacher Dr Ian Paisley:

Egypt – Moses forsook Egypt. Egypt offered leisure, pleasure (the pleasures of sin for a season) and it offered him treasure. Leisure, pleasure and treasure – they're all in the party interest. He laid them on the altar and instead he choosed to be an heir of heaven. He choosed the affliction of the people of God. *Moses* – his name is eternally linked with the lord of life and glory – what a reward compared with the beggarly elements of Egypt!

To Lawrence, therefore, these Sicilian socialists represent the chosen people about to break out of their Egyptian bondage, their enslavement by a tourist economy, by foreigners. And we remember that just two weeks earlier Lawrence had written that he and his wife were 'poor people' who knew what it was to be scared of hotel prices. Although he compares state socialism to a hotel in his essay 'Democracy', he here feels uncomfortable at being identified with the hotel dwellers, while the socialists appear as native free spirits outside hotel life. Wearing their bright red flowers, they are marked out, separated, chosen. They challenge the beggarly elements of Egypt – are beggars no longer – and do not hanker for its onions and garlic.

The flowers now 'Bloom along the Corso on the living, perambulating bush', but the poem's interrogative voice enacts the idea of presumption:

> Who said they might assume these blossoms?
> What god did they consult?
>
> Rose-red, princess hibiscus, rolling her pointed Chinese petals!
> Azalea and camellia, single peony
> And pomegranate bloom and scarlet mallow-flower
> And all the eastern, exquisite royal plants
> That noble blood has brought us down the ages!
> Gently nurtured, frail and splendid
> Hibiscus flower –
> Alas, the Sunday coats of Sicilian bolshevists!

The flowers aren't simply natural and organic – they are the product of culture, training, breeding, tradition. They are royal plants, 'gently nurtured' and associated with 'noble blood'. It is as though the socialists have expropriated, suddenly and completely, both nature and aristocratic culture. Interestingly, Lawrence combines primitivism with high culture: 'Rose of the oldest races of princesses, Polynesian/Hibiscus'. Here, the allusion is clearly to Gauguin, whose *Noa Noa* Lawrence had been reading six months earlier, and whose work was a major influence on Lawrence's painting. In a letter to Robert Mounsier (12 July 1920), he refers to Gauguin, to Maugham's *The Moon and Sixpence* and to Melville's *Typee*, and exclaims: "To think what has become of Melville's beautiful Typee! A million curses on European civilisation. It is collapsing, and it deserves to collapse. I spit on it." The socialists with their salvia and hibiscus flowers are outside hotels, outside European civilization by their association through the flowers with an ancient Polynesian aristocracy.

The reference to Eve ('Eve, in her happy moments,/Put hibiscus in her hair') follows this primitivist theme and is consonant with the supreme image of English puritanism – Adam and Eve in the garden before the Fall. This aligns the prelapsarian Eve with a Polynesian princess, but it then forces Lawrence to confront the argument deep in his own imagination between the radical idea of human rights and a conservative idea of tradition, duty, hierarchy, art:

The exquisite and ageless aristocracy
Of a peerless soul,
Blessed are the pure in heart and the fathomless in bright pride;
The loveliness that knows *noblesse oblige;*
The native royalty of red hibiscus flowers;
The exquisite assertion of new delicate life
Risen from the roots:
Is this how you'll have it, red-decked socialists,
Hibiscus-breasted?

The socialists are interrogated as to whether they embody a Jeffersonian idea of natural aristocracy, but there is a confusing transition from this to the echo of the Sermon on the Mount ('Blessed are the pure in heart') and to the quietistic meekness of 'The loveliness that knows *noblesse oblige*'. There would appear to be an irreconcilable argument in Lawrence's imagination between what in 'Democracy' he terms 'the singleness of the clear, clean self' and feudalism, hierarchy, aristocracy. Lawrence solves the problem by treating these irreconcilables as if they belong together, and cries:

> If it be so, I fly to join you,
> And if it be not so, brutes to pull down hibiscus flowers!

This is an echo of his letter of eleven days earlier to Eleanor Farjeon, in which he expressed a wish to 'really join myself to the revolutionary socialists now'.

Turning to the blazing scarlet spikes of the salvia flower, he exclaims:

> Or salvia!
> Or dragon-mouthed salvia with gold throat of wrath!
> Flame-flushed, enraged, splendid salvia,
> Cock-crested, crowing your orange scarlet like a tocsin
> Along the Corso all this Sunday morning.

Clearly this is Lawrence's dated and sexist phallic consciousness, and it is meant to supplement or complement the figures of Eve and of the Polynesian princesses. It prompts a shift in tone – to a type of macho taunting which may be strategic:

> Is your wrath red as salvias,
> You socialists?
> You with your grudging, envious, furtive rage,
> In Sunday suits and yellow boots along the Corso.
> You look well with your salvia flowers, I must say.

Lawrence now moves to an identification with the 'dawn-cock's comb flaring flower' which is a version of that wish to join the 'death struggle' which he had expressed in his letter to Eleanor Farjeon. It is hard for us now to read these lines – this is a romantic poetry of terrorism, of mass terror, of extermination:

> I long to be a bolshevist
> And set the stinking rubbish-heap of this foul world
> Afire at a myriad scarlet points,

A bolshevist, a salvia-face
To lick the world with flame that licks it clean.
I long to see its chock-full crowdedness
And glutted squirming populousness on fire
Like a field of filthy weeds
Burnt back to ash,
And then to see the new, real souls sprout up.

This is the climax of the poem, and it issues, I believe, both from the historical currents of the age and from that intransigence and destructiveness which are so much a part of the Protestant temperament. Six years later, Yeats was to end 'In Memory of Eva Gore-Booth and Con Markiewicz' with the lines:

We the great gazebo built,
They convicted us of guilt;
Bid me strike a match and blow.

Nourished as it is on the Book of Revelation, the Protestant imagination reacts to extreme pressure by imagining apocalypse, purging fire, a new order.

Confronting the spectacle of a mass political movement, an ideology which denies the importance and primacy of the individual, and which in this specific case sends out party members with dandyish buttonholes, Lawrence becomes a kind of demonic gardener fighting the 'wicked, obstreperous weeds' and attacking 'a cabbage-idealistic level of equality'. His puritanism identifies with their puritanism, but he cannot follow them in believing in equality. It is at this point that Lawrence moves the conflict in the poem to that between his romantic conception of his supreme individuality and the threat posed to that individuality by 'the louts along the Corso'. The vocal tone, it seems to me, is deliberately hysterical, as if he is enacting a realization that he must surrender his personality to the socialists:

What rot, to see the cabbage and hibiscus-tree
As equals!
What rot, to say the louts along the Corso

In Sunday suits and yellow shoes
Are my equals!
I am their superior, saluting the hibiscus flower, not them.
The same I say to the profiteers from the hotels, the money-fat-ones,
Profiteers here being called dog-fish, stinking dog-fish, sharks.
The same I say to the pale and elegant persons,
Pale-face authorities loitering tepidly:
That I salute the red hibiscus flowers
And send mankind to its inferior blazes.
Mankind's inferior blazes,
And these along with it, all the inferior lot –
These bolshevists,
These dog-fish,
These precious and ideal ones,
All rubbish ready for fire.

By separating the hibiscus flowers from the socialists and then lumping the socialists with the dog-fish, the profiteers, and 'all the inferior lot', Lawrence begins to climb out of his uneasy, sometimes hysterical querulousness, until he is able to solve the contradictions in his response by saying:

> And I salute hibiscus and the salvia flower
> Upon the breasts of loutish bolshevists,
> Damned loutish bolshevists,
> Who perhaps will do the business after all,
> In the long run, in spite of themselves.

In the calculated over-protestation here there seems to be a residual admiration for the bolshevist louts. And echoing Milton's opening paragraph to Book III of *Paradise Lost* ('but not to me returns / Day, or the sweet approach of Ev'n or Morn'), Lawrence moves into a stance of desperate puritan isolation:

> Meanwhile, alas
> For me no fellow-men,
> No salvia-frenzied comrades, antennae
> Of yellow-red, outreaching, living wrath

Upon the smouldering air,
And throat of brimstone-molten angry gold.
Red, angry men are a race extinct, alas!

Never
To be a bolshevist
With a hibiscus flower behind my ear
In sign of life, of lovely, dangerous life
And passionate disquality of men;
In sign of dauntless, silent violets,
And impudent nettles grabbing the under-earth,
And cabbages born to be cut and eat,
And salvia fierce to crow and shout for fight,
And rosy-red hibiscus wincingly
Unfolding all her coiled and lovely self
In a doubtful world.

This is Samson as impotent aesthete, wishing to be part of the God of Wrath, but helpless and powerless. And in a characteristic puritan hoisting movement, Lawrence concludes:

But yet
If they pull all the world down,
The process will amount to the same in the end.
Instead of flame and flame-clean ash,
Slow waters rotting back to level muck
And final humus,
Whence the re-start.

And still I cannot bear it
That they take hibiscus and the salvia flower.

It is a statement of loss and isolation, as if they have a power and a beauty he does not have access to, as if he cannot finally surrender his personality to comradeship and ideology and the dragonish dandyish beauty of the flowers. Like 'Snake', this poem is about wanting to lose self-conscious individuality and being unable to. If the desire for destruction seems with historical hindsight to be fascistic, it may in the context of Lawrence's culture and upbringing spring from the extremes of puritan subjectivity. In Joyce's terms, Catholicism is a coherent absurdity and Protestantism an incoherent absurdity. Here, in Lawrence's imagination, the incoherent clashes with the coherent; like Yeats's rose-poems, 'Hibiscus and Salvia Flowers' is a study in the temptations, dangers and attractions of the surrender of personal subjectivity to an élitist activism and an ideal of absolute beauty. In the end Lawrence feels that his freedom as an artist isn't necessarily threatened by the ideological commitment. It may be that the Sicilian socialists incarnate an aesthetic freedom he thought he owned absolutely and which was his by right – perhaps by 'noblesse oblige'. It is because of this subversive and disturbing challenge that he concludes:

> And still I cannot bear it
> That they take hibiscus and the salvia flower.

It is a poignantly self-critical conclusion to the poem, and one which confronts Lawrence with the need to relinquish his own hysteria and self-conscious posturing – with the need to reject the very rant out of which this beautiful poem springs.

Poetry and Power:
Robert Frost

Staked under box hedges, taut along the edges of ordinary middle-class gardens in smalltown America, pink plastic tapes mark the exact legal dimensions of each portion of real estate. Something chilling, something you can't quite identify, about that stretched pink tape. Each plot might be the site of an accident or Locke's idea of the individual soul – a precise autonomous identity, founded on private property, inscribed in title deeds, and forever trying to repudiate a lingering anxiety that might be the memory of some calamity.

This anxiety is a subject Frost shares with Dickinson, though his reticence often aims to conceal the paranoid personal and social insecurity she dissects:

> There came a Wind like a Bugle –
> It quivered through the Grass
> And a Green Chill upon the Heat
> So ominous did pass
> We barred the Windows and the Doors
> As from an Emerald Ghost –
> The Doom's electric Moccasin
> That very instant passed –

A sudden spasm of terror shivers through the puritan conscience, and this is metaphorically dramatized as the start of a battle between armies whose Indian scouts threaten the security of the private property 'we' own. This fear is the seething original ground of our being: it erupts without warning, melting the boredom of a small town in Massachusetts into an expressionist nightmare where fences turn into fugitives, houses become rivers and trees pant like a mob.

Frost's closed quatrains in 'Trespass' admit only a slight anxiety:

No, I had set no prohibiting sign,
And yes, my land was hardly fenced.
Nevertheless, the land was mine:
I was being trespassed on and against.

Whoever the surly freedom took
Of such an unaccountable stay
Busying by my woods and brook
Gave me a strangely restless day.

The trespasser may have been looking for fossils, 'in which there was little property right', but it was not the value of the fossils he stood to lose that worried Frost, it was the trespasser's 'ignoring what was whose'. He was threatening that clenched pride, that absolute certainty of ownership which is so fundamental to the culture of the United States. If the trespasser was the catalyst for the anxiety that frets beneath that apparently solid certainty, he was also capable of tactfully soothing the fears his intrusion on to Frost's private space had provoked:

Then came his little acknowledgement:
He asked for a drink at the kitchen door,
An errand he may have had to invent,
But it made my property mine once more.

By becoming a suppliant, the trespasser allowed the laureate of American individualism to assert property right.

Frost's status as national poet must in part be based on this tactic of acknowledging and then propitiating that North American unease about property and land ownership. 'The land was ours before we were the land's' means that we first acquired it as private property – as real estate – before we were able to bond with the land in the same way that the Indians whom we displaced once had. But this is a process Frost can't confront directly; instead he shunts it into a parenthesis – '(The deed of gift was many deeds of war)' – which serves as a rhetorical pause to launch the poem's triumphal invocation to the land:

vaguely realizing westward,
But still unstoried, artless, unenhanced,
Such as she was, such as she would become.

This version of Manifest Destiny wipes out Indian culture, which is why the trespasser can only examine and appropriate fragments of the fossil record, for there is no other relic from the time between the Upper Carboniferous Period, 300 million years ago, and the arrival of the Pilgrim Fathers.

Frost's land in 'Trespass' is almost without fences, but in 'Mending Wall' he and his neighbour reassert property rights by collaborating in the wall's repair:

I see him there,
Bringing a stone grasped firmly by the top
In each hand, like an old-stone savage armed.

Frost deploys this corny image of a caveman looming out of the darkness of prehistory in order to put a critical distance between himself and his more property-conscious neighbour. The ruse almost succeeds, until we consider just how European that cliché is. This is the culture that would create those aboriginal New Yorkers, the Flintstones, who are the comic remnants of one of the deepest puritan delusions.

This puritan dreamtime is one of Frost's assorted subjects in 'New Hampshire':

I call her old. She has one family
Whose claim is good to being settled here
Before the era of colonization,
And before that of exploration even.
John Smith remarked them as he coasted by,
Dangling their legs and fishing off a wharf
At the Isles of Shoals, and satisfied himself
They weren't Red Indians but veritable
Pre-primitives of the white race, dawn people,
Like those who furnished Adam's sons with wives;
However uninnocent they may have been

In being there so early in our history.
They'd been there then a hundred years or more.

John Smith is the English explorer (1580–1631) who was the principal founder of the first permanent English settlement in North America, at Jamestown, Virginia. Frost invokes him as a witness to the absolute right of all White Anglo-Saxon Protestants to be in North America – a right which stems from those autochthonous, 'pre-primitives of the white race' Smith claimed to have seen on his explorations.

This belief in the civilizing mission of WASP America – a population group Harry Truman called 'the good stock' – underpins both the European imagery Frost deploys at certain crucial moments and his numerous racist remarks. (For example, 'I prefer to contract my skin diseases from white people as being more likely to be white diseases.' Letter to Louis Untermeyer, 23 August 1920.) There is an ideological position concealed in the casual, touristy 'Cliff Dwelling' where he sees a cavern hole:

Where someone used to climb and crawl
To rest from his besetting fears.
I see the callus on his sole,
The disappearing last of him
And of his race starvation slim,
Oh, years ago – ten thousand years.

Because geography is a form of history, the poem is given no location; then the imaginary caveman is pushed back ten millennia, even though American Indians were cave-dwellers in much more recent times. Frost displaces his own fear – the anxiety that goes with ownership and property right – on to this possible pre-primitive, then wafts it away in that genially dismissive last line whose rhyme-word first softens and then soothingly abolishes any kind of bother.

Frost is a master of this rhetorical technique: using a vocal gesture, a pause, a parenthesis, a sudden sound, he conceals the gaps in his subject. In 'The Vanishing Red' it is the miller's weird, vicious, blocked-off laugh that simultaneously recognizes and conceals a gap in the historical record. The miller is supposed to have seen 'the last Red Man' in Acton, Mass., though:

> You can't get back and see it as he saw it.
> It's too long a story to go into now.
> You'd have to have been there and lived it.
> Then you wouldn't have looked on it as just a matter
> Of who began it between the two races.

If we could have been there – that is, been alive in the early nineteenth century when the poem is set – then we might be able to see the real subject of this poem, which is not the non-subject, the non-issue, of who began it between the two races. The apparent subject of the poem – the miller's murder of the Indian – is never described: it happens off-stage, like Duncan's murder, and this controls the poem's emotional sympathies. Instead, the poem seems to centre on the miller's curious laugh, which 'gave no one else a laugher's license'.

Hayden Carruth argues that what that laugh means is the 'heart' of Frost's poetic temperament: 'the blackest, bitterest despair in three hundred years of the New England tradition'. This is too generous to an evasion, for it suggests that we should sympathize with the executioner, not his victim. The real core of the poem is not the miller's laugh, but these lines which follow Frost's brushing off of who began it between the two races:

> Some guttural exclamation of surprise
> The Red Man gave in poking about the mill,
> Over the great big thumping shuffling millstone,
> Disgusted the Miller physically as coming
> From one who had no right to be heard from.

Originally the last line read:

> From a person who the less he attracted
> Attention to himself you would have thought the better.

Frost's revision shifts responsibility for a prejudiced attitude on to the miller, though that distinctly unjolly figure is really no more than a mask for Frost's Yankee beliefs and reticences.

Reuben Brower, one of the academics Frost flattered and manipulated, defends 'The Vanishing Red' in what purports to be a tough-minded conservative reading of the poem that mocks those 'tender readers who have read it not as a drama but as a defense':

Can it be, they all but ask, that Frost is in favor of shoving Indians down manholes in mills? What the poem catches – consecrates almost – is the old and respectable tradition of savagery in this country, the belief, not entirely unfounded, that Indians were not civilized. But the story-teller reimagines this feeling not 'as just a matter of who began it' but as freshly experienced in a 'guttural exclamation'. A moment of 'meanness', if you will, is grasped fully and that is the poem's 'moral'. To 'take rank hold' of any form of life is to have learned something about what we are and to prepare us for the return from *Walden*.

Brower views the poem as bravely entering into a moment of 'meanness' – a euphemism for racism – and he endorses the traditional (he calls it 'respectable') idea of white civilizers, Indian savages. The poem upholds that idea by identifying a historical process – those many deeds of war – with the sounds made by white technology. That great big thumping shuffling grindstone is the active memory of war,* and it substitutes for all that Frost dismisses as 'too long a story to go into now'. Instead of an unstoried narrative – itself a contradiction in terms – we have a symbolic noise which

*In Seamus Heaney's 'Churning Day' the churning process becomes subtly symbolic of historical suffering. There may be an allusion to Frost's 'The Vanishing Red' in these lines:

> The staff, like a great whisky muddler fashioned
> in deal wood, was plunged in, the lid fitted.
> My mother took first turn, set up rhythms
> that slugged and thumped for hours. Arms ached.
> Hands blistered. Cheeks and clothes were spattered
> with flabby milk.

By comparing the staff to a 'whisky muddler', Heaney refuses to allow it to exist simply as an authentic peasant artefact. He denies it innocence, just as Frost imputes sinister qualities to the milling process. The shuffling millstone becomes a critically placed, totemistic symbol of white 'civilization'.

makes the cramped, claustrophobic mill resemble a torture, or an execution, chamber.

The Indian's surprised guttural exclamation affects the miller with a physical disgust that prompts him boastfully to revenge himself on the last red man by revealing what lies below the manhole in the floor, and then – we read into the narrative gap – shoving the Indian into the millrace. The miller familiarly refers to the Indian as 'John', almost like an executioner who has a personal friendship with his victim which somehow modifies, but cannot interfere with, the regrettable professional task he must carry out. But John is allowed only that one exclamation, and this emphasizes his lack of any right to exist, an absence which reassures Brower and other readers.

This may seem decisively biased until we realize that the poem's actual vocalization, its subtle sentence-sound, plays against the traditional attitude it offers those lazy 'eye-readers', as Frost termed them. That vocal counterpoint is created by a cunning series of natural internal rhymes which allows John's single utterance to reverberate through the lines that follow. Thus the *uh*-sound in 'guttural' and 'surprise' is picked up by those same sounds in 'thumping shuffling' and 'disgusted'. It's as if the Indian reacts to the grindstone with an instinctive *ugh!* But because he is a dumb, almost non-person, he cannot react in such a direct manner – Frost's lines must encode his gut reaction. Angered by that reaction, the miller must get his revenge; and being boastful as millers traditionally are he throws open the manhole to show:

> The water in desperate straits like frantic fish,
> Salmon and sturgeon, lashing with their tails.

The manhole opens like the lid of a chest – see my riches! the miller might be gloating; I own nature, its creatures and its energies. Those energies may be cramped and 'desperate', but they have to be because the mill wheel couldn't turn without them.

This is surely the moral of 'Out, Out – ', where the men turn to their affairs after the boy's death under ether. The snarling, rattling buzz saw – a mechanized serpent – and the shuffling millstone are kin, they have to go on, no matter who dies. So the end justifies the means: for technology and progress to continue, people have to die, they have to lash frantically or be lashed frantically. The millrace is the current of history, the packed surge of human suffering, both becoming and necessity. Frost is justifying both the American industrial revolution and the early colonists' violent seizure of the land. Pain, he implies, is historically necessary.

What, then, does the manhole with the ring in it signify? It allows us to look down into a kind of sewer, then its ring jangles 'even above the general noise'. Ring-bangle or manacle? A trapdoor and below it a cramped ship's hold? Is the miller showing John a ship full of slaves? If so, he is exulting in his power over men and women, as well as over nature. The Indian is being forced to recognize the power which drives the wheel of state and is being told that he belongs down there with the wild, trapped fish. The miller owns him, too, and can do with him what he wants. The last line collusively exults in the miller's power: 'Oh, yes, he showed John the wheel pit all right.' We are left with a hardnosed Yankee understatement which is voiced by an onlooker rather than by the poet himself.

Despite this poem's acoustically coded criticism of pragmatic puritan values, Frost aimed to make himself become 'Yankier and Yankier'. Interviewed by a journalist in 1917, he was careful to present himself as 'a Yankee to the backbone', a puritan poet whose ancestors found New Hampshire in 1630: 'One of them was an Indian fighter, and a cunning one', Frost says. 'He invited the Indians to a barbecue. They stacked their arms, and he promptly killed them. Unfortunately for that ancestor, he didn't kill all of them. A few who were left came back after him on a Sunday morning after he'd finished praying, and got even.' This ancestor was Charles Frost, who was born in Tiverton, Devonshire, in 1631 and killed by Indians in 1697. Frost's biographer, Lawrance Thompson, notes that Charles Frost was a 'ruthless killer' whose body the Indians dug up immediately after burial, then carried to the top of a hill, now known as 'Frost's Hill', where they hanged it from a stake.

In his selection of Frost's letters, Thompson prints the previously unpublished poem 'Genealogy', where Charles Frost is remembered for having aspired:

> To wipe out the whole of an Indian tribe to order,
> As in those extravagant days they wasted the woods
> With fire to clear the land for tillage.

The poem ends with Charles Frost's reburial under a heavy stone:

> And there he lies in glory the ancestor of a good many of us.
> And I think he explains my lifelong liking for Indians.

This must be a coat-trailing irony, because earlier in the poem Frost describes the Indians who escaped the barbecue massacre as:

> An awkward remnant that would have lain, methinks,
> Even upon my somewhat sophisticated conscience
> Given to the sympathetic fallacy of attributing to savages
> The feelings of human beings,
> More heavily than those who were slain.

By 'conscience', Frost means 'memory': his ancestor's lapse of memory allowed the survivors to regroup and slay him in turn 'with great barbarity'.

Frost's attitude towards the Indians appears contradictory: in a letter to his socialist friend the poet and critic Louis Untermeyer, he recalls that as an adolescent he wrote a poem celebrating the 'bad night' the Spaniards gave the Indians when they drove them back from Tenochtitlán. Elsewhere Frost speaks of 'my Indian vindictiveness', a trope which sloughs off responsibility for a vicious emotion on to another race. On the other hand, Frost identified his theory of sentence-sound, which is as central to his poetic as Hopkins's theory of inscape is to his, with the American Indians:

> If we go back far enough we will discover that the sound of sense existed before words, that something in the voice or vocal gesture made primitive man convey a meaning to his fellow before the race developed a more elaborate and concrete symbol of communication in language. I have even read that our American Indians possessed, besides a picture-language, a means of communication (though it was not said how far it was developed)

by the sound of sense. And what is this but calling up with the imagination, and recognizing, the images of sound?

Frost made this statement in 1915, but four years later he thought differently. In a note to one of Frost's letters, Untermeyer states that a number of writers were 'causing a stir with books purporting to prove that the basic American rhythm was that of the Indian'. They argued:

> that our most indigenous poetry was in what they called the Amerindian song. Robert was one of those who maintained that, stirring as the Indian songs may be to the Indians, they were not, and could not be, part of our cultural heritage. He proved this by reading three different versions of one Indian chant which, according to the three translators, incorporated three different symbols and meant three different things.

Frost's nativism denies any Indian presence in what constitutes 'our' cultural heritage.

In a letter written in September 1915, four months after the interview in the *Boston Evening Transcript* where he stated that sentence-sound might be Indian, Frost explained that those sounds or 'sentence tones':

> are always there – living in the cave of the mouth. They are real cave things: they were before words were. And they are as definitely things as any image of sight. The most creative imagination is only their summoner. But summoning them is not all. They are only lovely when thrown and drawn and displayed across spaces of the footed line. Everyone knows that except a free-verster.

This is the European cliché again, but as Frost speaks and writes a European language, isn't it natural he should summon the cave image in trying to define the actual *Dasein* of that language? My hunch is that Frost identified free verse, which he hated, with Indian culture.

The two come together in a poem Frost disliked, Amy Lowell's 'Funeral Song for the Indian Chief Blackbird':

> Aï! Aï! Aï! Aï!
> The Morning Star and the Young Morning Star
> Are together in the sky above the prairie,

How far have you already gone from us?
Our blood drips slowly,
The wounds are closing,
It is time we pulled out the willow sprays
And left this place
Before the rising of the sun.

Frost was particularly hostile to these lines, confiding to Untermeyer in 1920: 'All I want to say about Amy is she had better enquire of the Smithsonian Institute if the Indian or any other American but H.D. (and she's an expatriate) wails in the two separate vowels "a" and "i" after the Greeks.' Although Lowell's poem is overlong, and as Frost says 'thin', its fairly deft free verse rings with sympathy for Indian culture. It is that sympathy which provokes Frost. He is annoyed that the Indians might mourn like the Greeks, because this challenges his central neoclassical ambition which is to relocate Virgil and Theocritus in North America.

With its standard props – buggy, horse, lantern, stove, load of grain – Frost's insistent homeyness may appear simply vernacular and nativist, like Andrew Wyeth's 'Wood Stove'. But behind this grainy populist surface there is a polished, wryly confident neoclassicism that locates Jefferson's ideal agrarian republic in slow-paced, often monosyllabic lines that have the look and texture, the restrained evenness, of Latin verse. 'For, Once, Then, Something' is written, as Richard Poirier notes in his remarkable study of Frost, in hendecasyllables, but who would spot the classical paradigm behind the apparently vernacular 'Truth? A pebble of quartz? For once, then, something.' This appears to be absolutely unbuttoned, casually spontaneous speech, though it is in fact formally perfect. It is Catullus in New England.

Frost's preference is for the monosyllable – sturdy, practical, honest, son-of-a-gun authentic, but never the simple index of his native pragmatism that it appears to be. Never quite, because a sequence of monosyllables can arrest the progress of a line and make it move forward very slowly indeed:

Is it too late
To drag you out for just a good-night call
On the old peach trees on the knoll, to grope
By starlight in the grass for a last peach
The neighbors may not have taken as their right
When the house wasn't lived in?

Forty-two monosyllabic words, only five bisyllables – the lines move very slowly, with a decorous formality that strains and stretches their simple diction too tightly. Frost aims to slow down the iambic line, almost to arrest its progress altogether, so that the sound of sense is taken beyond itself into the soundless heaven of the classics where we can count syllables but never hear them as they once were spoken.* It is hard to explain this sleight of hand, a trick which is most visible when it doesn't quite come off and so forces the lines to read like a translation from another language. In 'In the Home Stretch', Frost fails to give a marble solidity to the old peach trees on the knoll. The leisured speech of the couple is too obviously Theocritian and idyllic, especially as they have just moved house – a trauma that in folklore is deemed second only to a bereavement.

'The Wood-Pile', though, conjures a classical monument in the backwoods with immense assurance:

*Writing to Sidney Cox (19 January 1914), Frost explained the limitations of Robert Bridges's theory of poetry:

'He rides two hobbies tandem, his theory that syllables in English have fixed quantity that cannot be disregarded in reading verse, and his theory that with forty or fifty or sixty characters he can capture and hold for all time the sounds of speech. One theory is as bad as the other and I think owing to much the same fallacy. The living part of a poem is the intonation entangled somehow in the syntax idiom and meaning of a sentence. It is only there for those who have heard it previously in conversation. It is not for us in any Greek or Latin poem because our ears have not been filled with the tones of Greek or Roman talk. It is the most volatile and at the same time important part of poetry. It goes and the language becomes a dead language, the poetry dead poetry. With it go the accents the stresses the delays that are not the property of vowels and syllables but that are shifted at will with the sense. Vowels have length there is no denying. But the accent of sense supercedes all other accent overrides and sweeps it away.'

It was a cord of maple, cut and split
And piled – and measured, four by four by eight.
And not another like it could I see.
No runner tracks in this year's snow looped near it.
And it was older sure than this year's cutting,
Or even last year's or the year's before.

This is a risky, Wordsworthian banality in the frozen swamp, but the somehow unassuming cord of maple then takes on the qualities of a tomb or monument, even an entangled fasces:

The wood was gray and the bark warping off it
And the pile somewhat sunken. Clematis
Had wound strings round and round it like a bundle.
What held it, though, on one side was a tree
Still growing, and on one a stake and prop,
These latter about to fall. I thought that only
Someone who lived in turning to fresh tasks
Could so forget his handiwork on which
He spent himself, the labor of his ax,
And leave it there far from a useful fireplace
To warm the frozen swamp as best it could
With the slow smokeless burning of decay.

These lines may carry a slight allusion to Poussin's 'Et in Arcadia Ego', or perhaps Frost is following Cézanne and trying to paint Poussin from nature? Thus he drops the classical figures in Poussin's painting while retaining the spears ('stake and prop') and a tree.

Poussin made Rome his adopted home, and Frost's lines carry an almost invisible allusion both to that city and to three English poets who were inspired by it:

Go thou to Rome, – at once the Paradise,
The grave, the city, and the wilderness;
And where its wrecks like shattered mountains rise,
And flowering weeds, and fragrant copses dress
The bones of Desolation's nakedness
Pass, till the spirit of the spot shall lead

Thy footsteps to a slope of green access
Where, like an infant's smile, over the dead
A light of laughing flowers along the grass is spread;

And gray walls moulder round, on which dull Time
Feeds, like slow fire upon a hoary brand;
And one keen pyramid with wedge sublime,
Pavilioning the dust of him who planned
This refuge for his memory, doth stand
Like flame transformed to marble; and beneath,
A field is spread, on which a newer band
Have pitched in Heaven's smile their camp of death,
Welcoming him we lose with scarce extinguished breath.

Frost's cord of maple is a monument, a tiny pavilion in a frozen swamp, just as Shelley's Rome is paradise, grave, city, wilderness. Both are decorated with flowering weeds, both are being consumed slowly by time – 'slow fire upon a hoary brand', 'the slow smokeless burning of decay' – yet the very slowness of time becomes a metaphor for tradition and immortality. The images and intentions are identical, almost as though in writing his poem Frost is taking up a torch Shelley has handed him.

In 'Adonais' Shelley refers to a monument to a long-forgotten Roman called Cestius – 'one keen pyramid with wedge sublime' – which acts as a landmark in the cemetery and which inspired Hardy's poem 'Rome: At the Pyramid of Cestius near the Graves of Shelley and Keats'. Hardy praises Cestius for doing a 'finer thing' in death 'all silently':

In beckoning pilgrim feet
With marble finger high
To where, by shadowy wall and history-haunted street
Those matchless singers lie . . .

Frost's poem, though not obviously so, is as 'history-haunted' as Hardy's rather touristy verses about the Protestant Cemetery in Rome. Frost is equally fascinated by a monument and by the invisible creator of that monument (Cestius is virtually unknown;

the backwoodsman is anonymous and invisible, maybe even dead).

'Adonais' was published in 1821, Hardy's poem in 1901, Frost's in 1914. So 'The Wood-Pile' takes its place confidently as the expression of a long cultural tradition that begins in ancient Rome and finds renewal in a New England swamp. That renewal isn't just a matter of being the next poem in the line – it can be felt in the fact that Frost knows, but never says, that his poem is so much better than Shelley's strained elegy and Hardy's formulaic pieties.

Listening to Frost's lovely last line – 'With the slow smokeless burning of decay' – we let those two long 'O's draw the sound out till the poem slows to an absolute standstill. This is that sense of monumental permanence and classical fixity which Frost is asserting ('Ours is a more Senatorial democracy like the Republic of Rome', he wrote to President Kennedy). This New World neoclassicism overlooks Indian culture in order to reassure American readers that even in a swamp may be found traces of the Old World their ancestors left. 'The Wood-Pile' is therefore a version of that 'glory of a next Augustan age' Frost was to promise nearly half a century later in the lines he wrote for Kennedy's inauguration. It enhances the land with yet another artful 'storey'.

Frost prophesied the union of 'poetry and power' during the Kennedy presidency because he shared Yeats's dangerous ambition of recovering the poet's ancient right to full membership of the state council. Frost's presence on the platform at the Inauguration and his reading of 'The Gift Outright' at the ceremony became symbolic of this ambition to make the poet active in politics.

Commenting on the Kennedy inauguration, a journalist concluded an interview with Frost by saying: 'Those who attended the Inaugural will never forget the patriarchal figure of the poet on the platform, his hair white as snow, his voice as strong as the Republic itself.' In snowy Washington sunlight, among those dull, arrogant, neoclassical government buildings, the son of a failed Democratic machine-politician becomes his admirers and speaks for the republic. Frost's Augustanism is never far from militarism, although in his best poems he conceals his dislike of those 'sapheads' who are 'too liberal to fight'.* Thus 'The Most of It' may appear to resemble 'For Once, Then, Something' in its philosophic search for a value beyond subjectivity. The unnamed 'he' of the poem seeks an assurance that the world is not simply a mirror for romantic dreams. He wants 'counter-love, original response':

> And nothing ever came of what he cried
> Unless it was the embodiment that crashed
> In the cliff's talus on the other side.

With what plum assurance Frost launches that unusual word 'talus' at the reader. It's a French word which derives from 'talus', the Latin for 'ankle', but taken in the sense of the French word 'talon', meaning 'heel'. As Frost employs it, the cliff's talus is the mass of natural detritus lying at the bottom of the cliff. The very hardness of the word itself, rather than its literal meaning, complicates the epiphany which follows:

> And then in the far-distant water splashed,
> But after a time allowed for it to swim,
> Instead of proving human when it neared
> And someone else additional to him,
> As a great buck it powerfully appeared,
> Pushing the crumpled water up ahead,
> And landed pouring like a waterfall,
> And stumbled through the rocks with horny tread,
> And forced the underbrush – and that was all.

The buck's manifestation is grounded in 'talus' because that word links us back to European classicism and introduces specifically military associations (in the science of fortification it means 'the sloping side of a bastion or rampart').

This is the sense in which the word is employed in *Tristram Shandy* ('the talus of the glacis, and the precise height of the several banquets, parapets &c'). The term has associations with 'many deeds of war' – the War of the Spanish Succession in Uncle Toby's

*Frost made this remark in an interview in the *New York Herald Tribune* (9 September 1962) after his meeting with Khrushchev.

case – and Frost's description of the manner in which the great buck appears, pushing the lake water ahead of it, then landing on the shale, makes it appear like some kind of amphibious tank stumbling ashore 'with horny tread'. In such a context, that preening, lineny 'crumpled' water appears almost heraldic in its stylization.

'The Most of It' was first published in 1942, and though it was written in the late 1920s as a reply to a wilderness poem by Frost's friend Wade Van Dore, its publication within months of the Japanese attack on Pearl Harbor makes it read like a passage from a classical epic where the god of war emerges from under a tree-hidden cliff. Frost once defined being American as never having gone out of the country except to 'lick' another country. His buck is on its way to damage something, to get even. Where the appearance of the doe and buck in 'Two Look at Two' is the occasion of a chthonic message,

> As if the earth in one unlooked-for favor
> Had made them certain earth returned their love

the horny tread of this buck is more than sexual, more than earthy. There is a deliberately sinister, satanic ring to the phrase, for necessary revenge killings lie ahead.

This sinister quality which runs through Frost's work surfaces in an apparently innocuous pastoral sonnet, 'Putting in the Seed', which ends:

> How Love burns through the Putting in the Seed
> On through the watching for that early birth
> When, just as the soil tarnishes with weed,
> The sturdy seedling with arched body comes
> Shouldering its way and shedding the earth crumbs.

Just as the Indians in Charles Frost's day were felled like trees, so weeds and earth crumbs must give way to the sturdy seedlings. The final clenching, uplifting couplet finds the dragon's teeth of Manifest Destiny in what appears to be an innocent, ritual action where sex, agriculture and an evangelical hymn meet.

That combination of the homey and the sinister is present in many of Wyeth's paintings: it is difficult not to believe that Frost influenced them. Yet is 'sinister' the right term for his secret, cold, calculating, Yankee vision? Lionel Trilling, in a controversial tribute to Frost, called him a 'terrifying' poet, and in doing so annoyed many of the poet's patriotic admirers. The occasion was a birthday dinner for Frost in 1959, where Trilling spoke in honour of Frost as a poet, 'but also as a tutelary genius of the nation and as a justification of our national soul'. Trilling carefully set out his earlier reservations about Frost's poems: their 'manifest America' was rural, and rural in an 'aggressively moralized way'. Its appeal to many literary Americans lay in its rejection of the complexity, uncertainty and anxiety of urban life. Identifying himself as an urban intellectual, Trilling confessed that the magazine he most enjoyed writing for was *Partisan Review*, which was often regarded as having such an excess of 'city intellectuality' that it could scarcely be American at all. 'I know all that can be charged against the restless, combative, abstract urban intellect', Trilling said. 'I also know that when it flags, something goes out of the nation's spirit.'

He then argued that Frost was a tragic poet whose people were 'so isolated, so lightning-blasted, so tried down and calcined by life' that they became the carriers of that new, specifically American consciousness which D. H. Lawrence had identified in his study of classic American literature. Frost had succeeded in sloughing off the old European consciousness: the manifest America of his poems may be pastoral, the 'actual America is tragic'.

Trilling's speech was attacked by J. Donald Adams in the *New York Times Book Review*:

> Professor Trilling confessed that he thinks of Frost as a 'terrifying' poet, and that 'the universe he conceives is a terrifying universe'. Holy mackerel! Frost simply sees the universe as it is and accepts it. He isn't terrified by what he sees, and neither should we be. He takes it in his stride, which is one reason why he is in there pitching at 85; he has a private air-conditioning system denied to most of his younger contemporaries – and, as I said before, he got it from Emerson.

Adams's crude nationalism shows again in his remark that Trilling is lost in the 'Freudian wood'. Worse was to follow. The *New York*

Times published a page of letters which almost unanimously attacked Trilling in a similarly coarse, rasping manner. Writing from Troy, New York State, T. M. Guerin Jr employed Frostian imagery to denounce Trilling: 'I hope Robert Frost was having a nice plate of buckwheat cakes and Vermont maple syrup as he read Mr Adams's remarks. He couldn't have done better unless he had taken the so-called professor out to the woodshed.' This is the epistolary equivalent of being shown the wheelpit: the professor is led out to the woodshed for punishment. The vindictive crowing of Guerin and other correspondents saddened Trilling, who wrote that he was surprised by the 'low personal and intellectual tone' of the letters. What united the correspondents was a raw nationalism and a hostility to those critics who go 'whoring after European gods'. There is a thread of covert anti-Semitism in several of the letters, as well as a sadistic relish, like the growl of a smalltown lynch-mob.

Trilling's estimation of the poems was courageous, and in my view it was correct. Our admiration for them must struggle against our awareness of the monstrous national totem Frost became. There is bound to be a wary coldness in our admiration as we contemplate the terrifying history the poems shirk more often than they face, or insidiously justify rather than criticize. Like Yeats, a poet he admired and learnt from, Frost is a grunting caveman who approaches us with a club in one hand and a lyric in the other.

Dwelling without Roots: Elizabeth Bishop

Denken wir für eine Weile, Heidegger whispers. Let's think about a cottage in the Black Forest that has been dwelt in for 200 years by peasants. Such a building embodies 'the forces stemming from earth and blood'; rooted in history, land, *Volk*, language, it demonstrates the inauthenticity of transient habitation in modern buildings. This thick, phoney image issues from the imagination of a sinister conservative who identifies 'all genuine creators' with those political leaders who 'must be violent and willing to use power'. Artists and philosophers share a creative task – to lay the foundations for 'diese Führer' and give him the strength to be able 'to walk alone'. And when the Nazis seized power, Heidegger wrote that the *Volk* had won back the 'truth' of its 'will to be', its *Daseinwillen*. Hitler had led it away from 'rootless and impotent thinking'.

How easily Romantic ideas of authenticity, rootedness, traditional crafts, folklore, take on the stink of power politics and genocide. Heidegger admired the peasant shoes in Van Gogh's painting and liked to exchange his academic gown for *Lederhosen*. He enjoyed walks along woodmen's paths in the Black Forest, which he used as a metaphor for his thinking, arguing that Being declares itself in forest clearings. At the age of sixty-five he made his first visit to a foreign country – France – and later he made one trip to Greece. A deeply untravelled German nationalist, he died at the age of eighty-six and lies buried in a graveyard in Messkirch which he used to pass daily as a schoolboy. Walking his solitary thought-processes through the great forest, he exalted *Grund* – earthly ancientness and provenance – and hated technology. Technology designs buildings, not dwellings. It is incapable of bringing into being the mystical essence of building which is 'letting dwell'.

The word 'dwell' is a synonym for 'thinking', and thinking moves like a creeping root towards a cottage among trees. It returns us to that image of a thatched dwelling with a roof-tree, or 'tree of the dead', a kitchen table made of polished oak, ancient traditional implements in the still rooms. All this smells of acorns, but the essential concept of rootedness is one which many readers bring to poetry. And for Heidegger, poetry is the essence of language. It is 'where language *is*, where man is *bespoken*'. Language is 'the house of Being. Man dwells in this house.' Those who think and those who create poems are 'the custodians of the dwelling'. But the house, the dwelling, isn't an abstract concept – it is a Black Forest cottage whose walls are impregnated with race memories.

Is it possible to contemplate such an image without smelling the burnt flesh that clings to certain German place-names? And – to push the question further – doesn't this exaltation of the poet reflect two centuries of *European* aesthetics? If it does, how can writers come to terms with this tainted cultural inheritance? To rip up all those deep-laid roots like so much worn electrical cable is to place oneself in a minority and erect a makeshift building nowhere.

Elizabeth Bishop designs such a building in her poems, and a consideration of Heidegger's recuperation of traditional European concepts of the *volkisch* helps us appreciate her rejection of the dangerous cultural lumber which still weighs on the brains of the living. The concept of the peasant which Heidegger worked from is a tired one these days; in one of Western Europe's pervasive social myths, a White Anglo-Saxon Protestant businessman makes his own peasant costume from goatskins and acts out the part of noble savage. Old and exhausted three centuries after his conception in the mind of an energetic literary entrepreneur, Robinson Crusoe is leading a displaced existence in England, a country he feels no sentimental adherence to. It is simply:

> another island,
> that doesn't seem like one, but who decides?
> My blood was full of them; my brain
> bred islands. But that archipelago
> has petered out. I'm old.
> I'm bored, too, drinking my real tea,

surrounded by uninteresting lumber.
The knife there on the shelf –
it reeked of meaning, like a crucifix.
It lived. How many years did I
beg it, implore it, not to break?
I knew each nick and scratch by heart,
the bluish blade, the broken tip,
the lines of wood-grain on the handle . . .
Now it won't look at me at all.
The living soul has dribbled away.
My eyes rest on it and pass on.

The knife could be a sacred implement, like the 'aged utensil', a lamp, that acts as the lares and penates of the peasant cottage in Wordsworth's 'Michael'. In its previous existence on Crusoe's island, it was like one of those implements that are treated as objects of worship in primitive religions or celebrated in primitive paintings. Now the knife is only a dead thing: it is not a crucifix and has no meaning beyond its functional use.

After the publication of *Questions of Travel* in 1965, Bishop visited London and wrote to Robert Lowell that she had met:

> Oh so many poets – all the names at the bottoms of columns in those reviews, or at the bottoms of reviews – and most of whose poetry I can't tell apart. And all I'm afraid not terribly interesting. – I'm afraid you're the only poet I find very interesting, to tell the truth! There is a deadness there – what is it – hopelessness . . . that kind of defiant English rottenness – too strong a word – but a sort of piggish-ness! As if they've thrown off Victorianism, Georgianism, Radicalism of the '30s – and now let's all give up together. Even Larkin's poetry is a bit too easily resigned don't you think? – Oh I am all for grimness and horrors of every sort – but you can't have them, either, by shortcuts – by just saying it.

'Crusoe in England' gives this perception of English attitudes a dramatic voice.

Bishop had noticed that some fundamental change in the cultural climate was taking place – the colonial optimism which generations of readers had brought to Defoe's text was shrivelling as Britain began its protracted and clumsy adjustment to a diminished role as a post-imperial nation. In British pantomime in the 1980s, Man Friday was portrayed as a radical figure by black actors who challenged traditional stereotypes, and to the annoyance of many white conservatives and liberals Defoe's novel was withdrawn from school libraries in parts of Britain. For the moment, that text is a piece of colonial propaganda which cannot be disentangled from the stubborn remnants of the world view it helped shape.

Bishop's Crusoe is a wan and pathetic figure who knows that he belongs in a maritime museum:

> The local museum's asked me to
> leave everything to them:
> the flute, the knife, the shrivelled shoes,
> my shedding goatskin trousers
> (moths have got in the fur),
> the parasol that took me such a time
> remembering the way the ribs should go.
> It will still work but, folded up,
> looks like a plucked and skinny fowl.
> How can anyone want such things?

Like Van Gogh's peasant shoes and the contents of that cottage in the Black Forest, Crusoe's iconic costume will be exhibited in a folk-museum where the flute and the knife will acquire obvious meanings: art and barbarism. This is the end of the imperial male, of those 'uncontrolled, traditional cries' that oppose 'rootless and impotent thinking'. It is also an affectionate parody of Larkin's resigned grimness.

Bishop delights in makeshift, temporary dwellings furnished with minimal possessions and occupied by fragile voices that lack the ability to make things happen in the public world. The building in 'Jerónimo's House' is no stone cottage with an ancient floor sanctified by the dead feet of many peasant generations; instead, it's an ironic fairy palace made of perishable clapboards, a 'gray wasps' nest/of chewed-up paper/glued with spit'. It is a leafy, ferny habitation with wicker chairs, tissue-paper roses, paper decorations, an old French horn whose ancientness is denied by its recent coat of 'aluminum paint'. Looking at this house at night, you would think it abandoned, but on closer inspection you can see and hear:

> the writing-paper
> lines of light
> and the voices of
> my radio
>
> singing flamencos
> in between
> the lottery numbers.
> When I move
> I take these things,
> not much more, from
> my shelter from
> the hurricane.

It's all so beautifully flimsy and deracinated and benign. The poem has the airiness of flowing script on airmail paper or voices singing on the airwaves.

Bishop is unique among Anglo-American poets in possessing a type of third-world imagination which bases itself in squatters' camps and shantytowns, and which refuses all grandiloquent gesture and phrasing. Instead of the rooted phallus, the female sexual organ dwells in this trailing exploration of 'My home, my love-nest'. The paper wasps' nest glued with spit – an image varied and developed by the tissue-paper roses and the writing paper – concretely symbolizes the female organ. A man lives inside the house not in the manner of a magisterial poet in a lonely, dominating tower, but as a voice inside a warm and fragile shelter that gives what protection it can against the hurricane of history. Heidegger's peasant cottage, like the stone ski-hut he owned and made into a philosophic symbol, is a figure born of the professor's stormy demand for 'authentic' leadership and lonely power. The deliberately lightweight details that blow like fluff through Bishop's laidback lines are types of that 'accidence' Yeats expelled from his verse.

Heidegger celebrates the apparently natural and traditional in order to naturalize a violent politics – a strategy based on European culture's fallacious distinction between nature and society. Bishop refuses to recognize any such distinction, and delights in presenting organic images as artificial consumer objects. Some day a history of the relationship between the poetic image and commercial advertising may explore this type of ironic consumerism. Such a study might begin with the wry soft porn of that moment in *Don Juan* where Byron presents Haidée and Juan taking a package holiday on an Aegean island:

> And the small ripple spilt upon the beach
>   Scarcely o'erpassed the cream of your champagne,
> When o'er the brim the sparkling bumpers reach,
>   That spring-dew of the spirit, the heart's rain!
> Few things surpass old wine; and they may preach
>   Who please – the more because they preach in vain.
> Let us have wine and woman, mirth and laughter,
> Sermons and soda water the day after.

Bishop, like Byron, deploys tourist verse in a deliberately unsettling manner that unites colonialism with foreign travel. Heidegger spent most of his long life refusing to be a tourist, and Bishop is simultaneously aware of the objections to the tourist poem as a type of literary expropriation and the dangers implicit in the concept of being rooted in one place.

Her imagination links consumption with tourism and imperialism, and in 'Brazil, January 1, 1502' she moves from the image of a lizard with a wicked tail as red as a (non-natural) 'red-hot wire' to the entrance of the Conquistadores:

> Just so the Christians, hard as nails,
> tiny as nails, and glinting,
> in creaking armor, came and found it all,
> not unfamiliar:
> no lovers' walks, no bowers,
> no cherries to be picked, no lute music,
> but corresponding, nevertheless,

to an old dream of wealth and luxury
already out of style when they left home –
wealth, plus a brand-new pleasure.

These armed males hum '*L'Homme armé* or some such tune' as they rip into 'hanging fabric' like that in Jerónimo's house. They rip this ferny fabric with their swords in pursuit of Indian women, whose bird-like voices are forever retreating behind the ferns and lianas. The symbolism is developed in 'The Hanging of the Mouse', where the hanged mouse's feet curl into little balls 'like young fern-plants'. This is a primitivist image of a harmless, organic innocence that is always vulnerable to harsh treatment by a masculine public world.

With its epigraph from Kenneth Clarke's *Landscape into Art* – 'embroidered nature . . . tapestried landscape' – 'Brazil, January 1, 1502' points to the consumerist link between colonial violence and art. This is the display of Crusoe's knife and flute which we as readers admire and extract a brand new pleasure from. Art and the human eye are not innocent, and this shows in the way Bishop insistently socializes nature. In 'Electrical Storm', for example, the '*Crack!*' of thunder is a 'tinny sound, like a dropped tumbler', while the hail that follows its splintering smash is like artificial pearls:

Dead-white, wax-white, cold –
diplomats' wives' favors
from an old moon party.

The images delight in their social existence and relish a luxurious corruption. Bishop is developing the Marxist point to Auden's brilliant, flip question, 'Am I/To see in the Lake District, then,/ Another bourgeois invention like the piano?' It is a camp moment, an exulting revelation of the artificially natural. And Bishop, like Auden and Wilde, textures her writing with an ironic exquisiteness.

This refined aestheticism has led many critics to view Bishop's work as refusing all accredited political themes, though her poems identify unobtrusively with poor peasants and workers. Imaginatively, she belongs with the 'confused migration' of the million squatters in 'The Burglar of Babylon'. She is against the big houses whose soggy legal documents enforce the rights of squatters' children 'in rooms of falling rain'. Similarly, her refusal to endorse a feminist position has been interpreted as a rejection of the values associated with feminism, though her poems can be read as subversive of 'a most virile presence,/plus all that vulgar beauty of iridescence'. A lesbian who refused to go public, she imbues her verse with a luxurious eroticism that can be felt in her sometimes exclamatory cadencing and fascination with oily smells and swampy, scratchy, mallowy and creamy textures.

These lines from 'Electrical Storm' suggest a shared sexual guilt and sense of threat:

> We got up to find the wiring fused,
> no lights, a smell of saltpetre,
> and the telephone dead.

And the closing image, with its final clutch of heavy stresses, is moist with a tingling erotic recollection:

> The cat stayed in the warm sheets.
> The Lent trees had shed all their petals:
> wet, stuck, purple, among the dead-eye pearls.

On the other hand this poem may be simply about a thunderstorm, not about making love. The reticent nature of Bishop's imagination makes me reluctant to read it this way, but I suspect there is a recollection here of what Keats terms 'the honeyed middle of the night'. Her eroticism is altogether more complex, though, for there is a sense of affronted or at least confronted pleasure in the closing lines, where those multiple adjectives are both decisive and threatening.

Keats's *jouissance*, his labial delight in warm, gooey textures, can be felt in many of Bishop's South American poems. By contrast, her poems of the moral north where she grew up prefer the calcified, Wyeth-like texture of clapboard farmhouses and churches 'bleached, ridged as clamshells'. These northern and southern climates are set against each other in 'Seascape', which is sunny, Catholic and sensuous until the eye is drawn to a 'skeletal lighthouse in black and white clerical dress'. This vigilant Calvinist knows that heaven is not like flying through the air or swimming in warm water:

> but has something to do with blackness and a strong glare
> and when it gets dark he will remember something
> strongly worded to say on the subject.

These lines are an exercise in comic *faux naif*, and throughout her work Bishop's populist fascination with primitive painting plays against the high patrician decorum of her verse. At times, these apparent opposites work together, and in 'Manuelzinho' there is an almost feudal quality in the mutually dependent and familial relationship between employer and employee, which resembles a version of the aristocrat's pact with the peasant to oppose middle-class ideas of progress and equality.

There is a joke against mechanistic progress at the end of 'The Bight', where the dredger working beyond the dock brings up a 'dripping jawful of marl':

> All the untidy activity continues,
> awful but cheerful.

These lines are aimed at Whitman's populism, and in their fastidious correspondence of rhyme-sounds they incorporate and put down the vulgar optimism that ignores art's formal properties. Bishop's reference to Baudelaire, like her use of 'one' in this poem and her preference elsewhere for 'aeroplane' over 'airplane', 'firefly' for 'lightning bug', and 'he gave it to me', instead of 'he gave it me', may seem to mark her out as a paleface who looks to European culture and is dismissive of the native American grain. English readers tend to regard her as an anglophile who rejects any kind of redneck relevance, and in recent years critics of her work have attacked its apparent lack of ideological commitment. But Bishop's poems fly beyond the nets spread for it by the kitsch aristos and the spraygunning punks. In 'Santarém' her third-world imagination celebrates a fecund mish-mash of races and cultures, and implicitly rejects a WASP mentality:

After the Civil War some Southern families
came here; here they could still own slaves.
They left occasional blue eyes, English names,
and *oars*. No other place, no one
on all the Amazon's four thousand miles
does anything but paddle.

There is no nostalgia for racial purity or hierarchy here, and Bishop's tough-minded rejection of modernism's dark reactionary side is apparent in 'Visits to St. Elizabeths', which confronts that ugly monster Ezra Pound, whose anti-Semitism is frequently glossed over elsewhere.

Although its title may seem somewhat dated, 'Songs for a Colored Singer' celebrates black American speech with the most delicate sympathy and love. To call Bishop anti-racist would be conscriptive, but we need to notice the quietly amused joy she takes in mocking those blue eyes, English names and oars scattered along the Amazon. The planters who tried to master nature and enslave black people have been absorbed back into the jungle; for Bishop, this is a benign process, because it abolishes the false split between nature and culture that she ironizes elsewhere in her poems. This is her strategy in 'The Bight', where the light is refracted through a hypothetical Baudelaire whose synaesthetic observation transforms the blue water into 'marimba music'. The marimba is a type of African 'xylophone' that was adopted by Central American and jazz musicians. In this context, it reminds us of Baudelaire's relationship with Jeanne Duval, the black woman to whom he wrote poems; it is employed as a mischievously miscegenating term that refutes the chill ethnic exclusivism of the scene's blueness and whiteness.

Bishop's imagination prefers to dwell on warm, mulchy images, which she uses to create a type of *Dasein* that serves a generous politics of innocence and merging humanity. To reveal the ontic character of reality is to risk experiencing the oppressiveness of a monumentally concrete otherness, a nature that appears to be untouched by socialization. And that ontic character is expressed in the opening lines of 'The Bight':

At low tide like this how sheer the water is.
White, crumbling ribs of marl protrude and glare
and the boats are dry, the pilings dry as matches.

But Bishop must smuggle social processes and artefacts into this image of sheer *Grund* by comparing its dryness to matches, a gas flame, that hypothetical marimba music. Her camp wit toys with various *faux naif* pathetic fallacies in order to deny the authenticity of nature and insist on its artificiality. Like Wilde, she has absolutely no belief in natural purity.

At first savouring, her beautifully observed image of fireflies beginning to rise

up, then down, then up again:
lit on the ascending flight,
drifting simultaneously to the same height,
– exactly like the bubbles in champagne

seems to be a version of Byron's appetitive delight in marine champagne. But Bishop intends that her readers align this image with certain images from Hopkins's sonnet 'Spring', whose risky first line – 'Nothing is so beautiful as Spring' – she prints as epigraph. Hopkins compares a thrush's song to clothes being rinsed, then wrung through a mangle, and he also notes the 'glassy' texture of new leaves on a pear tree. Both images identify natural phenomena with human, technological processes – laundering and glass-making. They do so partly because the social stresses of the industrial revolution made Hopkins wish to perceive a fundamental identity between the two:

I was looking at high waves. The breakers always are parallel to the coast and shape themselves to it except where the curve is sharp however the wind blows. They are rolled out by the shallowing shore just as a piece of putty between the palms whatever its shape runs into a long roll.

This is a subtle version of the argument from design, whose merging of nature and artifice also appeals to Bishop. In 'A Cold Spring' greenish-white dogwood infiltrates the wood, 'each petal burned, apparently, by a cigarette-butt'. The voiced hesitation helps to heal the split between culture and the organic world, and the champagne fireflies express a similarly hedonistic sense of relaxation.

This polarity is left hanging at the end of 'The Moose', a loose-limbed narrative poem that investigates Bishop's persistent theme of dwelling. The moose is 'homely as a house/(or, safe as houses)', and it represents that affinity between nature and human design implicit in the concept of dwelling. Its appearance releases a 'sweet' sensation of joy in the passengers, who crane backwards when the bus moves on:

> the moose can be seen
> on the moonlit macadam;
> then there's a dim
> smell of moose, an acrid
> smell of gasoline.

The two smells are linked – technology in the wilderness, wilderness in technology – and we would be wrong to think that Bishop deplores the smell of gasoline. Oil is a sacral symbol of dwelling in her poems, and in 'Filling Station' she employs it as an emblem of *Dasein*, an emblem that is insistently artificial, unnatural, technological, commercial:

> Oh, but it is dirty!
> – this little filling station,
> oil-soaked, oil-permeated
> to a disturbing, over-all
> black translucency.
> Be careful with that match!
>
> Father wears a dirty,
> oil-soaked monkey suit
> that cuts him under the arms,
> and several quick and saucy
> and greasy sons assist him
> (it's a family filling station),
> all quite thoroughly dirty.

> Do they live in the station?
> It has a cement porch
> behind the pumps, and on it
> a set of crushed and grease-
> impregnated wickerwork;
> on the wicker sofa
> a dirty dog, quite comfy.

For Bishop, the sacred chrism of Being is a tin container of Esso motor oil, and the insistent oiliness of these lines makes the cement building a 'comfy' dwelling imbued with the familial essence of *Gemeinschaft*.

By contrast, the vulnerably alienated man-moth returns to 'the pale subways of cement he calls his home', where he exists as an undwelling shadow with one 'possession' – a single tear that represents his fragility and spiritual riches. Like the mouse who is about to be hanged, or the coiner in *Great Expectations*, the man-moth is the victim of institutionalized cruelty. A figure from an expressionist cartoon, he flickers through an urban landscape of buildings that are not dwellings.

This may be the symbolic significance of the wasps' nest in 'Santarém':

> In the blue pharmacy the pharmacist
> had hung an empty wasps' nest from a shelf:
> small, exquisite, clean matte white,
> and hard as stucco. I admired it
> so much he gave it to me.

In this tourist poem, 'mongrel' river boats are mixed in with blue eyes and English names. The pharmacy is 'blue'; the wasps' nest is 'white', instead of 'gray' like the wasps' nest in 'Jerónimo's House'. A fellow passenger of the speaker calls it an 'ugly thing' at the end of the poem. Is it a dwelling or a building? Is it a figure for that mistaken critical view of Bishop's poems as chill, tight, anglocentric artefacts?

The image draws very deliberately on two technical processes –

copper smelting ('matte') and plastering ('stucco') – and by humanizing the object in this way Bishop refuses to take the idea of natural purity seriously. This refusal is a form of radical camp that unpicks the cultural complacencies which produce images of 'embroidered nature' in European painting and poetry. By dissenting from this consumerist manner of viewing the natural world, Bishop refuses to align her poem with a dominating acquisitiveness. Very subtly, she questions the power politics which the Western aesthetic tradition so often conceals.

Mr Cogito and the Nation: Zbigniew Herbert

Edmund Burke said that Poland must be regarded as 'situate on the moon'. Alfred Jarry defined it as '*nulle parte*'. Ever since the First Partition of 1772 Poland has been scourged and walked over by its more powerful neighbours. When Molotov signed a non-aggression pact with Ribbentrop, a secret protocol effectively partitioned the country for the fourth time and ensured that as a result of the September Campaign that followed, Poland, in Molotov's words, 'had ceased to exist'. Poland was the Dead Man of Europe or the Christ of Nations. Now that it is at last a free sovereign nation again, there is a danger that we will forget the vast historical suffering that stretches before and beyond Mickiewicz's prophecy:

> For the Polish Nation did not die. Its Body lieth in the grave; but its spirit has descended into the abyss, that is into the private lives of people who suffer slavery in their own country . . . For on the Third Day, the Soul shall return again to the Body; and the Nation shall arise, and free all the peoples of Europe from slavery.
>
> (trans. Norman Davies)

Reading Zbigniew Herbert, we discover a classical imagination that is remarkable for the fineness of its desperation. These printed texts are like underground messages that are being passed to us from the graveyard of Europe. Rigorously sceptical, they perpetually question their existence as printed texts, and in this they resemble the famous slogan that hung outside the Hotel Lambert in Paris after the Great Emigration of Poland's leaders in 1831–2. That slogan read: 'First we must exist, before deciding how to exist.' In Herbert's poems the writer from Nowhere is No one – a Cartesian spectre called Mr Cogito whose thought processes never lead to the consoling infinite I AM. To call Mr Cogito Herbert's poetic persona is to clothe him in the myth of the individual; instead, Cogito is the poet as non-person speaking invisibly and silently in the empty daylight. He is the voice of an underground or 'naturally mobile' nation.

Herbert, who now lives in Paris, joined the Polish resistance in his late teens. His poems speak for Europe:

> I saw a man who had been tortured
> he now sat safely in the family circle
> cracked jokes ate soup
> I looked at the opened mouth
> his gums – two bramble twigs stripped of bark
> I saw his whole nakedness
> the whole humiliation

'What I Saw', the poem in which these lines occur, was published in Gdańsk in 1957, but the censors did not permit its subsequent publication in book form. The effect of censorship can be felt everywhere in Herbert's poems, and it contributes to their pervasive sense of anonymity:

> is this the last act
> of the play by Anonymous
> flat as a shroud
> full of suppressed sobbing
> and the snickering of those
> who heave a sigh of relief
> that again it has worked out
> and after clearing away the dead props
> slowly
> raise
>
> the blood-drenched curtain

These are clandestine lines, a speech-risk taken in a void by an imagination that is remarkable for its Swiftian refusal to settle for anything. Herbert is faithful 'to uncertain clarity', and he strips away certainties, illusions, ideals, any form of romantic feeling.

Looking at two rooms of Rousseau memorabilia in one of the travel sketches in his collection *Barbarian in the Garden*, he notes a dirty collar in a showcase and 'a hat, a pen and the arm-chair in which the author of *The Confessions* expired. The arm-chair is conjectural. But since no counter-claimant has emerged, it is justly an object of veneration. On the wall an engraving portrays Rousseau's last moments with the alleged last words of the philosopher praising greenery, nature, light and God, and his longing for eternal peace. The aria is long, phoney and operatic.'

Herbert's refusal of phoney romantic emotion is part of his fidelity to historical suffering and to the necessary anonymity that accompanies it. In 'Old Masters' he remarks simply that these painters 'went without names', and then calls on them 'in hard moments of doubt' to ensure that he is deaf to the temptation of fame. The prayer is for the writer to be as exact and invisible as a principle, but for that principle to be as human as all the buried, unique, anonymous lives that make up the soul of Europe. This refusal of the cult of personality in either its Stalinist or bourgeois liberal forms becomes the ground of Herbert's invocation:

I call upon you Old Masters

Painter of the Rain of Manna
Painter of Embroidered Trees
Painter of the Visitation
Painter of the Sacred Blood

For all their refusals of a romantic nationalism and a Catholic faith, Herbert's lines have a pointed, more-than-secular intensity. Stripped of punctuation, his lines stand out on the page like fragments of a litany that is taking place under arc lights, somewhere in dockland.

Many writers in Poland and other European countries thought in 1946 that pre-war culture and its traditions had little relevance to what they had recently lived through. Punctuation and other formal practices were questioned, and from this a writing emerged which in my view is closer to immediate speech than to the controlled linearity of a punctuated printed text. Historical events are solid and immediate – only in hindsight can they be shaped into patterns and given a progressive syntax. But Herbert's poetry doesn't 'move' in that programmatic manner – instead it is a poetry of pure presence, as volatile and stringent as this moment here, now. As Procrustes says in one poem, 'progress demands victims', and for the writer who doesn't believe in giving 'a single form to disgustingly varied humanity' it is necessary to find a manner of creating poems which flies in the face of social engineering. This means that the poem cannot power a forward movement through the belt-drive of commas, semicolons and full stops. It must simply utter itself.

With the gradual recovery of John Clare's unpunctuated poems by the cultural memory of Britain, we can begin to detect how a standard punctuation enforces the dominant power of certain institutionalized values – the editorial process to which all printed texts are subject is sometimes a necessary part of the individuating creative process, at others a form of cultural imposition and censorship. Because Herbert's poems are speech acts they seek to break with and subvert official forms. They issue from the natural anarchism of oral tradition, from a way of talking which tears out the state apparatus of punctuation. If this attitude can be construed as romantic we need to note that Herbert speaks with an uneasy wariness from what Norman Davies terms 'the Positivist-Conciliatory-Realist Camp'. Presenting himself as the anonymous European intellectual Mr Cogito, he begs a non-existent God: 'forgive me also that I didn't fight like Lord Byron for the happiness of captive peoples that I watched only risings of the moon and museums'. Byron here stands for the Polish Romantics, the Insurrectionary Idealists who were opposed by the Positivists. Herbert's positivism is wary and sceptical, though, and he does not recommend a commonplace pragmatism to his readers. With bitter generosity, he incarnates the multi-culturalism of that wonderful vanished state of Poland-Lithuania, and the result is an international poetry which combines a freefloating cosmopolitanism with a demanding sense of local responsibility.

This conscientiousness is articulated in 'Mr Cogito – the Return', where Cogito decides to return to his homeland, the treasure-house 'of all misfortunes', and sees the frontier, a ploughed field, 'murderous shooting towers/dense thickets of wire'. These lines are effective in context, but here and elsewhere in the volume I'm worried by the translators' use of adjectives. Indeed the theological intensity of Herbert's imagination usually overcomes my resistance to the occasionally uncertain use of cliché and to archaic words like 'amidst'. This is particularly troubling in the noble and stoical letter to Ryszard Krynicki where Herbert contrasts the 'holy speech' of poetry with 'the babble of the speaker's platform the black foam of newspapers'. The juxtaposition of living speech with junk rhetoric and official *écriture* is blurred by that phrase 'the black foam of newspapers', which sounds like a dead, if magniloquent, poeticism.

Herbert's vision emerges from a total scepticism about historical significance and personal identity, and in order to appreciate his poems we need to jettison both the idea of progress and the consensual notion of a fixed transcendental subject. We must fix in our minds the knowledge 'that art hélas cannot save', and remind ourselves that 'ignorance about those who have disappeared/ undermines the reality of the world'. It is then, in the very next poem, that Herbert flings us a term that has itself virtually disappeared from critical discourse, a word that in England suffers the unfortunate fate of being employed almost exclusively by the Reactionary-Patriotic Camp – that small, brittle word 'taste':

> Who knows if we had been better and more attractively tempted
> sent rose-skinned women thin as a wafer
> or fantastic creatures from the paintings of Hieronymous Bosch
> but what kind of hell was there at this time
> a wet pit the murderers' alley the barrack
> called a palace of justice
> a home-brewed Mephisto in a Lenin jacket
> sent Aurora's grandchildren out into the field
> boys with potato faces
> very ugly girls with red hands

Detailing a rhetoric 'made of cheap sacking', a syntax 'deprived of beauty of the subjunctive', Herbert insists in 'The Power of Taste' that 'aesthetics can be helpful in life'. It is taste:

Yes taste
that commands us to get out to make a wry face draw out a sneer
even if for this the precious capital of the body the head must fall.

This most exacting aestheticism informs the brilliant poem 'Mr Cogito and Maria Rasputin – an Attempt at Contact', where Cogito finds himself in California one hot Sunday and, as he leafs through a newspaper called *The Voice of the Pacific*, reads of the death of Rasputin's daughter. It seems that, like the rest of us, Cogito had spent many years of happy ignorance as to the existence of Maria Rasputin, but he now learns that she had been a Hollywood starlet who made her début in a silent film called *The Jolly Sailor Jimmie* and then slumped into variety shows, 'second-rate music halls', cabarets. She made two unsuccessful marriages, was nearly crushed by a bear in a circus act, and in rejecting a publisher's offer to write a fictitious autobiography which was to be called *Lucifer's Daughter* behaved more tactfully 'than a certain Svetlana'. Herbert's displaced vision of trivia, dreck, vulgar absurdity and an invisible personal life contains an obsessive section in which Cogito meditates on the leather object which Maria Rasputin holds in her photograph. Unable to determine what it is she has carried through wildernesses and 'deserts of cities', he lists the various fragments of the national essence it might be – a samovar from Tula, a tooth of Saint Cyril, war and peace, a congealed lump of earth, an icon. This list of possible solutions to the mystery enables Herbert to move to his unexpectedly poignant conclusion, where Maria Rasputin is invoked as 'Laura of no one'. At this moment, that essential anonymity – an insistent selflessness – becomes mysterious, because it takes us out of a series of placeless Californian banalities into both Cogito's immediate thought-processes and the risked statement: 'only the boxwood and the birds/speak of eternity'.

Herbert's fascination with 'the disappeared', his relentlessly historical imagination, transforms his collection of brief travel writings, *Barbarian in the Garden*, into a tersely intelligent sequence of prose poems. As he remarks in 'Albigensians, Inquisitors, Troubadors', the martyrs of destroyed religions 'are not canonized'; we need to attend closely to the series of connections Herbert makes between the cave painters of Lascaux, the Bushmen artists wiped out by the Boers, the Templars and masons and others who have been pushed into the 'abyss' of history. The Poles have created innumerable secret societies – for example, the Philomats and the National Freemasonry in the nineteenth century – and this partly explains Herbert's fascination with various underground or submerged cultures. He identifies with those cultures that have been obliterated from 'the religious map of the world' because they help him encode Polish history. Deploying this symbolic code, he is able to beat the censor, and he also avoids the navel-gazing obsessiveness of the romantic nationalists.

Herbert's respect for individual cultures can be felt most compellingly in his remarks about *langue d'oc*, the language of European poetry in the twelfth and thirteenth centuries 'until conquest reduced it to the rank of a dialect'. Noting that Dante originally intended writing the *Divine Comedy* in *langue d'oc*, he states:

> If we can identify a single word which would be the key to a dead civilization, like *kalos kagathos* for the Greeks, and *virtus* for the Romans, such a word for the South would be *paratge*, declined innumerable times in the troubadors' poems, and meaning honour, integrity, equality, condemnation of brute force, and respect for individuals.

One of the constituent qualities of *paratge* is 'honour', and in recommending this concept Herbert reveals that there is an aristocratic element to his imagination, as there is to Conrad's. His writing is remarkable for its sophisticated integrity, unillusioned lucidity and profoundly unsentimental vision of European culture and history.

The Soldier and the Prince: Zbigniew Herbert

Elegy of Fortinbras
for C.M.

Now that we're alone we can talk prince man to man
though you lie on the stairs and see no more than a dead ant
nothing but black sun with broken rays
I could never think of your hands without smiling
and now that they lie on the stone like fallen nests
they are as defenceless as before The end is exactly this
The hands lie apart The sword lies apart The head apart
and the knight's feet in soft slippers

You will have a soldier's funeral without having been a soldier
the only ritual I am acquainted with a little
There will be no candles no singing only cannon-fuses and bursts
crepe dragged on the pavement helmets boots artillery horses drums drums
    I know nothing exquisite
those will be my manoeuvres before I start to rule
one has to take the city by the neck and shake it a bit

Anyhow you had to perish Hamlet you were not for life
you believed in crystal notions not in human clay
always twitching as if asleep you hunted chimeras
wolfishly you crunched the air only to vomit
you knew no human thing you did not know even how to breathe

Now you have peace Hamlet you accomplished what you had to
and you have peace The rest is not silence but belongs to me
you chose the easier part an elegant thrust
but what is heroic death compared with eternal watching
with a cold apple in one's hand on a narrow chair
with a view of the ant-hill and the clock's dial

Adieu prince I have tasks a sewer project
and a decree on prostitutes and beggars
I must also elaborate a better system of prisons
since as you justly said Denmark is a prison

I go to my affairs This night is born
a star named Hamlet We shall never meet
what I shall leave will not be worth a tragedy

It is not for us to greet each other or bid farewell we live on archipelagos
and that water these words what can they do what can they do prince

The corny, the overexposed, the anthology piece, the national heritage sign or shrine – we can all list examples of these revisited boredoms. *Hamlet* and the *Mona Lisa* are two of the most outstanding, and Zbigniew Herbert has confronted them both.

In 'Mona Lisa' he crosses 'seven mountain frontiers' –

barbed wire of rivers
and executed forests
and hanged bridges

in order to stand in front of Western Europe's supreme cultural cliché. What he sees is a frightening image 'hewed off from the meat of life/abducted from home and history'. The displaced transcending image is 'smothered with a scarf of glaze' and is entirely outwith and beyond its original social moment.

Matthew Arnold performs a similar action in his essay 'The Study of Poetry', where he simultaneously withholds canonical greatness from Chaucer and then confers it upon him: 'His poetry transcends and effaces, easily and without effort, all the romance-poetry of Catholic Christendom; it transcends and effaces all the English poetry contemporary with it; it transcends and effaces all the English poetry subsequent to it down to the age of Elizabeth.' This idea of art expresses a secure idea of national grandeur and it flattens social, political and literary history. The critical act of affirming the one great author, the single perfect image, wipes out whole generations of artists. To the writer who is not imbued with a national or nationalist confidence, the historical void which this act of canonization designs is threatening, like a piece of weaponry:

between the blackness of her back
and the first tree of my life

lies a sword
a melted precipice

The *Mona Lisa* is separated from Herbert by a huge historical gap. His lines register that sinister hole with enormous bitterness, because this ahistoricism, or anti-historicism, is really a trope that conceals the heavy artillery of empire, of successful power. And his attitude to the image and the trope is complicated because he both envies and despises the Western bourgeois enjoyment of art, leisure, historical absence.

Sensing that attitude, I approach 'Elegy of Fortinbras' warily – tempted in the face of so much inattention to Herbert's work to call it 'great', but knowing how that much derided adjective drains history from texts.

My first sense of *Hamlet* as a twentieth-century political drama came from seeing the haunting Soviet film of the play in Belfast in the mid-1960s (the film was directed by Grigori Kozintsev, the script was by Pasternak, the score by Shostakovich). In the – with hindsight – unreal quiet of that city, the film threw the spectre of Stalin's terror across the screen. And after that experience Olivier's film was a hollow embarrassment. Later I learnt from Shostakovich's memoirs that the censors banned a stage-production of *Hamlet* in the 1930s because Stalin hated it. Reading Pasternak's poem 'Hamlet in Russia', we can see how the stage-fright of the actor playing Hamlet is a symbolic code for the relationship of the artist to the Stalinist state, and Herbert's poem develops this theme. Clearly, the Soviet Union, the figure of Stalin, his successors, are central to Herbert's poem, but to locate it we need to consider *Hamlet* in Poland. Here, the distinguished Polish drama critic Jan Kott must be our guide.

Kott notes the play's canonical similarity to the *Mona Lisa* and then describes its stage-history in Poland, where it was staged for the first time in Lwów in 1797, two years after Poland lost its independence. The actor who took the title role and directed the play, Wojciech Bogusławski, had been a prominent participant in the Kościuszko insurrection three years earlier. The failure of that insurrection brought about the fall of Poland. In this production, Denmark became Poland and Claudius Catherine the Great/Frederick/Maria-Theresa, the three monarchs who partitioned Poland.

The first Polish Hamlet, Kott notes, appeared in *Horsztyński*, a historical drama by Słowacki written in the 1830s:

> This Polish Hamlet, Szczesny-Kossakowski by name, is the central figure of the play. He has a fine aristocratic lineage; his father commanded the Polish army and his uncle was a bishop. Both the father and the uncle are authentic historical figures. Both were hanged during the Kościuszko Insurrection for treason and servitude to Catherine of Russia. The time of the play is the eve of the Insurrection. Szczesny hates his father, the traitor to Poland, but his Hamlet-like 'To be or not to be', 'To act or not to act', is, at the same time, the choice between the long tradition of the nobility of old Poland and joining the mob of cobblers and tailors who, in their admiration for the French Revolution, are only too eager to hang the aristocrats. The first Hamlet in Polish drama is unable to make the choice.

Both this early nineteenth-century version of *Hamlet* and the first Lwów production of Shakespeare's play must inform the presentation of Hamlet and Fortinbras in Herbert's poem.

In 1904, Kott notes, Stanisław Wyspiański described Hamlet as 'Poor boy with a book in his hand'. Wyspiański – a painter, dramatist and designer much admired by Gordon Craig – made the Polish Hamlet walk round the renaissance galleries of Kraków's Royal Castle: 'The scenario of history imposed on the Polish Hamlet at the turn of the century a duty to struggle for the nation's liberation. That particular Hamlet used to read Polish romantic poets and Nietzsche.' Herbert's Fortinbras might be a tough-minded anti-romantic, an exemplar of what James Joyce termed 'the classical temper'. He might be rejecting Hamlet's elegant romantic posturing, his nationalistic excess.

In 1956, Kott attended the opening night of *Hamlet* in Kraków. This production took place at the time of the 20th Congress in Moscow, three years after the death of Stalin and just before what Kott terms 'the stormy October in Poland', the period of the thaw. Evoking the atmosphere of that moment, Kott remarks: 'The lines that everyone knew by heart, that were until now only literature, suddenly sounded frightening, almost shocking . . . *Hamlet* became from the first scene to the last, a political drama. Of all Shakespeare's words the most audible was "watch". At Elsinore someone is hidden behind every arras.' Kott describes how Rosencrantz and Guildenstern behave like secret police agents, and suggests that this is how Shakespeare saw them: 'He certainly knew well who murdered Marlowe and why.' In Kraków, Hamlet's 'To be or not to be' may signify 'To act or not to act', because the Polish Hamlet of 1956 was both 'an angry young man and a rebellious communist'.

For Kott, Fortinbras is central to a political *Hamlet*. He has broken the chain of crime and revenge, and restored order to the Danish kingdom. This order may be understood as 'the restoration of moral law', or as the 'neue Ordnung in Europa'. Fortinbras may be one thing, he may be the other – this uncertainty of interpretation is the adhesive irony that holds together the character of Herbert's Fortinbras. As Kott points out, the difficulty is that in Shakespeare's text Fortinbras – 'man of the strong arm' – is only broadly sketched: 'Who is this young Norwegian prince? We do not know. Shakespeare doesn't tell us. What does he represent? Blind fate, the absurdity of the world, or the victory of justice?' Reading Herbert's poem, we have no producer to impose a definite meaning on the text – instead, we need to float various meanings. Is Hamlet an insurrectionary idealist? – Is Fortinbras a positivist, a pragmatist? Is this a version of the young, romantic Joseph Conrad's correspondence with his sceptical uncle, Tadeusz Bobrowski? Is Hamlet merely Fortinbras's biased view of the prince?

For Kott, the rest is not silence: 'The rest, or at least, the very end, is the coming of Fortinbras.' And here Kott would seem to be echoing Herbert's 'The rest is not silence but belongs to me.' Maybe Fortinbras is the politician who has to pick up the pieces? He embodies two political clichés – 'the bottom line', 'at the end of the day'. He is nothing if not a realist. Perhaps he will reform the prison system? Or perhaps he will build bigger prisons and fill them with more and more detainees?

Fortinbras knows that Hamlet's state funeral will be an excellent propaganda opportunity which will help create the myth of Hamlet, that 'star named Hamlet'. And in English, 'hamlet' is a little village like Bethlehem. The prince's charisma is both secular and religious. His canonization will assist Fortinbras's control of the state.

Perhaps for the reader who views *Hamlet* as securely embedded in a literary canon that is above politics, this may seem a merely idiosyncratic and peripheral reading. Here, we may note that Coleridge seized on its propagandist possibilities when he was making notes for his lecture on the play. Commenting on the opening scene, he noted 'Shakespeare's tenderness with regard to all innocent superstition: no Tom Paine declarations and pompous philosophy.' He then wondered 'whether it will not do to speak of the honest pride of our Englishmen – Milton, Shakespeare, Bacon, Newton, and now Wellington – and how the glorious events of the day all are (as?) deducible from the attack on England'. At the time – it was May 1809 – Wellington was beginning his invasion of southern France, after driving Soult out of Spain. Perhaps Wellington is Fortinbras? His name looks out of place, like a non-sequential name in a quiz or an intelligence test. But for Coleridge writing under the pressure of war, he is another great name to add to the list of national greats.

Herbert's Fortinbras, like Wellington, is both soldier and politician, but at moments his voice has a lyric cadence that makes him more than the tough, terse man of action and cynical operator:

> but what is heroic death compared with eternal watching
> with a cold apple in one's hand on a narrow chair
> with a view of the ant-hill and the clock's dial

Like an apostrophe to the office furniture, this is power seen from the inside, without the self-regard of the megalomaniac who reminds us that it's lonely at the top. The last poignant lines are religious in their cadence and texture:

> It is not for us to greet each other or bid farewell we live on archipelagos
> and that water these words what can they do what can they do prince

The trailing, incomplete close is reminiscent of the beginning and end of Eliot's 'Marina':

> What seas what shores what grey rocks and what islands
> What water lapping the bow
> And scent of pine and the woodthrush singing through the fog
>
> What images return
> O my daughter.
>
> . . .
>
> What seas what shores what granite islands towards my timbers
> And woodthrush calling through the fog
> My daughter.

Perhaps in the end Fortinbras sounds romantic and mystical, not armourplated? Perhaps he, too, has succumbed to the dream and the myth? He and Hamlet are kin, they need each other.

Dimensions of the Present Moment: Miroslav Holub

In one of Miroslav Holub's most subtle poems, a group of children are being given a history lesson. When was Napoleon born? their teacher asks. A thousand years ago, the children say. A hundred years ago, the children say. Last year, the children say. Then teacher asks what Napoleon did:

> Won a war, the children say.
> Lost a war, the children say.
> No one knows.
>
> Our butcher had a dog
> called Napoleon,
> says František.
> The butcher used to beat him and the dog died
> of hunger
> a year ago.
>
> And all the children are now sorry
> for Napoleon.

It's a Švejkian irony that mocks every authoritarian personality cult – Napoleon might be code for Stalin or for one of his minions in the Eastern Bloc. By demonstrating how easily and how accidentally our ideas of the past can be manipulated, the poem very cunningly invokes a legendary figure in order to deny historicity. 'Napoleon' simultaneously draws on and expels history, just as in its bare, stripped-down structure it appears not to be a poem at all.

Holub is an anti-poet because he refuses to endorse the romantic cult of the poet as hero. We sentimentalize the past – all those doggy Napoleons – and we sentimentalize the poet, substituting the priest of a sacred mystery for the designer of 'a machine made of words', as Holub's beloved William Carlos Williams puts it. Like Williams,

Holub contemplates 'the disrespectfully grey, insolent/frontal bone of fact', and throughout his career he has consistently ironized the European legacy of romanticism and charismatic leadership. He denies the role of poet, arguing that a poet exists only when he or she is writing a poem, and he rejects the concept of individual scientific genius in favour of science, the first 'truly collective planetary human enterprise'. Unlike Byron, he would never boast of being 'rather famous' in his time or of being 'the grand Napoleon of the realms of rhyme', though he shares with the noble lord a dislike of pomp and power.

Holub belongs to a dissident community of 'wakers up', as intellectuals were known in nineteenth-century Czechoslovakia. He is a tireless awakener of the comatose and servile, all those 'milliards' of people who lie low silently in his poem 'The Prague of Jan Palach'. He shakes up his readers in whatever country, and with a terse classical enlightened wit insists that we learn a humility that can oppose the onslaughts of 'powerful, prevailing imbecility, verbal or otherwise'. The means of resistance are poetry and science, and Holub has unique access to both. He is a distinguished immunologist who has published over 130 scientific papers and is now chief research immunologist at the Institute of Clinical Medicine in Prague; he is also a prolific poet with an international reputation. His imagination has a strict, undogmatic openness and wit, that distinctive form of ethical joy we find in Aeschylus. He speaks for the classical idea of Europe, a Europe that is also a continent of war and massacre and numbing one-party states. To read Holub in the 1990s as so many of those states move towards democracy is to realize that here is another Czech writer who has lived in truth and spoken it wryly and very firmly. His post-modernist poems have a democratic patience and wisdom that is both bracing and humbling. Like Zbigniew Herbert, Holub submits European history and culture to a rigorously sceptical investigation that both denies our more cherished illusions and offers something other than a stoic void in their place.

The nature of Holub's offer might be found in 'Brief Reflections on Killing the Christmas Carp', where he imagines that a 'far better creature' would surely be one that would stretch out and say something, for instance:

> These are my happiest days; these are my golden days.
> Or
> The starry sky above me and the moral law within me,
> Or
> And yet it moves.

Maybe we glimpse nothing here? Because Holub is adept at taking away with one hand what he gives with the other. For him, song is 'just as final' as life and death:

> and equally without allegory,
> without transcendence
> and without fuss.

Holub is forever undermining the portentous and isolating the cruel folly of human illusions, but his high irony has a restless quality, an adrenalin risk-factor which never settles for a merely adversarial position.

In his collection *Vanishing Lung Syndrome*, he takes the idea of the body politic into regions no one has dreamt of exploring until now. The collection is divided into four sections – 'Syncope', 'Symptom', 'Syndrome' 'Synapse' – and many of the poems also have clinical titles. In the title poem, 'Vanishing Lung Syndrome', Holub begins with a man lost in a crowd and fighting for breath. Through a series of medical and literary images, he imagines the anonymous man's distressing condition and concludes:

> Inside there may be growing
> an abandoned room,
> bare walls, pale squares where pictures hung,
> a disconnected phone,
> feathers settling on the floor
> the encyclopaedists have moved out and
> Dostoevsky never found the place,

lost in a landscape
where only surgeons
write poems.

This is both an image for an identifiable disease and a brilliant late twentieth-century version of the body politic. The abandoned house is a Europe wrecked by war and massacre, an image of a culture destroyed, but the apparent negation in the closing lines works to offer what it ostensibly takes away – the idea of poetry surviving. At the very last moment, a deconstructive rhetorical gesture modulates into its opposite.

Holub has always rejected the idea that poems are sacral vessels or icons, and long before it became fashionable to speak of the death of the author he imagined a Homer who casts no 'biographical shadow', an author 'so unsuccessful/that maybe he didn't exist at all'. In the prose-poem 'Although' he suggests that:

> although poets are most needed when freedom, vitamin C, communications, laws and hypertension therapy are also most needed,
>
> although to be an artist is to fail and art is fidelity to failure, as Samuel Beckett says,
>
> a poem is not one of the last but one of the first things of man.

Noting that there is no worse emptiness than a house in ruins, Holub moves to a sceptical affirmation:

> But in its aimlessness, in its desperate commitment to the word, in its primal order of birth and re-birth, a poem remains the most general guarantee that we can still do something, that we can still do something against emptiness, that we haven't given in but are giving ourselves *to* something.

A house in ruins, a desperate commitment to the word, are both present in the closing section of 'Vanishing Lung Syndrome', and they aim to delineate a possible hope untainted either by sentimental optimism or the punitive aporias of subsidized deconstruction.

The poems collected in the magnificent volume *Before and After* prepare the ground, not so much for a change of style as a change of mood, and this must signal the effect of *perestroika* on the Eastern Bloc. To compare the new poems with the poems in *Before and After* is to notice with delight how Holub's stringent pessimism is occasionally displaced by something renewed and miraculous. In a remarkable poem, 'Heart Transplant', which should be read alongside the essay 'Giving Us Heart' in *The Dimension of the Present Moment*, he describes how a new heart 'bedded in melted ice' is brought to the operating table like some trophy from 'the Eightieth Olympiad of Calamities':

> Atrium is sewn to atrium,
> aorta to aorta,
> three hours of eternity
> coming and going.
>
> And when the heart begins to beat
> and the curves jump
> like synthetic sheep
> on the green screen,
> it's like a model of a battlefield
> where Life and Spirit
> have been fighting
>
> and both have won

This is Holub speaking for the new Europe, and it is impossible to read these lines without feeling that a most remarkable intellect has bidden you witness a miracle.

That sense of the miraculous – a zestful, deadpan openness to marvels – pervades Holub's essays. They celebrate something we might term 'creativity' but which he prefers to describe differently: 'For me "creativity" is too luxurious a word, too richly coloured. What I know is the will for new things and the enjoyment of new things, and these are identical in science and art.' For Holub, a poem should be 'short, instantaneous and rewarding on the spot', just like a good scientific paper.

It is this instantaneous quality allied to the will to enjoy new things that underpins the classical temper of Holub's mind. James Joyce defined classicism as a 'constant' state of the artistic mind – a temper of 'security and satisfaction and patience' that was not the manner of any fixed age or country. Holub, like Joyce, possesses a great international imagination, and like Joyce he celebrates Daedalus, the patient craftsman, rather than Icarus, the overweening romantic. He can be a marvellously comic writer – his essay 'Visible Microbes' is a hilarious masterpiece, while his essay on Lincoln has a cherishing tenderness that belongs to the spirit of Joycean comedy.

The most haunting essay in the collection is 'Perhaps They'd Better'. It depends for its effect on the careful deployment of scientific information about retinoblastoma, a condition that affects one out of 18,000 children and can spread from the optical nerve to the brain and kill. A retinoblastoma can be removed but in its place another and more mysterious 'genetic horror' is likely to appear: patients surviving succumb to bone cancer between the ages of fifteen and seventeen. With a group of fellow scientists, Holub listened to a reading of a report on this condition by the molecular geneticist Webster Cavenee. This type of bone cancer is 3,000 to 4,000 times more frequent in patients surviving retinoblastoma than in the rest of the population. Hearing this, one scientist commented, 'Perhaps they'd better . . .' Holub muses: 'Perhaps they'd better . . . No doubt the aposiopesis was the most terrible thing about this sentence, although the word "better" was also rather improper and internally unsuitable. Internally, we agreed only with the word "perhaps".' Here Holub takes us deep into an ethical problem – the passing of judgement, the use and abuse of power. He concludes by saying that surgery should be carried out because molecular genetics advances so quickly that twelve years is a sufficient period for further developments in 'the art of the solvable'.

But he also offers another conclusion, which is an uncharacteristically personal response to the terrible knowledge he has communicated:

> leaves were falling from the trees outside, revealing the bare essence of wood, wood that looked sad but was full of vascular bundles distributing vital hormones, no matter how large the sadness or how total the leaf-fall.
>
> And from a distance, from a great and invisible distance, echoed the voices of children who played some game and were cheerful, in spite of everything, in spite of everything distant, great and invisible.

I am not saying this to use lyricism as a cosmetic or a camouflage. I strongly resent lyricism as adhesive tape over the mouth. But there are moments when lyricism still does reach further, beyond the 'better' and the aposiopesis.

For such a classical imagination, this is a heartrendingly lyrical conclusion. But how beautifully it's crafted. And how wonderfully these books enhance the first spring of the new decade.

Hiding Itself in Itself: Tadeusz Różewicz

In *Nations and Nationalism*, Eric Hobsbawn speaks of the 'new independent Wilsonian petty states' which came into existence after the Allied victory in the First World War. Poland, historically one of Europe's most civilized nations, was numbered among those new states. After 150 years of partition by Russia, Germany and Austria it enjoyed two decades of independence. Tadeusz Różewicz was born in Radomsko, in eastern central Poland, in 1921. His poetry is saturated in the experience of the Second World War: his brother was shot by the Gestapo in 1944, and Różewicz served in the Home Army (the Polish resistance). Belonging to an optimistic generation whose hopes were destroyed by the German invasion of September 1939, Różewicz writes out of a deep sceptical distrust of all forms of national culture. He studied art history in post-war Kraków, but his experience of the war made him doubt the object of his studies: 'I was full of worshipful admiration for works of art (the aesthetic experience having replaced the religious), but at the same time there grew within me a contempt for all aesthetic values.'

Różewicz doubts the act of writing, and instead jots down random clumps of signs. He chucks lists at the reader, casual inventories:

> They heaped over him a mound
> of arrivals and departures
> of space and time
> of men objects events
> butter coffee newspapers
> of plush green albums
> bromide flowers
> and artificial laughter

By piling up the inert and the official, Różewicz lets the reader contemplate the invisible hand of massive political power as it kills language and freezes speech. His poems are attempts at survival in an environment that is monumentally insincere, a place whose public rhetoric and buildings are coated with a dead, formal glaze. But the poems, because they are anti-poems, are not romantically 'authentic' reactions to the lies of the public world. Often they seem to exist as revolutionaries and resistance fighters live: anonymously and illegally. In them language endures a brief reprieve. They have the clipped, intense feel of phrases exchanged in wartime. They don't promote or express personality – instead they exist as clandestine speech, wary phrases, oblique gestures. These messages from underground start and stop like jammed radio signals.

Where it exists, the individual emotion seems not to be the possession of the writer, so that each impersonal lyric feels clamped by something external – history, politics, the metal sinews and coiled wires of the state. As Różewicz remarks in 'My Poetry', his poetry 'loses even against itself'. It hides 'itself in itself' and explains nothing. This makes Różewicz the laureate of anti-matter, a shadow poet who writes about empty space and randomness – Mallarmé's subjects – in a manner radically different from those styles that belong with a cult of the artist as hero. Like that refugee from Nazi Germany Kurt Schwitters, Różewicz designs collages on a void. He takes bus tickets, theatre tickets, shopping lists, captions from posters and newspapers, and places them with extreme and insouciant care into a formal arrangement which appears entirely informal:

> they came to him
> grabbed his suitcase
> others snatched it from them
> into his hands they slipped cards
> handbills street-plans
>
> cards bearing the names of hotels
>
> they walked beside him behind him
> in front of him

repeated names
cried and spoke with their hands
lifted their hands
folded and unfolded their hands
a man in a white shirt
made a sign of the cross

These lines from 'Et In Arcadia Ego' superimpose a collage of *écriture* upon Poussin's painting, and they connect feelings of angst and paranoia with a religious emotion (does the man crossing himself look like someone in front of a firing squad?). A tourist arrives in Naples like a child being born and christened – it's all so sudden, hostile, strange, enticing. Being inside any social or historical moment is like being tossed into a crazed tumble-drier – the individual consciousness, in so far as it exists, is a bundle of accidental sense impressions that is forever being pushed around and turned inside out.

Because he is hostile to the official and canonical, Różewicz must deconstruct whatever is meant by 'culture':

we live on an island
peopled by a handful of creatures
we are left with a few closest to us
but they too depart
each in his own way
they take with them
vacuum cleaners insipid paintings
women children
motors fridges
a stock of information
ashes pseudonyms
remnants of an aesthetic
a faith

Like an image from pop art – say Richard Hamilton's *$he* – these lines are meant to be expendable; they refute the permanent and lapidary. Różewicz articulates a view of art, society, language, which regards the idea of consensus as a myth and which is intent on exposing the thumbprints of power smeared on every artefact.

In 'Blind and Dumb Criticism' Barthes attacks the obscurantist myth of 'commonsense' and 'feeling', and shows how many critics posit an ideal of culture as 'nothing but a sweet rhetorical effusion, an art of using words to bear witness to a transient moistening of the soul'. Różewicz's verse strips away sweet rhetoric, and long before Barthes he enters what that critic terms 'writing degree zero'. He designs a 'non-style or an oral style' which frees itself from the frozen classical or romantic gestures of the printed word. His poems therefore have a tentative, throwaway, intensely vulnerable look to them – they seem to tell the reader, 'I'm like that bit of paper you see on the street. It blows about in the dust. A tank is passing. Read me. Or don't. It doesn't matter. I don't care.' This poet incognito or ignotus doesn't shed tears. Instead, 'he tears easily/like newsprint/ roughly patchily'. And so the poet becomes the poem, becomes the vulnerable physical object our eyes register.

Barthes speaks of dissolving the greasiness of 'natural' language – that is, language that feigns ignorance of its own nature as language – and always in Różewicz there is a strict ironic consciousness which eats away at that greasiness and at its concept of the Author. Words are shit, Różewicz insists, and poets are not the shepherds of Being:

cries songs words too many words
baroque churches of words
dust rustling of papers
and if he is not there
only a cloud a whirl
of noise burning white
an exploding and fading ball
a magician's glass ball

It's as if Różewicz is inverting that too-famous couplet from 'Adonais' ('Life like a dome' etc.) and saying with Barthes, let's be rid of the myth of the Great Writer, that mausoleum of high moral values. We mustn't kid ourselves by joining and supporting the Institution of Literariness.

That institution also produces the pastoral poet, and in doing so it often crushes an isolated, fugitive imagination under the weight of public attention and expectation. Like Różewicz, John Clare is an essentially oral poet who mixes speech moments with bits of inert official or poetic diction. His lines at the end of 'The Flitting' – '& still the grass eternal springs / Where castles stood & grandeur died' – have an affinity with Różewicz's 'Grass':

> patiently I spread
> in the cracks of silence
> I wait for the walls to fall
> and return to earth
>
> then I will cover
> names and faces

Like Clare's poetry, these lines speak for Anon.: they seem to rise out of the proletariat in order to repossess all that was stolen and distorted by the thick hands of power.

Clare writes out of the experience of being socially marginal, and in 'To the Snipe' there is a deep quietism that speaks for that sense of being powerless before history which permeates the work of Różewicz. This experience of historical dispossession implies the negation of personal identity (as in Clare's 'I Am'), as well as the negation of culture, community, a shared past:

> you ask about
> the more significant events and dates
> in my life
> ask others
>
> my biography almost came to an end
> on several occasions
> some better some worse

This poetry of studied negation is a version of Mandelstam's argument in his essay 'The End of the Novel', where he remarks that the Napoleonic epos which caused the 'stock value of the individual in history to rise in an extraordinary manner' is now over.

Mandelstam states that the future development of the novel will be 'no less than the history of the atomisation of biography as a form of personal existence'. And he bases his diagnosis on the fact that in the twentieth century, Europeans are 'plucked out' of their own biographies like balls from the pockets of billiard tables. This image is reminiscent of the sceptical analogy with billiard balls which Hume employs to describe the concept of cause and effect – Hardy adopts it when he describes the faces of his characters standing out against the background of Egdon Heath like balls on a billiard table.

Hume, Hardy, Mandelstam, Różewicz, all concur in doubting causation biography, personal identity:

yes
this leaf
from my son's schoolbook
contains my biography
there's still a little space left
there are some blanks

I crossed out just two sentences
but added one
in a little while
I shall write in a few words

Różewicz's search for an absolute transparency of style articulates the moment of the poem as a kind of nothing that happens nowhere in particular, as if his personal biography disappears each time he sets words on paper – sets words in scorn of words to create an invisible anti-poetry which we seem not to read but to look through at some terrible fact. A fact that can never be pinned down, described, or sung.

Różewicz's imagination appears to be grounded in Wittgenstein's famous dictum 'Whereof we cannot speak thereof we must be silent', and it is therefore appropriate that his definitive translator into English, Adam Czerniawski, should have written a brilliant prose poem, 'Words', which cunningly displaces an English landscape by quoting Wittgenstein and recalling a moment from Polish history. A teacher of philosophy, Czerniawski brings a rigorous and incisive intelligence to the poems. Often they have the dry, shell-like quality of philosophic puzzles – on the page they have a geometric or Cartesian appearance, like bits of Meccano randomly assembled. All of them are responses to the task of creating 'poetry after Auschwitz', and each poem carries a built-in recognition of the impossibility of that task. Różewicz is a type of Sisyphus watching each poem roll back down Parnassus:

> I'd been writing a good while
> suddenly I noticed
> no pen in my hand

Poems exist by not existing: their invisible writing is the product of an antithetical imagination that is overlooked by the facts of modern history and the presence of the state's hired reader, the censor. We read them as if they were messages smuggled out of prison.

Różewicz's anti-romanticism leads him to invert poetry's traditional articulation of sweet sounds together – he makes the domestic lyric sound like a chainsaw. In 'Warmth' he turns the poem about home and family on its head:

> Since it's so cold
> in the world
> that men stare
> so coldly
> even
> one's own children
>
> you might as well
> use a pot full of hot coffee
> to warm your hands
> the moment they wake
> they speak in accents of tin and rust
> they buzz and hiss

All cosy options and sentimental conscriptions are closed off by this imagination.

A poetry that pulls the rug from under itself is always provisional and unfinished – it is founded on a denial of the vatic and a refusal of personality. Each poem is like a diagram of a self-destruct mechanism. The reader's eye operates it, cancelling the poem in the very moment of its existence. There's a sudden stop – no moment of revelation before the blankness:

> The poem
> is finished
> now to break it

She Did Not Change: Philip Larkin

Social history and the lyric poem appear to be poles apart. Politics and culture are always melting into different shapes, but the lyric speaks for unchanging human nature, that timeless essence beyond fashion and economics. Reading the opening lines of Larkin's 'Afternoons':

> Summer is fading:
> The leaves fall in ones and twos
> From trees bordering
> The new recreation ground .

we catch the characteristic accent of the medieval English lyric and are reassured by something that endures beyond the sadness of leaves falling. The new recreation ground and 'estateful of washing' fade into the background, and out of an elegiac sense of time passing a permanent and essential quality emerges – that devout, rather bony Englishness Larkin celebrates or questions in many of his poems. The sad lyricism is rooted in a culture, but the poem's plaintive terseness encourages us to elevate the emotion into a universal value and to miss Larkin's real theme – national decline. The autumn leaves fall in ones and twos, rather like colonies dropping out of the empire, while the poem's tonal melancholy evokes the seeming permanence of a personal emotion that also happens to be universal. After many an autumn, we watch another fading season and feel sad.

The young mothers whose beauty has thickened feel that 'something' is pushing them to the side of their own lives, and this is a metaphor for a sense of diminished purpose and fading imperial power. Incipient middle age is like a return to the middle ages, to the English people's faint, marginal, early history. The poem's lonely voice promises an exit from history into personal emotion, but that private space turns out to be social after all. This lyric poem is therefore a subtly disguised public poem, for it comments on a social experience.

Larkin wrote 'Afternoons' in late 1959 and it is an elegy both for a decade and for an historical experience. The wind that is ruining the young women's 'courting-places' in a Hull park is a trope, just like Macmillan's use of the same figure in his famous 'wind of change' speech, except that Larkin's attitude is opposed to the historical process the Conservative Prime Minister was describing. Larkin loves the unchanging, and in his Jubilee quatrain he locates its symbolic presence with devotion:

> In times when nothing stood
> but worsened, or grew strange,
> there was one constant good:
> she did not change.

Facing this poem in the *Collected Poems* is a lacklustre complaint about ageing entitled 'The Winter Palace' which makes the disguised metaphors of 'Afternoons' explicit. Ageing is like being a monarch besieged by revolutionaries. Change is a revolutionary process, the completed revolution is death. But the lyric voice – 'Summer is fading', 'Westron winde, when wilt thou blow' – remains constant within mutability, like the monarch. Much as Larkin was bored by *The Faerie Queene*, he has more in common with Spenser than might appear. Both are English Protestant royalists whose nationalism was intensified by their experience of Ireland.

In the deep, or not so deep, recesses of Larkin's imagination, there is a rock-solid sense of national glory which reveals itself in 'The March Past', a poem about a military band which he wrote in Belfast in 1951. The loud martial music produces:

> a sudden flock of visions:
> Honeycombs of heroic separations,
> Pure marchings, pure apparitions.

The poet is overcome by a 'blind',

Astonishing remorse for things now ended
That of themselves were also rich and splendid
(But unsupported broke, and were not mended) –

The Yeatsian word 'remorse' (Larkin quotes 'When such as I cast out remorse' in his introduction to *The North Ship*) points to the synergy of nationalism and lyricism in his imagination. It is, of course, a transposed nationalism – fiercely pro-imperial, unlike Yeats's anti-colonial lyrics. And yet for all his repudiation of Yeats, Larkin's career is a version of the old magician's – instead of flowing hair and bow tie, baldness and bicycle clips and the Library Association tie. Instead of the Abbey Theatre, Hull University Library.

Public Larkin acts a part, cultivating a sober-suited persona with a gloomy-tender private side. But that private side is another form of concealment, for it enables him to issue public statements disguised as lyric poems. The skilled and self-conscious performer makes institutional life appear heroic, because life in the 'first slum of Europe' has to retain a vision of that greatness, those pure marchings and apparitions, which a now-drab island once gave to the world. Because things rich and splendid are now at an end, life on the island is unheroic, routine, toadlike. The present – October 1953 in 'Triple Time' – is 'traditionally soured', a time 'unrecommended by event'. Beyond it stretch 'our last/Threadbare perspectives, seasonal decrease'.

Characteristically, Larkin naturalizes his embittered sense of cultural decline as seasonal, the falling of leaves. Where he feels an optimism or joy in the present, nature is socialized through traditionally English imagery – trees thresh like 'unresting castles', white blossoms create lost lanes of 'Queen Anne's lace'. Most daringly, the 'sense of falling' in 'The Whitsun Weddings' becomes an 'arrow-shower' like the clothyard arrows in Olivier's film of *Henry V*. The poem summons both the play's patriotism and that of the film (it was made during the Second World War), but the reference is typically oblique. Perhaps only readers of a certain generation – those brought up on Victorian children's literature – will recognize that bows and arrows, just as much as cricket bats and oak trees, are icons of patriotic devotion in English culture.

In 'Long Lion Days' the midday 'hammer of heat' is a martial memory of imperial high noon, not just a poetic apostrophe to a heatwave. And this resembles the fusion of sunshine, empire and Edwardian nostalgia in 'At Grass':

> Silks at the start: against the sky
> Numbers and parasols: outside
> Squadrons of empty cars, and heat,
> And littered grass: then the long cry
> Hanging unhushed till it subside
> To stop-press columns in the street.

This is on one level a field of battle – squadrons, littered grass, the long cry of victory travelling across time and distance into newspapers and history books. The horses are emblems of the heroic as they are in Yeats and in his brother Jack's drawings and paintings, but in the poem's present – January 1950 – they are observed almost by a sniper's eye:

> The eye can hardly pick them out
> From the cold shade they shelter in,
> Till wind distresses tail and mane;
> Then one crops grass, and moves about
> – The other seeming to look on –
> And stands anonymous again.

The phrase 'cold shade', like 'distresses', is classical – this is the underworld of dreary shades that move through the waste dominions of the dead in the *Aeneid*. The horses are heroic ancestors – famous generals, perhaps, who can now 'stand at ease' but who are also vulnerable, anonymous and largely neglected. Only the groom and his boy tend them now. Like the last vestiges of traditional hierarchy, these servants 'with bridles in the evening come' – the closing line's elegiac, slightly archaic cadencing beautifully imparts a strange sense of threat.

As Janice Rossen points out in *Philip Larkin: His Life's Work*, this poem marks a turning-point in Larkin's style, but unfortunately she is unable to see his style as more than the product of personal neurosis. She states that the racehorses symbolize 'something' about success and failure, and neglects to notice that the threatening atmosphere of the closing lines is Larkin's response to modern social democracy. His élitist distaste for British mass society shows in the contrast he draws between the 'slovenly crowd' in *A Girl in Winter* and the 'more highly strung' horses which seem to belong to 'a higher breed altogether'. Where Yeats's crowd in 'At Galway Races' is 'all of the one mind', like a completely cohesive society united by a single belief, Larkin's crowd is only 'half-attentive'. It is this lack of unity of social being which he mourns in 'At Grass' – it exists somewhere in the Edwardian past, an idealized memory against which 1950s England appears dull, pinched, banal and second-rate. And despite his notorious dislike of 'abroad', Larkin's celebrations of island life are shot through with an intense loathing of his own insularity. That insularity – its sealed cosiness, its bleak disgusted bareness – is not a subject the poems appear to address because Larkin disguises it as a form of self-consciousness, the poetry of the autonomous self.

The connection between the personal and the national life is made through the idea of power and its loss. The self desires full and undivided sovereignty but fears a diminution of its personal freedom through marriage. Larkin's long, nagging, troubled argument against marriage is almost like a public agonizing about national sovereignty. He sets out to defend his personal autonomy – the 'realm of me', to adapt Emily Dickinson – and he employs the different attics, flats and single rooms he inhabits as symbols of that sacred privacy. But by carrying his search for autonomy to the limit, he subjects it to potentially destructive stresses. At first autonomy wins, and in 'Dry Point' he exclaims against marriage:

> What ashen hills! what salted, shrunken lakes!
> How leaden the ring looks,
> Birmingham magic all discredited,

And how remote that bare and sunscrubbed room
Intensely far, that padlocked cube of light
We neither define nor prove,
Where you, we dream, obtain no right of entry.

This clean, sunny, secure room is the ideal autonomous self, but in 'Mr Bleaney' the ugly functionalism which the adjective 'padlocked' carries in 'Dry Point' becomes the metaphoric coffin of 'one hired box'. This is not simply a prolepsis for death – it defines the queasy, lonely discomfort of the self that doubts the value of its independence.

If Dickinson's poetry may be read as a struggle to achieve and preserve female autonomy, Larkin's poems are often sceptical assertions of male autonomy, a state 'we' neither define nor prove because as males we have always enjoyed it. Or have we enjoyed it? Isn't there something frowsty or fusty or just downright awful about the little cell where each of us preserves his ego?

Larkin raised this question jokily in a letter to Barbara Pym: 'why are single rooms so much worse than double ones? Fewer, further, frowstier? Damper, darker, dingier? Noisier, narrower, nastier?' This complaint was made in 1969, but in 'Counting', written in the mid-1950s, he is more triumphalist in his assertion of 'one':

Thinking in terms of one
Is easily done –
One room, one bed, one chair,
One person there,
Makes perfect sense; one set
Of wishes can be met,
One coffin filled.

But counting up to two
Is harder to do;
For one must be denied
Before it's tried.

One is ace and masculine, two is trouble and female, though singleness is rejected – at least temporarily – in 'Poetry of Departures':

I detest my room,
Its specially-chosen junk,
The good books, the good bed,
And my life, in perfect order.

This self-hatred is prompted by a spasm of admiration for someone else's 'audacious' rejection of job and career, but that admiration is then cancelled in favour of what can only be construed as a camp gesture:

But I'd go today,

Yes, swagger the nut-strewn roads,
Crouch in the fo'c'sle
Stubbly with goodness, if
It weren't so artificial,
Such a deliberate step backwards
To create an object:
Books, china, a life
Reprehensibly perfect.

Here Larkin fuses his art and his life – his solitude is an 'artificial' gesture, a self-conscious and deliberately reactionary conclusion which reworks the earlier statement 'I detest my room' and quietly exults in the reproofs it aims to provoke. The poem doesn't so much develop an argument as retrace its steps in order ironically to adopt a more complex and more honest perspective. But the honesty of that perspective is really a form of lesser deception, for Larkin comes clean by admitting that his solitariness is a pose. He has merely substituted one mask for another.

In an early notebook poem which Rossen quotes, Larkin speaks of 'art's plain room' and this is another version of his favourite symbol, the sunscrubbed room that excludes 'you', the other, the threat. The symbol is more than simply personal and more than campily self-conscious, because to the outsider it is bound to appear as the expression of a culture and a history. Larkin speaks not for the imperial male – too transcendental a subject that – but for the English male, middle-class, professional, outwardly confident, controlled and in control. The history of that distinctive personality has yet to be written, but anyone who has observed it as a phenomenon, as a distinctive pattern of behaviour and attitude, is bound to see Larkin as a secret witness to what it feels like to be imprisoned in a personality that 'something hidden from us chose'. Thus Larkin's favourite romantic value, 'solitude', designates the consciousness of the autonomous English male professional. It refers not to physical isolation, but to a consciousness which has been moulded by upbringing and education to manage and govern. Such personalities, with their committee skills, power lusts and filing-cabinet voices, are seldom attractive, but what is so lovable about Larkin's persona is the evident discomfort he feels with the shape of the personality he has been given. Angry at not being allowed to show emotion, he writhes with anxiety inside that sealed bunker which is the English ethic of privacy. He journeys into the interior, into the unknown heart – the maybe missing centre – of Englishness.

This exploration of a way of feeling – or not feeling – is the subject of *A Girl in Winter*, where he places the foreigner, Katherine, inside a middle-class southern English family in order to explore the limitations of the culture he loved. Katherine is intimidated by the sixteen-year-old Robin's 'almost supernatural maturity', by the finished quality of his public-school manners which overwhelm her with 'a sense of barren perfection'. This is a version of the reprehensible perfection of 'Poetry of Departures', and it is developed through Katherine's reaction to the welcome Robin's family give her on arrival. They welcome her 'undramatically, even casually, as if she had come from the next village'. Disappointed, Katherine feels that there is no 'intimacy' among them: 'the whole thing resembled a scene in a hotel lounge'.

As an outsider from a European country Larkin never names and shows no interest in evoking, Katherine is puzzled by Robin's personality and by his motives in asking her to visit:

> It couldn't be natural for anyone of sixteen to behave like a Prince Regent and foreign ambassador combined. It just wasn't possible. Besides, if (ghastly thought!) by the thousandth chance it *was* natural, it would mean that he would never have asked her. They would be so entirely opposite in

every way that — And again, to be so entirely independent, yet so gracious – and Robin's movements were always beautifully finished and calm – well, it would mean that *people*, mere friends, mere other personalities, would hold no interest at all for him.

This must be what the use of 'natural' means in 'Posterity' – 'One of those old-type *natural* fouled-up guys' – where there is again a foreign perspective on an English personality. Here 'natural' means in reality 'artificial', because it describes a code of manners, a way of acting in public which leaves the private human being utterly enigmatic and detached.

Larkin's unusually ruffled, spontaneous prose sets Katherine's consciousness, her unstudied passion, against Robin's English reserve which she tries to understand for the mask it is: 'And therefore this reserve, this sandpapering of every word and gesture until it exactly fitted its place in the conversation, this gracious carriage of the personality – this was not natural, or at the most it was a manner, so familiar by now that his thoughts and motives could change freely behind it.' Katherine wants to see what is behind the mask, she wants to understand the core of his privacy and to know what his detached, enigmatic freedom really is. She has perceived that in any social situation he is never wholly present. This distinctively English combination of presence and detachment is well described by Roy Harris in a recent essay on the state of the English language. Harris notes: 'For the British, communal life is bearable only on the understanding that one may withdraw from it, temporarily or permanently, into another world of inviolable, timeless privacy.' The natural reserve of the English male (British is too wide a term) expresses the sense that any communal activity – say a family gathered to greet a foreign guest – is both temporary and inferior compared to that inviolable, because padlocked, cube of light which is completely self-sufficient. The French call this quality *morgue anglaise*, and in the novel Katherine identifies it almost as a puzzle, a logical construct which conceals either emotion or the absence of emotion.

As a novelist, Larkin wants to explore this enigma, but as a poet he knows this is the form of consciousness he's stuck with. He is caught in the trap of being unable to adopt an alternative way of feeling because to do so would mean relinquishing his native language and his Englishness. In *A Girl in Winter* he tries to solve this problem by giving a foreign perspective on English 'natural' reserve, but he refuses to give Katherine any foreign words or to describe the events that subsequently bring her back to England as a wartime refugee. She thinks, feels and speaks entirely in English. There are hints that she is German, but she may be connected with a poem Larkin wrote during the war:

> Like the train's beat
> Swift language flutters the lips
> Of the Polish airgirl in the corner seat.
> The swinging and narrowing sun
> Lights her eyelashes, shapes
> Her sharp vivacity of bone.
> Hair, wild and controlled, runs back:
> And gestures like these English oaks
> Flash past the windows of her foreign talk.

These lines from poem XII in *The North Ship* express more than sexual attraction. It is as if the English oaks are being left behind by the Polish airgirl's fast, vivacious talk, as if she speaks a language of the passions that Larkin is unable to understand. His later hostility to foreign languages ('deep down I think foreign languages irrelevant' he told one interviewer) isn't present in this poem, which expresses something of the emotional release he found in listening to jazz and blues records. But it would never do, he told his Hull friend Jean Hartley, 'to marry a foreigner'. It was difficult enough to understand the minds and hearts of fellow members of the English middle class. Difficult and also unsatisfying, because of the English prejudice against emotions, the belief that they are somehow foreign.

In Larkin's personal mythology, black American musicians become icons of the emotions and cheer his glum, solitary rationality. In 'The Persistence of the Blues' he remarks that somehow 'in this most characteristic music of the American Negro has been imprisoned an inexhaustible emotional energy. You can go on playing or listening to the blues all night.' In a brilliant phrase, he calls Billie Holliday's latterday voice 'at once charred and scorching', and he rejects the idea that black Americans had the blues because they were 'naturally melancholy'. They had the blues because they were 'cheated and bullied and starved'. Nevertheless, they have a 'relaxed vitality' white America lacks. This may seem to express a sense of his own inferiority, except that Larkin believes that black musicians exist to entertain the whites: 'the tension between artist and audience in jazz slackened when the Negro stopped wanting to entertain the white man', he argues in *All What Jazz*. The white audience must be in control, because if they are not, modernism and Black Power will inevitably follow.

This deep-seated idea of control emerges briefly in *Jill*, when the lovesick John Kemp looks out of a train window at trees being tossed 'recklessly' by the wind. He meditates on love fulfilled and unfulfilled and looks again at the tree tops: 'What control could he hope to have over the maddened surface of things?' Larkin wants everything to submit to the rational exercise of power, but the result is a desperate attraction to something which is apparently other than that power, to the wildness *and* control of the Polish airgirl's flowing hair. Listening to jazz records he is able to indulge emotion like a private hobby, rather as if he is the Housman of Auden's sonnet, who keeps tears like dirty postcards in a drawer. In this way he can both enjoy a snug security and have access to mechanically reproduced emotion – emotion that can be switched off and on at will and so be controlled in the way that trees in a high wind and personal relationships cannot be.

In *Jill*, John Kemp hopes that he will be able to have that essential space for the establishment of personal autonomy, a room of his own: 'with a fire and the curtains drawn, where he could arrange his few books neatly, fill a drawer with his notes and essays (in black ink with red corrections, held together by brass pins), and live undisturbed through the autumn into the winter'. Unfortunately, he has to share a room with an upper-class lout whose 'panoplied and trampling' existence he comes to admire but who disturbs his dream of hibernating in his study. Examining the symbol of solitary room with jazz record playing, we can see that this is a version of Defoe's profound cultural myth of Crusoe and Friday on the island. Elizabeth Bishop recognized this, and her subtly ironic long poem 'Crusoe in England' affectionately mocks Larkin:

> I often gave way to self-pity.
> 'Do I deserve this? I suppose I must.
> I wouldn't be here otherwise. Was there
> a moment when I actually chose this?
> I don't remember, but there could have been.'
> What's wrong about self-pity, anyway?
> With my legs dangling down familiarly
> over a crater's edge, I told myself
> 'Pity should begin at home'. So the more
> pity I felt, the more I felt at home.

The glum, tetchy, agonized questions, the self-conscious self-pity, the drably and quizzically fatalistic 'I suppose I must' sound like Larkin at his most insular. Bishop's foreign perspective anatomizes a type of terminal Englishness that feels lost and tired and out of date.

Larkin likes to set up apparent opposites – room with fire blazing, cold wind and darkness outside – and this appears to express his insularity and independence. In *A Girl in Winter* Robin and Katherine meet during the war – he is thrawn, nervous, edgy, while she feels only an 'abstract kindliness' towards him. Her solitary bedsit is described like this: 'there was a fire, that he paid to keep burning; she had hot coffee she could give him; there was so much laconic mutual help, while outside lay the plains, the absence of the moon, the complete enmity of darkness'. A fire and hot coffee, outside the cold plains. It is a lyric moment that offers an epiphany for the natural fouled-up personality the older Robin has revealed – his emotional nullness and undeveloped heart. The cold plains of his personality are inside the room.

A similar vision appears many years later in Larkin's discussion of Emily Dickinson's poems: 'somewhere within them there is a deep fracture, that chills the harmless properties into a wide and arctic plain where they are wedged together eternally to represent a life gone irrevocably wrong'. As the ships' horns cry in 'Arrivals, Departures': '*come and choose wrong*'. The source of this primal sense of mistaken choice – a secular version of original sin – is hard to identify, but it is addressed in an unpublished poem which begins with the vulnerable, rather overprecise line: 'Love again: wanking at ten past three'. He then tries to discover why love 'never worked for me':

> Something to do with violence
> A long way back, and wrong rewards,
> And arrogant eternity.

It is difficult to decide what these lines refer to, and though it is tempting to read them as invoking a Hughesian primitivism as a metaphor for historic violence, this seems unlikely. The urge towards self-knowledge is blocked off even as it is apparently obeyed, and the poem oddly combines an admission of masturbation with reticence, as if there is something that can't be faced.

Perhaps the phrase 'arrogant eternity' can be linked to the image of deep blue air in 'High Windows' – an image which sets the windows of Larkin's top-floor flat against the imagined paradise of youthful sexuality. The idea of arrogant eternity is a version of Larkin's secret idea of the poet, an idea that runs counter to the argument he advances several times in his critical prose that poets should have a 'direct relationship' with the reading public, as Kipling, Housman and Betjeman had. This relationship depends on 'normal' vision, syntax, language, because poetry is 'an affair of sanity, of seeing things as they are'. The days when 'one could claim to be the priest of a mystery are gone'. Larkin's rational commonsense materialism, his insistence that poems should give pleasure, appears both modest and polemically anti-modernist, but he has an altogether more ambitious concept of the poet that Milton, Shelley and Yeats would have approved.

From Milton's 'high lonely tower' to Shelley's starlit 'evening tower' to Yeats's self-conscious recuperation of Milton and Shelley in *The Tower*, the line is clear and apparently terminal. No poet since Yeats has laid claim to the mystic symbol of platonic poet in his ancient tower. No one has had the nerve, except Larkin. Typically, he disguises his appropriation of the symbol by appearing to invoke another kind of building in these lines:

By day, a lifted study-storehouse; night
  Converts it to a flattened cube of light.
Whichever's shown, the symbol is the same:
  Knowledge; a University; a name.

From the library of which he was custodian to that emblem of personal privacy in 'Dry Point', the symbol remains constant – each is a cube of light. The poet and the librarian are one, the library and the rented flat are identified.

In the early 'Best Society' Larkin again occupies the symbol:

Viciously, then, I lock my door.
The gas-fire breathes. The wind outside
Ushers in evening rain. Once more
Uncontradicting solitude
Supports me on its giant palm;
And like a sea-anemone
Or simple snail, there cautiously
Unfolds, emerges, what I am.

These lines are reworked in 'Vers de Société', which again rehearses the argument in 'Best Society' that virtue is social, solitude selfish. In the later poem, Larkin rejects the time he's spent in society, time that should have been 'repaid':

Under a lamp, hearing the noise of wind,
And looking out to see the moon thinned
To an air-sharpened blade.

The lunar blade is a daring echo of Yeats in his visionary tower, a version of Sato's sword in 'The Table':

Chaucer had not drawn breath
When it was forged. In Sato's house,

Curved like new moon luminous, moon-luminous,
It lay five hundred years.

Like Yeats, Larkin wants to make his pen into a sword and fuse violence with 'arrogant eternity'. His sometimes violent rancour is a version of Yeats's passionate hatred and is webbed in with his youthful ambition to be a 'great' writer.

In 'Best Society' the autonomous, fully empowered self unfolds like a sea anemone or a snail, and this marine imagery anticipates his cunning use of the tower symbol in the second poem in 'Livings', where the keeper of the light rejoices in his solitude:

Rocks writhe back to sight.
Mussels, limpets,
Husband their tenacity
In the freezing slither –
Creatures, I cherish you!

Here, the disguised platonist exults in his freedom. The poet in the seaport of Hull is reincarnated as a custodian of light who is also 'guarded by brilliance', another version of the padlocked light-cube. The high windows of the poet's flat and his library are also a version of the lighthouse-tower, as is the 'high room' in the unfinished 'At Thirty-one, when Some are Rich'.

Larkin reworks the symbol in 'The Old Fools' – 'Perhaps being old is having lighted rooms/Inside your head' – and alters it slightly in 'Friday Night in the Royal Station Hotel':

In shoeless corridors, the lights burn. How
Isolated, like a fort, it is –
The headed paper, made for writing home
(If home existed) letters of exile: *Now*
Night comes on. Waves fold behind villages.

The hotel is like a fort in some nameless colony or like a lighthouse above darkening waves. The poem displaces an English provincial city and makes its author momentarily into an exile. This bold deployment of *ostranënye* which transforms the Victorian hotel into a place of mystery and danger is essentially colonial, rather than European.

The maritime fastness of Hull, its bracing dinginess and unique atmosphere of being somehow Yorkshire and north European and entire unto itself, is essential to Larkin's public–private persona:

> Isolate city spread alongside water,
> Posted with white towers, she keeps her face
> Half-turned to Europe, lonely northern daughter,
> Holding through centuries her separate place.

This deeply-felt cantata celebrates the great, graceful, pointless Humber Bridge, which every day sends a few cars out into Lincolnshire. Larkin obviously had his doubts about the structure – 'this stride into our solitude', he calls it – but he uses the opportunity to express his sense of his own poetic mission, his commitment to what Coleridge in his poem to Wordsworth terms 'the dread watch-tower of man's absolute self'. The strangeness and the isolation and the white towers in Larkin's cantata reach back to Milton's star-gazing platonist and to the visionary Protestantism both poets share. In 'Bridge for the Living' Larkin casts himself as a watchman in Zion who longs to echo Isaiah's words: 'My lord, I stand continually upon the watchtower in the daytime, and I am set in my ward whole nights.' On watch, a prophet, he speaks for the nation:

> And past the poppies bluish neutral distance
> Ends the land suddenly beyond a beach
> Of shapes and shingle. Here is unfenced existence:
> Facing the sun, untalkative, out of reach.

These lines from 'Here' identify the value of solitude with a vision of the North Sea, so that Hull – a 'terminate and fishy-smelling/ Pastoral of ships up streets' – and the hinterland of Spurn Head build an emblem of England.

In Larkin's tower-poem, 'Livings II', there is a bracing and delighted sense of being completely isolated, totally islanded:

Barometers falling,
Ports wind-shuttered,
Fleets pent like hounds,
Fires in humped inns
Kippering sea-pictures –

The lighthouse is exchanged in 'The Card-Players' for the 'lamplit cave' of another kippered inn, where Jan van Hogspeuw, Old Prijck and Dirk Dogstoerd celebrate the 'secret, bestial peace!' Like the royalist and misogynistic dons in 'Livings III', the three grotesques are cronies who symbolically express a type of desolate selfish comfort which Larkin is torn between hating and hugging. Like Bleaney they embody a revulsion against his own insularity with its prejudices and recessive professional Englishness, but as their caricatured names are Dutch rather than English Larkin is able to offload his self-disgust on to the foreign.

For all this poem's invocation to rain, wind and fire, no one reading Larkin can fail to notice that there is a gruelling, punitive, desperately joyless quality to his imagination. Though he can be warmly reverential, often the England he addresses is a cold country inhabited entirely by hard-working Anglo-Saxon Protestants who wear cheap, ugly clothes and drink beer. This is the England of 'Show Saturday', a place of small towns and allotments where it is forever 1947, though sometimes it feels like 1347; and as Rossen points out, the alliterative line 'Watchful as weasels, car-tuning curt-haired sons' might be a line from *Piers Plowman*. She suggests that this resemblance to Langland makes the image appear 'timeless' and so fails to notice that Larkin is in fact offering a distinctively nationalist point of view. Often the poems provide images for the sentiments Norman Tebbit expressed at the start of his political career:

> Nor as a small densely populated island with a closely integrated population living cheek by jowl sharing common ethics, ambitions and standards – and prejudices too – can we afford to import large numbers of immigrants who neither share nor care for those ethics, ambitions or standards – and with prejudices of their own – nor can we allow them to set up foreign enclaves in our country.

Larkin's snarl, his populism and his calculated philistinism all speak for Tebbit's England and for that gnarled and angry puritanism which is so deeply ingrained in the culture. Recognizing this, Larkin called himself 'one of nature's Orangemen', adopting the mask of an Ulster Protestant, a sort of Belfast Dirk Dogstoerd, in order to ironize his own philistinism. Yet that attitude was itself a strategy because it enabled him to conceal the knowledge that he had created many outstandingly beautiful poems. In that distinctively embarrassed English manner he had to bury his pride in his artistic creations under several sackfuls of ugly prejudices.

One of his deepest prejudices was against women, and in a rigorous account of 'Deceptions' Rossen analyses Larkin's most famous attic image:

> For you would hardly care
> That you were less deceived, out on that bed,
> Than he was, stumbling up the breathless stair
> To burst into fulfilment's desolate attic.

Rossen argues that this 'equable' view of the rapist as personally unfulfilled ignores the fact that the source in Mayhew's *London Labour and the London Poor* clearly shows that someone is eventually going to profit from the girl's ruin and abduction into prostitution. The poem also neglects to mention the rapist's violence and domination, and Rossen further argues that the 'callousness' it exhibits and the 'sadism' it in part condones ought to be seen as a limitation in Larkin's art.

Rossen's study is valuable for this insight into Larkin's misogyny and for the many quotations from his unpublished letters and notebooks which she discusses. Larkin wrote to Barbara Pym that he felt deeply humiliated at living in a country which spent more on education than defence, and this emotion must underlie his assertion of male autonomy in the poems. Although Rossen is unsympathetic in her attempts to understand the roots of the writer's block Larkin suffered, she shrewdly notes that in addressing his stalled creativity as a subject for poems he began to forge 'a distinctive, ingenious sort of pessimism'. Her biographical speculations are often clumsy and her critical comments usually amount to dull descriptive paraphrase, but by drawing on so much unpublished material she is able to extend our understanding of the very cunning and very wounded personality of a poet whose sometimes rancid prejudices are part of his condition, part of the wound. Watching the east coast of England from his lighted tower, he dreams of escaping from that imprisoning self: 'Such attics cleared of me! Such absences!'

Laureate of the Free Market? Ted Hughes

The nature poet reports back to society from the wild. He does not address us as citizens or preach the civic virtues, nor does he express opinions about public events or political issues. Celebrating a time before history, he is the rhapsodist of the wet and the wilderness, the feral and untamed. Almost invariably, the nature poet is aggressively masculine, a hunter and gatherer who lives instinctually and denies what Hegel terms the 'daylight gods', the forces that rule civic, self-conscious, rational life. The nature poet returns us to the *dei inferii*, to the gods of the underworld and the life of the tribe.

For more than three decades now, Ted Hughes has been read as a poet who writes about the natural world – its 'violent impending presence', in Alvarez's phrase – and ignores the public sphere. Every creature in his bestiary rejects the secular, the urban, all that we mean by *Gesellschaft*. Yet nature poetry is always a form of disguised social comment. It may face the campfire and the darkness of the cave, but its back is to the daylight.

Hughes's appointment as Poet Laureate in 1984 aligned his poetry with the British state and revealed some of the contradictions that have stretched and pulled his imagination during a prolific writing career. A patriot who dislikes the British Empire, a domineering Anglo-Saxon Protestant drawn to a relaxed Catholic Celticism, a monarchist fascinated by the molten energies of the free market, Hughes seems at times to be a type of Yeatsian changeling who has taken up temporary residence as an English poet. The apparently natural forces he celebrates are symbolic metaphors for a series of historical struggles – Reformation, Industrial Revolution, First World War – which echo and combine in Hughes's radically unsettled imagination. And for all his professed hostility to technology, many of his poems are laments for Britain's decline as a great manufacturing power:

One morning
The shuttle's spirit failed to come back
(Japan had trapped it
In a reconstructed loom
Cribbed from smiling fools in Todmorden).

In their animist vision of machinery, these lines from 'Mill Ruins' in *Remains of Elmet* resemble one of Hughes's masterpieces, 'Tractor'. Like Kipling, one of his earliest literary models, he expresses a distinctively British belief in the creaturely nature of heavy industry.

This primitivist sense that material reality and the manufactured objects it contains are suffused by spirits and demons is the holy ground on which Hughes raises his standard against big business, multi-national corporations, the European Community. He nourishes a dream of Albion before the invasions, and in a note to *Remains of Elmet* remarks that the Calder Valley where he was born was the 'last British Celtic kingdom to fall to the Angles'. This Yorkshire valley, west of Halifax, was for centuries considered 'a more or less uninhabitable wilderness', but in the 1800s it became 'the cradle for the Industrial revolution in textiles' and the upper Calder became 'the hardest-worked river in England'. Rooted like D. H. Lawrence in dissenting culture, Hughes follows Lawrence both as a literary model and as a writer who tried to relocate the self-justifying act of individual witness in a primordial wilderness.

The population of the Calder Valley – Luddites, Anabaptists, renegade Methodists, Wesleyan field preachers, successive waves of Irish and other immigrants – is the seething original ground of his imagination, and it is significant that in a Faber publicity-release he says that he was born in Mytholmroyd, a small mill-town 'very near Haworth'. Topographically, he aligns his imagination with the Brontë sisters – the Yorkshire children of a Cornish mother and an Irish immigrant father who joined the evangelical wing of the established Church. For all his gut patriotism, Hughes does not search out static and exclusive definitions of Englishness. He notes that his father-in-law, Jack Orchard, spoke with 'a very deep African sort of timbre', the result possibly of pockets of 'North-African genes' along the Cornish and Devon coasts. And his admiration for Dylan Thomas is linked to the fact that physically Thomas appears to have been a representative of the 'old Moorish strain of blood in South Wales'. This is race theory against race theory, a batty form of learning that expresses a deep discomfort with what Lawrence termed 'my whiteness and Englishness and myself'.

Hughes is an intensely uncomfortable writer – driven and earnest like a street preacher – and the sense of strain that underpins his lunging, extempore lines is a type of homelessness, a hungry sense of not belonging anywhere. It is as if his poems are cries from the dawn of the English working class, that relatively recent formation which was created out of declining social groups. And even as he speaks for the surge and stress of that process, he tries to escape into a dreamtime before history. His aesthetic primitivism embodies this wounded search for a primordial wholeness.

The big bang of the Industrial Revolution is also identified with another huge social trauma – the First World War – and Hughes's continuing treatment of this subject makes him appear like a shocked survivor of that war. He grew up in a community which seemed to be in permanent mourning for the war dead, and in a powerful recent poem, 'Dust As We Are', he elegizes his silent 'salvaged' father, one of only seventeen survivors of an entire regiment destroyed at Gallipoli:

> He took up his pre-war *joie de vivre*.
> But his displays of muscular definition
> Were a bleached montage – lit landscape:
> Swampquakes of the slime of puddled soldiers
> Where bones and bits of equipment
> Showered from every shell-burst.

For Hughes, the First World War refutes the concept of progress, and so he turns away from a compromised, barbaric civilization to an imagined world that is both innocent and feral. Like all primitivist artists, he offers a critique of social progress and designs images of an unfallen, new and natural world that predates society and ideology. This is the utopian vision of 'October Dawn':

Then, sound by sight
Will Mammoth and Sabre-Tooth celebrate

Reunion while a fist of cold
Squeezes the fire at the core of the world.

The animal theme in Hughes's verse is an expression of his wish to exit from history, and here he comes close to Nietzsche's argument in 'The Use and Abuse of History' where he asserts that an animal lives 'unhistorically' because it goes into the present 'like a number' without leaving 'any curious remainder'. It cannot dissimulate: 'it conceals nothing; at every moment it seems what it actually is, while thus can be nothing that is not honest.' Nietzsche's use of 'honest' betrays the Lutheran origins of his assertive style of thinking, while Hughes's fierce identification with the momentous instant, the now of action and perception, belongs to a type of Protestant discourse that rejects all that is formal and institutional in favour of something Nietzsche and Hughes term the 'elemental'.* By breaking with history, Hughes enables a poetry of free individual conscience, a risky and radically subjective form of writing. But here he immediately re-enters history and exposes the hidden ideology of the natural and elemental.

Central to his imagining of the animal world is a famous story by a survivor of the First World War – *Tarka the Otter* by Henry Williamson. Hughes read this children's classic at the age of eleven and continued to read and reread it for the next year. The story is crucial to his poetic vocation, to his whole existence even, because for many years now he has lived 'on Tarka's river, the Taw, in the middle of Devon'. In a memorial tribute to Williamson given at a service of thanksgiving in 1977, Hughes praises Williamson, whom

*In the *Institutes* Calvin attacks bishops and cites Hilarius Pictaviensis: 'One thing I advise you – beware of Antichrist, for you have an improper attachment to walls; your veneration for the Church of God is misplaced on houses and buildings; you wrongly introduce under them the name of peace. Is there any doubt that they will be seats of Antichrist? I think mountains, woods, and lakes, prisons, and whirlpools less dangerous; for these were the scenes of retirement or banishment in which the prophets prophesied'.

he had known personally, for his 'icy' sense of the moment, his worship of 'energy' and ability to catch 'the pathos of actuality in the natural world'. Aligning him with D. H. Lawrence, Hughes deftly raises and dispels Williamson's Nazi politics in order to argue that his 'untamed' freedom expressed his social vision: 'He worshipped the clear, undistorted spirit of natural life – and this led him to imagine a society based on natural law, a hierarchic society, a society with a visionary leader.' Indulgently, Hughes speaks of the 'razor's edge' of Williamson's particular type of 'political idealism'.

Williamson had an obsessive admiration for Hitler, and according to Diana Mosley was 'intensely loyal' to her husband, the Blackshirt leader Oswald. He was briefly interned during the Second World War and on his release made no secret of his Nazi sympathies. It was once said of Mosley that he was the 'only Englishman who was beyond the pale', but it is difficult not to see Williamson as a fellow member of that exclusive coterie. He gives off a bad smell, a smell that needs to be analysed and placed before his work can be considered. Hughes links Williamson's 'later beliefs' with 'much of what many came to regard as his later mistakes', but he argues that those beliefs were founded in an essentially valid perception of certain social and spiritual values. Williamson the writer drew on his memory of 'the stable, happy world of some of the big old estates, where discipline, courtesy, tradition, order, community and productive labour flourished in intimate harmony with a natural world that was cherished'. This memory shaped his rejection of what Hughes terms 'the worst side' of democracy: 'the shoddy, traditionless, destructive urban emptiness that seemed to him to be destroying England, in its ancestral wholeness and richness, as effectively as the work of a deliberate enemy'. Elsewhere Hughes speaks of 'our psychotic democracy . . . our materialist, non-organic democracy', and the Burkean or Eliotian side of his imagination can express a disgusted hatred of contemporary society. Here he would seem to belong among a few angry aristocrats on the far right, though such furious disgust is also a quality of the primitivist imagination, which can mobilize it to express radical opposition to aristocratic hierarchy. As Hughes has noted, Blake's tiger is the force of popular revolution, and there is a powerful populist current in Hughes's writing which conflicts with its aristocratic dimension.

In the memorial oration for Williamson, Hughes allows us a glimpse into the cave life of his own imagination. Williamson becomes an imaginative avatar – his 'Demon had a black side, even a diabolical side', but he was also an instinctive being with a 'fierce, fiercely alert, bristly look' like an otter. He was a 'North American Indian dreamer among Englishmen'. The gruelling tone of Hughes's eulogy lifts his oration to a level of desperate exaltation. His archaic traditionalism, his recuperation of aristocratic *virtù* and a social stability that never existed, appear at bay in the modern world, angry and cornered. It's as if Hughes is possessed by some wild, wounded spirit, as though he incarnates the pain of belonging to a successful nation. The wound, the neurosis, the hang-up, is difficult to approach and hard to describe, but it is more than personal and needs no reduction to the public facts of his personal life. Hughes allows us insights into the secret imaginative life of the nation, but these get obscured by the prying attention that is given to his relationship with Sylvia Plath.

The insistent feudalism of Hughes's first volume, *The Hawk in the Rain*, may be read as a protest against the materialism and consensus politics of Macmillan's Britain, or it may express a desire to recover an earlier grasp of power and sovereignty. Hughes would agree with Hazlitt's remark in his essay on *Coriolanus* that the language of poetry 'naturally falls in with the language of power':

And there rides by
The great lord from hunting. His embroidered
Cloak floats, the tail of his horse pours,
And at his stirrup the two great-eyed greyhounds
That day after day bring down the towering stag
Leap like one, making delighted sounds.

These lines conclude 'A Modest Proposal', a love poem where the lovers are compared to two wolves meeting in a wood. And in another celebration of love as aristocratic power, 'Wind', the house where two lovers sit 'deep' in chairs in front of 'the great fire' has earlier rung 'like some fine green goblet'. The goblet is a metonym for a medieval castle, which symbolizes the heroic dimension that has momentarily displaced quotidian reality.

Typically, Hughes aims to cancel out the modern world through a momentous, ephemeral intensity of feeling, and in another love poem, 'Two Phases', he compares himself to Caractacus, the ancient British chieftain who resisted the Romans and was taken captive to Rome where he was pardoned by Claudius because of his dignified conduct. Caractacus, unlike Boadicea, does not figure in the historical memory, and neither does Queen Eleanor, whom Hughes mentions in a note to *Moortown Diary* (she introduced cattle from the South of France 'to supply beef and hides for the Fleet at Dartmouth'). The note merges monarchy, a prize bull, the Fleet, but what is revealing is Hughes's easy assumption that his readers will recognize precisely which Eleanor he means. His mind moves instinctively from nature to monarchy:

> We stand; leaves have not timed the summer.
> No clock now needs
> Tell we have only what we remember:
> Minutes uproaring with our heads
>
> Like an unfortunate King's and his Queen's
> When the senseless mob rules;
> And quietly the trees casting their crowns
> Into the pools.

In 'September' the lovers are doomed monarchs who belong in the pages of Burke's *Reflections*. Hughes would revive the age of chivalry, and like Burke he is not afraid to deploy a kitsch language and imagery in the service of monarchy:

> When all the birds of Roxburghshire
> Danced on the lawns, and all
> The Salmon of the Tweed cavorted
> Over the Garden Wall
>   *Gold as the Honey Bee*

A helicopter snatched you up.
The pilot, it was me.
The props, like a roulette wheel,
Stopped at felicity
Soft as the Thistle's Crown

These lines are from 'The Honey Bee and the Thistle', a poem written to celebrate the wedding of Prince Andrew and Sarah Ferguson. For Hughes, salmon, prize bulls, falling leaves, bees and thistles are naturally royal.

Luckily, Hughes's temperamentally wild and impatient imagination is constrained by rhyming quatrains, and this discomfort shows in those early poems which adopt formal metres and stanzas. He loves horizons, open space, the impacted bunching of strong monosyllables – 'short fierce fuse' ('The Jaguar'), 'sudden sharp hot stink of fox' ('The Thought-Fox'). Drawing on Whitman and Robinson Jeffers, his lines stride out most confidently in free verse:

I climbed through woods in the hour-before-dawn dark.
Evil air, a frost-making stillness,

Not a leaf, not a bird, –
A world cast in frost. I came out above the wood . . .

The 'iron light' in the poem and the horses' megalith stillness point towards the cult of the horse in Celtic Britain, and there is a romantic Celticism in the concluding lines of 'The Horses':

In din of the crowded streets, going among the years, the faces,
May I still meet my memory in so lonely a place

Between the streams and the red clouds, hearing curlews,
Hearing the horizons endure.

In 'The Horses', the curlew in Yeats's 'Paudeen' is crossed with an echo of 'The Lake Isle of Innisfree' ('on the roadway, or on the pavements grey/I hear it in the deep heart's core'), and Hughes then gives his final line a distinctively North American turn by invoking 'horizons'. He would appear to share with Margaret Thatcher a belief in 'the great open site of human freedom', a pioneering idea of

England as a wilderness inhabited by mammoths and sabre-tooth tigers.

His outlook has in many ways the solitary, committed toughness and risky certainties of the self-employed, and his unique ability to locate a North American type of wilderness poetry in England endorses, however unconsciously, Thatcher's famous remark when she was Prime Minister that 'there is no such thing as society'.

The entrepreneurial energy and puritan striving in Hughes's poetry work to produce what, in a discussion of Shakespeare's language, he terms his 'dream of an ideal vernacular', and that ambition underlies the phrase 'hour-before-dawn dark'. Although it is close to Shakespeare's 'world-without-end hour' (Sonnet 57), this compound noun anticipates the improvised vernacular of Hughes's mature style. This is not a settled idiom appropriate to 'big old estates'; rather it follows the hectic, unstable language that Shakespeare floated on the mercantilist values of his society. Hughes admires what he calls the 'backyard improvisation' of Shakespeare's verse, his way of taking dialect 'to the limit', and this all-off-the-top-of-the-head inventiveness and authenticity is also embodied in the heroic figure of his father-in-law, Jack Orchard, whom he describes in *Moortown Diaries* as belonging to 'that tradition of farmers who seem equal to any job, any crisis, using the most primitive means, adapting and improvising with any old bit of metal'. This is very close to Hughes's admiration for Shakespeare's language, which has 'the air of being invented in a state of crisis, for a terribly urgent job, a homely spur-of-the-moment improvisation out of whatever verbal scrap happens to be lying around, and this is exactly what real speech is'. The unstudied inventiveness of speech, farming, vernacular poetry, is the opposite of alienated labour and implies a hunter-gatherer or a war economy, a state of urgent improvisation which is really a myth for individual private enterprise. That myth is embodied in the bull Hughes drew for the cover of *Moortown Diary*, an image that echoes cave paintings and naïve art. And this utopian primitivism – an appeal to a world before economics – also empowers Hughes as a children's writer.

His visceral populism informs his pessimistic history of the language as a civilized decline from the buzz and rap of Elizabethan speech to the 'crippled court-artifice' of Restoration speech which was then passed on to 'the military garrison of the Empire, where the desirable ideal of speech for all Englishmen became the shrunken, atrophied, suppressive-of-everything-under, bluffing, debonair, frivolous system of vocal team-calls which we inherit as Queen's English'. Angrily, Hughes identifies with the struggle of regional vernacular forms of English against standardization and state centralization, and his obsessive images of caged wild animals express that struggle. This means that Hughes, like Hopkins, who powerfully influences his early poems, on some level wants to overthrow existing power-structures. The stoat in 'Strawberry Hill' emerges 'thirsting, in far Asia, in Brixton', and it symbolizes the opposition of Asian or Afro-Caribbean English to garrison standard English.

In many poems, Hughes articulates that northern English sense of having been colonized by the east Midlands dialect, of being dominated by London and Oxbridge. His second volume, *Lupercal*, aims to challenge southern power by designing heroically English figures on recognizably Yeatsian principles. Thus Dick Straightup is identified with stony hills and the 'dust of Achilles and Cuchulain'. He has passed eighty winters on the 'windy ridge' of England, can swallow 'the twelve-pint tankard at a tilt', and is legendary in Heptonstall. Like Edward Thomas's 'Lob', he is an heroic ancestor out of folklore whose portrait is paired with the caricature figure in 'The Retired Colonel', who provokes a simple question and a thumped answer out of Yeats or Williamson:

> And what if his sort should vanish?
> The rabble starlings roar upon
> Trafalgar. The man-eating British lion
> By a pimply age brought down.
> Here's his head mounted, though only in rhymes,
> Beside the head of the last English
> Wolf (those starved gloomy times!)
> And the last sturgeon of Thames.

Nelson is an English version of Cuchulain/Pearse, the 'rabble starlings' are Yeats's moorhen – Hughes sides with the heroic and archaic against ordinary citizenship, compromises, the small mercies of civil life. Here, Yeats's Irish nationalism fuels an alternative English nationalism which naturalizes imperial power as lion, wolf, sturgeon, or else imagines the hunter-gatherer in a yellowing topee.

Hughes's dedicated heroism, his search for an ennobling ancestry, draws him to the figure of Robert Farrar (or Ferrar), who was burnt at the stake during the reign of Queen Mary. Farrar was Bishop of St David's and his uncompromising Protestantism is described in Foxe's *Book of Martyrs* and celebrated in the last poem in *The Hawk in the Rain*. By family tradition, Hughes's mother is descended from Farrar, and a local history records that the future bishop was born at Ewood Hall in the Calder Valley. If this ancestry helps to define the Protestant cast of Hughes's imagination, it may also contribute to the persistent idea of decline in his writing. In 'Things Present' the tramp in the sodden ditch dreams that his 'sires had towers and great names', and this Yeatsian image of past heroism and present humiliation must be a response to the British experience in the 1950s. But what sort of response? Hughes is clearly not an imperialist, yet he holds to a gut belief in power and sovereignty – he is in Hazlitt's terms concerned to glorify authority and elegize its decline.

His admiration for a dogmatic executive simplicity and certainty in 'Hawk Roosting' hardly fits the social climate of Macmillan's England: 'There is no sophistry in my body:/My manners are tearing off heads.' These lines may show the influence of T. H. White's *The Goshawk*, which was published in 1951 and combines an English patriotism with the far-right attitudes of the late 1930s:

> It was drowsy in the kitchen, with the music and rain outside. I was stroking a murderer, a savage. Gos knew that might had always been right, that the Vikings slew the last two kings of Northumbria because the Gokstad ship could come so strongly in from sea, that William had cavalry at Hastings as Edward III had archers on the wings at Crécy, that the press barons of the year I was writing about were right about re-armament in spite of the *New Statesman*. It was a sad truth, but we still lived in the Middle Ages. The *New*

Statesman was a platonic organ unfortunately, which believed in logic and 'right and wrong' and the world of noun-plus-verb ideas. Hitler and Mussolini, Gos and the irreclaimable villein kestrel, seals that preyed on salmon and salmon that preyed on herrings that preyed on plankton that preyed on something else: these knew that God had given a law in which only one thing was right, the energy to live by blood, and to procreate.

This passage savours many of the Viking, medieval and natural images which were to be deployed in Hughes's verse. Both writers share a primitivist belief in 'the energy to live by blood', and like Williamson they set natural violence and instinct against human senses 'dulled by civilization'. They demonstrate, too, that the Yeatsian imagination has its equally emotional English counterpart – a bloody mulch of heroic names, battles, bits of history, ancient weapons.

In a sense, these imaginations are not separate and distinct – there is a hidden, collusive, almost occult relationship between them. This imaginative interdependence is explored in the epilogue to *Gaudete*, where Lumb appears on the west coast of Ireland after his immolation in Devon and whistles to an otter which comes out of the sea. Three girls watch its 'foreign eyes, its wide whiskers'. Later they bring a black waterproof notebook Lumb left on a rock to a priest who thinks that 'something supernatural' has happened and becomes faint. Then he sees the notebook and remembers the otter and the 'strange way' it had come out of the sea lough because a man whistled. The notebook contains a cycle of poems, and this passage works to identify waterproof notebook, otter and poems. It is a version of the thought-fox, but more complex and self-conscious.

The Irish setting is both an acknowledgement of Yeats's imaginative presence and a more personal means of recognizing that it was after a visit to Ireland in 1966 that Hughes emerged from a three-year-long writing block. The otter is also the reincarnation of the 'fierce bristly' Henry Williamson, and Lumb's whistling is an allusion to Bishop Farrar, who was accused at his trial of whistling to a 'seal-fish' which he saw 'tumbling' in Milford Haven. Thus the Reverend Lumb is a phallocentric symbol ('lumb' is Yorkshire for 'chimney') who unites ancestry, natural instinct, the supernatural.

The name also alludes to Lumb Bank, the stone mill-manager's house now used for writing courses by the Arvon Foundation which Hughes set up in 1969. And although the symbol is both overdetermined and too personal, it does point to the deep structures of Hughes's imagination.

The otter is more than otter, just as the hawk expresses more than hawkness:

> The sun is behind me.
> Nothing has changed since I began.
> My eye has permitted no change.
> I am going to keep things like this.

The overstatement may be intended to ironize the hawk's cosmic conservatism, though the rejection of 'sophistry' – code for liberal humanism and consensus politics – is repeated in 'Thrushes':

> No indolent procrastinations and no yawning stares,
> No sighs or head-scratchings. Nothing but bounce and stab
> And a ravening second.

Hughes exults in a feral creativity – 'Mozart's brain had it, and the shark's mouth' – and this admiration for the unswervingly predatory aligns the natural world with the nation in 'Pike'. The pond is 'as deep as England' and the pike are 'immense', perhaps like submarines or battleships. They lurk in a 'legendary depth' that is both elemental and mythic-historical, like Dick Straightup. The powers that create fear in this poem are atavistic forces rising from deep in the nation's soul, even though we are led to believe that the still spooky darkness is a form of natural supernaturalism way beyond the social world.

This occult nationalism is the subject of 'Crowego', where Crow drinks Beowulf's blood, wraps himself in his hide, and 'communes with poltergeists out of old ponds'. For Hughes, Crow is a totem of England, and so, too, is the otter in a poem whose subject was suggested by a Yeatsian experiment with a ouija board. 'An Otter' is also indebted to Williamson and T. S. Eliot and shows how Hughes aims often to combine the feral with an Anglican royalism. The otter is like 'a king in hiding' and the allusion to 'Little Gidding' is made explicit in 'Nicholas Ferrer' (sic), where Hughes momentarily softens into admiration for the 'blue calm' of Anglo-Catholicism.

Temperamentally, though, his imagination rejects the middle way with its undogmatic sense of balance, its compromises or sophistries. His best poems are creatures of the extreme, dragon's teeth, armed invaders:

Against the rubber tongues of cows and the hoeing hands of men
Thistles spike the summer air
Or crackle open under a blue-black pressure.

Every one a revengeful burst
Of resurrection, a grasped fistful
Of splintered weapons and Icelandic frost thrust up

From the underground stain of a decayed Viking.
They are like pale hair and the gutturals of dialects.
Every one manages a plume of blood.

Then they grow grey, like men.
Mown down, it is a feud. Their sons appear,
Stiff with weapons, fighting back over the same ground.

The frosty, Icelandic thistles embody certain atavistic energies and express that cult of the nordic which is so central to the imagination of British Protestantism. As Carlyle demonstrates in *On Heroes, Hero-Worship and the Heroic in History*, there is a thread that links dialect, folklore, superstition, heroic ancestry: '*Frost* the old Norse Seer discerns to be a monstrous hoary Jötum, the Giant *Thrym, Hrym*; or *Rime*, the old word now nearly obsolete here, but still used in Scotland to signify hoar-frost. *Rime* was not then as now a dead chemical thing, but a living Jötum or Devil.' The entrepreneurial side of the British imagination identifies with the nordic, or 'the Teutonic blood' as Gaskell's mill-owner in *North and South* terms it. Vikings are really a proleptic cultural code for Protestant individualism, and they are always invoked in order to justify certain contemporary, not past, values.

Hughes unravels the code in 'The Warriors of the North' where the northern invaders arrive:

> To no end
> But this timely expenditure of themselves,
> A cash-down, beforehand revenge, with extra,
> For the gruelling relapse and prolongueur of their blood
>
> Into the iron arteries of Calvin.

Always Hughes thinks in terms of splits and polarities – salt-bleached warriors against the 'elaborate, patient gold of the Gaels'. The warrior energies are prolonged, distorted, changed to a constrained boredom in the neologism 'prolongueur,' as their wild blood is channelled into Calvinism. The poem is in part a protest against the work-ethic and the cash nexus, an attempt to push back beyond the Industrial Revolution and the Reformation into a heroic northern wilderness of rape and pillage. It sets one form of violence against another, but it ratifies both. Hughes has constructed a myth in which the Germanic/puritan/masculine is eternally at war with the Celtic/Catholic/feminine. The myth is an attempt to explain the hurt of history, but it is impossible not to wonder if it isn't also a means of expressing historical guilt. The metal scream of the pig in 'View of a Pig' and the similarly metallic rat-scream in the short story 'Sunday' are cries out of British history. Like Geoffrey Hill, Hughes is obsessed by the pain which his historical state has inflicted in countless wars. His choice of Crow as a controlling symbol enables him to subsume the ravens on that bloody national site, Tower Hill, into this rather too capacious rhetorical device. There is an ancient butcher's block somewhere near the centre of his imagination: these poems speak for the uneasy conscience of a nation which during his lifetime has ceased to be a leading world power. But the conscience is both more and less than tortured – it is exultant:

> Out of the blood-dark womb, gallops bowed the horseman of iron.

The blood-crossed Knight, the Holy Warrior, hooded with iron,
  the seraph of the bleak edge.
Gallops along the world's ridge in moonlight.

The iron rider – St George? industrialist? colonist? – glitters with weaponry as he 'follows his compass, the lance-blade, the gunsight'. He is a Cromwellian figure, a colonel who is destined never to retire, a heroic tank commander, a facile symbol overloaded with significance. Like so many of Hughes's myth poems, 'Gog' suffers from a lack of social and temporal location – it achieves too easily an empty and fulminous universalism that only a devotee could admire. And perhaps because of the contradiction there is in any attempt to examine certain imaginative polarities self-consciously, the poem fails to unpick that knotted obsession with heroic violence. Had Yeats written 'Gog' we would have no difficulty in relating it to a nationalist mythology which glorifies and justifies political violence, but because England and violence are so often regarded as opposites the poem stays obscure, indeed it colludes with its own obscurity.

But perhaps this leashed-in energy and frustration expresses the struggle within England between north and south? In an interview with Robert Faas Hughes discussed his first language – the West Yorkshire dialect – remarking that whatever other speech we grow into, 'your dialect stays alive' in a kind of inner freedom, a 'separate little self'. His original dialect, he affirms, connected him intimately and directly to middle-English poetry. Therefore the Wodwo, even though he addresses the reader in standard English, is the spirit of middle English and is intended as a populist emanation, opposed to the élite speech of the ruling class. But this voice is lost and uncertain:

                    I suppose I am the exact centre
but there's all this what is it roots
roots roots roots and here's the water
again very queer but I'll go on looking

The roots – etymological, cultural – seem to have floated loose, so that the Wodwo has the innocent, vulnerable puzzlement of a figure in one of Golding's fables. Hughes has moved him from the margins of *Sir Gawain and the Green Knight* only to problematize his centrality in a poem which progressively sheds standard punctuation and initial upper-case letters. The wild man of the woods emerges briefly into print and then vanishes into blankness. He drops back into orality like a fugitive dialect.

On tape, Hughes's reading voice is a shifting mix of several accents – Yorkshire, American, Devon, with some standard flattening – and its hypnotic growly depths belong to the verse-speaking style of Pound and Yeats. This is shaman-chant, tribal music, but wildly eclectic and displaced. If we could hear Hopkins reading his poems the effect might be similar, for his poetic voice also synthesizes several regional accents. Hughes's reading voice absorbs and dominates, gathers his listeners into itself and won't let them escape. This may be one reason why, unlike Larkin, he is so conspicuously unquotable. His poems are meant to happen in the moment; they are one-off oral events, speech acts which distrust the fixity of print. The poems are built on a ritual cadencing that overrides the rational contents of individual words and lines. It's as if Hughes has been endlessly redrafting the same poem, so that each version is a temporary and provisional utterance only. It has a casual throwaway quality that refuses the idea of a canonical permanence. And in this his poems are writings to the moment, puritan journalism, all that's represented by Hazlitt's rejection of his past writings as 'mere words, waste-paper' which have none of 'the glow, the creative enthusiasm, the vehemence, and natural spirit' they had when he wrote them. Rejecting a Horatian *aere perennius*, these poems seem to recycle themselves as though they are part of a natural ecological process.

The difficulty is that so many of Hughes's poems – particularly those in *Crow*, *Cavebirds*, the Prometheus sequence – slide away like rain off a duck's back. The condition of their intense moments – their sudden, sharp, hot fox-stinks – is that they must disappear and leave no trace. The page may be printed, but we're immediately drawn on to the next page, then the one after that. Hughes thinks often in sequences, so his poems tend to melt into each other. They seem tossed out in passing by an imagination that is both prodigal and modest, never bothering to revise a poem once it is in print (though the last line of 'Snow Drop' – 'Her pale head heavy as metal' – has been changed in the *Selected Poems* to the more formal and less tender 'Her pale head as heavy as metal').

This visionary spontaneity is a form of born-again puritan earnestness that is integral to Yorkshire dissent. It can be found in the journal of the Methodist preacher John Nelson, who was born in Birstall in the West Riding in 1707 and who describes how at the age of nine he was 'horribly terrified' by thoughts of death and judgement when he was alone. Listening to his father read the twentieth chapter of *Revelation*, he testifies that 'the word came with such light and power to my soul, that it made me tremble, as if a dart was shot at my heart'. Hughes naturalizes this experience of being saved in 'The Trance of Light':

> The upturned face of this land
> The mad singing in the hills
> The prophetic singing of the rain
>
> That fell asleep
>
> Under migraine of headscarves and clatter
> Of clog-irons and looms
> And gutter-water and clog-irons
> And clog-irons and biblical texts
>
> Stretches awake out of Revelations
> And returns to itself.

Like all the poems in *Remains of Elmet*, this is a self-conscious examination of his dissenting background, probably indebted to E.P. Thompson, who quotes John Nelson in *The Making of the English Working Class*. But the pervasive solitude of Hughes's verse, its fears and bold effects, link it directly to puritan discourse, to a culture where it is not uncommon to dream, as John Nelson did, of a snake-haired Satan walking between Gomershal-hill Top and Cleckheaton. This is Protestant folklore, part of the atmosphere of the

West Riding, and it vibrates in Hughes's imagination, producing grotesque visions and occult dramas.

Hughes has justified the violent surfaces of his poems by explaining that his generation was too young to have fought in the Second World War. Sympathizing with the New Lines poets, many of whom had served in the armed forces, he told Robert Faas that those poets had had enough 'of the dark gods, enough of the id'. Yet it is impossible not to view Hughes's fascination with elemental energy as expressing an impatience with the post-war consensus. That rage against peace and civility erupts in 'A Motorbike', where the machine is left unused in an outhouse throughout the war. When the war ends, the men are taken 'prisoner' by peace: 'The shrunk-back war ached in their testicles/And England dwindled to the size of a dog-track'. Then a 'quiet young man' buys the motorbike and with difficulty kick-starts it into life. Like a hibernating beast, it erupts out of its six-year sleep:

> A week later, astride it, before dawn,
> A misty frosty morning,
> He escaped
>
> Into a telegraph pole
> On the long straight west of Swinton.

The last line needs either a comma or a line-break after 'straight', which looks initially to be an adjective but takes a heavier stress when we realize it is a noun, and this creates a pause before 'west'. With a clumsy, over-emphatic directness, the poem presents the youth's death as a symbolic protest against what Hughes has termed 'our psychotic democracy', 'our rationalist humanist style of outlook'. It is a Mishima-like rejection of 'spiritless materialism'.

Coincidentally, the volume in which this poem was first published, *Moortown*, appeared in 1979, and 'Motorbike' may express an impatience with what are now regarded as the 'fudge and mudge' policies of the 1970s. Hughes speaks for the freebooting private sector, with its hostility to state interference and control. Aesthetically, this economic philosophy expresses itself in a type of elemental super-realism which begins with Defoe and continues in the factoids of Norman Mailer, the sculptures of Duane Hanson and the gleaming Kodakcolour paintings of Robert Cottingham.

This superbright puritan aesthetic shapes the title sequence, 'Moortown', which was republished ten years later as *Moortown Diary*. This is Hughes's most assured, most perfect work; it is written with a brilliance that rides on the admission that these 'pieces' are not 'poems'. Instead, they are 'improvised verses', casual journal notes, 'fleeting' snapshots. Both this insistence on immediacy and the use of the journal-form align these poems with puritan discourse. Such apparently provisional texts aim to record the moment of direct experience, or what Hughes calls 'the authentic fingerprints of the day itself'.

In the preface, Hughes states that in the early 1970s North Devon was an 'ancient farming community' still undisturbed by industrial development or an 'immigrant population'. North Devon felt like an 'island', and though Hughes does not draw the parallel, he becomes Crusoe to his father-in-law's Friday – Jack Orchard has a 'gangly long broad Masai figure'. Farming was soon to be changed from a 'deeply satisfying, self-reliant', if sometimes 'gruelling' way of life into a 'jittery, demoralized, industrial servitude' at the mercy of 'foreign politicians'. These poems therefore elegize an island economy and polemicize the Common Market. They aim to exist as direct physical actions – 'Mud-water spurts as the iron bar slam-burns/The oak stake-head dry' – and they insistently demonstrate how the force of individual enterprise reclaims the wilderness. Human actions and natural forces – wind, rain, storm – are identified, not within the poem, but as the actual poem itself:

> The wind is inside the hill.
> The wood is a struggle – like a wood
> Struggling through a wood. A panic
> Only just holds off – every gust
> Breaches the sky-walls and it seems, this time,
> The whole sea of air will pour through,
> The thunder will take deep hold, roots

Will have to come out, every loose thing
Will have to lift and go. And the cows, dark lumps of dusk
Stand waiting, like nails in a tin roof.

The cows are like nails, the fields like a tin roof, because nature, simple technology and poem are seamlessly one. Everything fits.

This may appear to express the desire to occupy a primal natural world before 'industrial servitude', but Hughes is really giving vent to the forces – the 'struggle' – which have created capital. In 'Socialism: Utopian and Scientific', Engels argues that active social forces work 'exactly like natural forces: blindly, forcibly, destructively, so long as we do not understand, and reckon with, them'. Engels uses storms as metaphors for uncomprehended social forces, while in Hughes's verse natural forces are both actual phenomena and metaphors that express active social energies. In *Capital*, Marx describes the 'self-expansion' of capital, its 'blind, unrestrainable passion', 'its werewolf hunger for surplus labour', and his metaphors are echoed unconsciously in Hughes's poems, which realize them literally as seasonal phenomena. For Marx and Engels, the constant revolutionizing of the instruments of production is a poetic process – 'All that is solid melts into air' – and the melting drive of the *Moortown* poems enacts this constant movement. Hughes's poems are always in process, never complete. They express that 'everlasting uncertainty and agitation' which in the *Communist Manifesto* are defined as the distinguishing features of 'the bourgeois epoch'.

By this argument, the viscid slither of a 'gawky black calf/ Collapsed wet-fresh from the womb' in 'Birth of Rainbow' is a celebration of the absolute newness of commodity production on a March morning that begins with 'a blustery violence of air, and a soaked overnight/Newpainted look to the world'. A similar, if much more constrained superrealist admiration for the newly produced can be seen in these lines from an anonymous eighteenth-century poem called 'A Description of the Spring in London':

Now new-vamped silks the mercer's window shows,
And his spruce 'prentice wears his Sunday clothes;

> His annual suit with nicest taste renewed,
> The reigning cut and colour still pursued.

These mercantilist lines identify spring with fashionable new clothes, and Hughes similarly merges nature and production in these lines which describe how he helps a ewe give birth to a dead lamb:

> Then like
> Pulling myself to the ceiling with one finger
> Hooked in a loop, timing my effort
> To her birth push groans, I pulled against
> The corpse that would not come. Till it came,
> And after it the long, sudden, yolk-yellow
> Parcel of life
> In a smoking slither of oils and soups and syrups –
> And the body lay born, beside the hacked-off head.

The parcel, its oils, soups, syrups, all belong to the sphere of human, not animal, labour. By a visceral pun on labour – birth pains, the physical work of acting as midwife – Hughes identifies the human and the natural.

This is the great ambition of literary primitivism – to merge the social with the natural so that neither is backdrop to the other. Primitivist painters therefore ignore perspective and so infuse their images with an animist oneness. In Hughes's 'February 17th' the 'oils' aren't simply bodily fluids – they are oil paints. Everything is integrated – art, work, nature – in a supreme act of physical prowess that is like pulling himself up to the ceiling with one finger.

For Hughes, material reality embodies the spiritual; the two are inseparable. In 'Tractor', he demonstrates how the materialization of spirit begins with a machine frozen like the wartime motorbike:

> The starter lever
> Cracks its action, like a snapping knuckle.
> The battery is alive – but like a lamb
> Trying to nudge its solid-frozen mother –
> While the seat claims my buttock-bones, bites

With the space-cold of earth, which it has joined
In one solid lump.

In this frozen wilderness, mechanical parts are imagined as being like living organisms – a snapping knuckle, a nudging lamb. The engine is now the 'black throat' of an animal or monster into which Hughes squirts 'commercial sure-fire':

– it just coughs.
It ridicules me – a trap of iron stupidity
I've stepped into. I drive the battery
As if I were hammering and hammering
The frozen arrangement to pieces with a hammer
And it jabbers laughing pain-crying mockingly
Into happy life.

There is a juddery, ouija-board intensity to these lines. We are witnessing rather more than the application of an aerosol can to frozen points:

And stands
Shuddering itself full of heat, seeming to enlarge slowly
Like a demon demonstrating
A more-than-usually-complete materialization –
Suddenly it jerks from its solidarity
With the concrete, and lurches towards a stanchion
Bursting with superhuman well-being and abandon
Shouting Where Where?

Now hitched to a heavy plough, the tractor steams with sweat, 'Raging and trembling and rejoicing'. A wodwo, a monster, a giant. The hands that steer it are cased inside 'armour gloves', so the poet is both farmer and medieval knight, a Gawain or a green knight.

This ambitious wish to draw together history, the natural environment and human enterprise can be seen most clearly in *River*, a collection of poems by Hughes which was published in 1983 with funding from British Gas and the Countryside Commission. The volume is a commercial for British Gas's environmental friendliness, though it also celebrates fish-farming, a process now regarded as ecologically damaging. The glossy appearance of *River* and the colour photographs it contains make it resemble a coffee-table book. Like the high-gloss pocket volume *Flowers and Insects*, it draws attention to its saleability, its existence as commodity. Both volumes have a bright, new-painted look, and the opening line of 'Tern' – 'The breaker humps its green glass' – is a characteristically instantaneous vision that unites the literal and the figurative, the natural and the technological. The alienated space between them is abolished as the action of the sea is expressed as a form of labour – it 'humps' the glass and makes work appear natural.

If such ostensibly 'natural' images can be construed as forms of disguised ideology, what is the driving force of this imagination? Like those anti-intellectual German intellectuals who celebrated intuition, self, immediacy, Hughes would seem to be enacting a will-to-power in his verse. This passage from one of Nietzsche's letters expresses that will:

> I hurried out to a nearby hilltop, called Leusch . . . found a hut up there, a man who was slaughtering two kids, and his young son. The storm broke with immense force, with wind and hail. I felt an incomparable elation, and I knew for certain that we can rightly understand nature only when we have to run to her, away from our troubles and pressures. What to me were man and his unquiet will! What were the eternal 'Thou Shalt', 'Thou shalt not'! How different the lightning, the wind, the hail, the free powers, without ethics! How fortunate, how strong they are, pure will, without obscurings from the intellect!

Pure will, the free powers without ethics, this is the imaginative charge of Hughes's verse. His poems embody what Nietzsche terms a 'physical style of thinking'. By pretending to look away from the packed cities of Britain and continental Europe, they tell many uncomfortable truths about our civilization.

A Visionary Nationalist: Geoffrey Hill

Unlike Philip Larkin and Ted Hughes, Geoffrey Hill tends to appeal almost exclusively to an academic audience. Yet his poetry, too, has a populist element and is hostile to collectivism. His second collection of poems, *King Log*, was published in 1968, that year of student radicalism and disappointment. Hill's title is reactionary in its implications and derives from Aesop's fable of the frogs who desired a king. In my edition of L'Estrange's royalist version of Aesop, the fable runs like this:

> The Frogs, living an easy, free life everywhere among the lakes and ponds, assembled together, one day, in a very tumultuous manner, and petitioned Jupiter to let them have a King. Jupiter ridiculed the request; and, throwing a large Log down into the pool, cried, 'There is a King for you.' The sudden splash which this made by its fall into the water at first terrified them so exceedingly that they were afraid to come near it. But in a little time, seeing it lay still without moving, they ventured, by degrees, to approach it; and at last, finding there was no danger, they leaped upon it; and, in short, treated it as familiarly as they pleased. But not contented with so harmless a King, they sent their deputies to petition again for another ruler, for this they neither did nor could like. Jupiter next sent them a Stork, who, without any ceremony, began to devour and to eat them up, one after another, as fast as he could. Then they applied themselves privately to Mercury, and begged him to speak to Jupiter in their behalf, that he would be so good as to bless them again with another King, or restore to them their former Sovereign. 'No,' says he; 'since it was their own choice, let them suffer the punishment due to their folly.'

From this fable, a Victorian cleric, the Reverend G. F. Townsend, draws the moral: 'Resist not, for slight reasons, constituted authorities.' And he adds that Aesop's fable 'inculcates lessons of loyalty, and fosters that pirit of obedience so dear to the hearts of Englishmen'. Townsend speaks with the voice of the status quo, and he would no doubt have agreed with those British judges who assert that the interests of the state are identical to those of the political party in power.

Although Hill's conservative imagination endorses the cleric's simple-minded concept of national loyalty, it is possible to read much of his verse as a protest against what Hugh Haughton terms 'the indignity of King Log'. Haughton argues that Hill seems to yearn 'for real authority and real title, the kind of transcendence embodied in a language of kingship derived from the past and earlier power-relations'. It is a serious charge, and though Haughton argues that Hill resists the temptation to succumb to 'his glamorous rhetoric and grand style', it is significant that none of the other contributors to *Geoffrey Hill: Essays on his Work* – the first critical study of his writing – raises the difficult political issues implicit in the poetry. Haughton's fellow contributors all believe in the magical transcendence of art, and the cover of this volume expresses that archaic humanist cop-out. It reproduces a recent portrait of Hill in the act of composition: brow furrowed, pencil poised, the poet sports a rust-red silk scarf over a black shirt and wears a large ring mounted with a chunky ruby. The painting is clumsy but it does express how seriously Hill takes himself and the stupefied awe his critics feel for him.

One of Hill's most notable champions is Christopher Ricks, and we may approach this volume by applying the critical principles which Ricks enunciated in a recent consideration of Empson's work in *The London Review of Books*. There Ricks praised his critical master for speaking 'with the direct personal commitment that, prior to the current scientism and theoreticity, used to be thought germane to the understanding of literature'. Having established his authority for the act of direct critical witness, Ricks went on to quote a stray remark of Empson's about Hugh Kenner, and then added, 'This [i.e. Empson's remark] precipitates not Ooh but Ah.'

Let us indulge Professor Ricks for a moment. Supposing critical judgements – and judgements about judgements – may be reduced to a series of sounds like 'ooh' and 'ah', what 'direct' and 'personal' vocal reaction is precipitated by *Geoffrey Hill: Essays on his Work?* The Ricksian 'Ah'? A McGregorish 'Nope'? A Belfast 'Yuk'? Or the

'Pprrpffrrpfff' of a Leopold Bloom? You can take your pick of these further descriptions, but in my view the Fabian Dubliner's reaction most nearly approximates to the hollow truth of the matter. Not since the unremembered days of *Reconstructing Literature* have I had to hunch over a collection of dull, dim essays straining to articulate they know not what. The volume's self-reflexive murkiness seems symptomatic of a more general malaise, and it is hard to remind oneself that it is simply the product of a small group of academics who have lost all touch with an audience and a society. It appears to express some deeper and more terrifying sickness:

> Loud thunder to its bottom shook the bog,
> And the hoarse nation croak'd, 'God save King Log!'

Pope's couplet refers to Ogilby's 1651 version of Aesop's fables, and Hill's use of that fable in his second volume inevitably attaches a disabling reminder of the *Dunciad* to Peter Robinson and his assembled chorus of scholars. There is something cosy and desperate in their yawping enterprise.

It could be that Ricks, in his essay '*Tenebrae* and at-one-ment', is deliberately baiting 'the current scientism and theoreticity', but his discussion of hyphens – yes, hyphens – in Hill's work must represent the nadir of traditionalist close textual analysis. To read Ricks on the hyphen is to taste that abject world of trivializing critical duncery which filled Pope with such savage despair. Assonating from one loose sentence to the next, Ricks's mannered style preens itself in a fussily rebarbative manner – 'extend to and attend to', 'tonally and totally', 'at once ended and endless', 'does effect a true fusion because it does not strive for a "true-fusion" '. There is no glimmer of a critical intelligence in this type of infantile paronomasia: 'The hyphen has the capacity which Hill sees as "an essential quality of Swift's creative intelligence: the capacity to be at once resistant and reciprocal". "Their spades grafted through the variably-resistant soil" (*Mercian Hymns*, XII): there the variably-resistant hyphen at once joins and divides, at once grafts and grafts through.' Similarity is difference, difference is similarity – anything is like anything else, Ricks's non-argument suggests. And more disturbingly, it also suggests that Hill and Swift are different but similar. Like most of Hill's critics, Ricks takes the poet at his enormous self-estimation, and the result is a reputation hyped by a series of adulatory comparisons. Hill is like – and therefore on the same level of achievement as – Eliot, Yeats, Mandelstam, Lowell, Blake, Pasternak. Ricks's arid, nimbling critical manner pretends to discover a mystic complexity in pure platitude and bathos:

> The hyphen cannot but acknowledge, in the moment when it conceives of two things coming together, that they are nevertheless two not one, just as Hill's need not exactly to spell but to articulate the word 'atonement' differently when he means at-one-ment is tacitly an admission that the two, the same and not the same, will always be magnetically held apart and held together by being like-poles.

Kipling's McAndrew discerned a calvinistic predestination in 'the stride o' yon connectin' rod', and Ricks appears to identify some type of medieval Catholic solder or theological magnetism in Hill's use of hyphens. He concludes by exclaiming, 'But as a child his first recorded word was "jam-jar" '. This deadly bit of trivia is meant to offer a final bucolic epiphany, for even the preliterate child was vouchsafed an atoning primal hyphen.

Ricks's essay is a piece of self-indulgence instinct with that reactionary Anglo-Catholicism which T. S. Eliot managed long ago to foist on Protestant England. His trapped critical outlook prevents him from confronting the essentially *Blut-und-Boden* nature of Hill's imagination – an imagination in love with the dark age of the Spanish counter-reformation. Even Gabriel Pearson (a founder-editor of *New Left Review*) succumbs to the kitsch feudalism that flaws so much of Hill's verse. 'The critic', writeth Pearson, 'enters the poet's castle, having given his little tinkle or sounded his annunciatory horn, with some foreboding that he is to be humiliated or scorned.' This is Jamesian camp, and throughout his essay Pearson struggles to sound the high, exquisite, immaterial note of James's prefaces. Art is daunting, mysterious, difficult of access – the critic must manner himself into it with a great deal of oohing and ahing, and with much affected reverence for the superior mage who built the castle and installed the dungeons.

Sometimes the critic cometh on ye tiptoe, like Master Jeremy Hooker, who begins his essay, '*For the Unfallen*: a Sounding', with the tremulously respectful:

> To adapt a phrase from 'Of Commerce and Society', Geoffrey Hill in *For the Unfallen* is a poet who exposes the muddle of Europe's dreaming. I may perhaps be excused for beginning boldly and generally, by abstracting from parts of this poem, an overview of his apprehension of the history to which the poems are, in part, a highly critical response; density and complexity must come soon enough to an argument that tries to remain faithful to the very concentrated poetry in this book and at the same time to say something useful about it.

Hooker's idea of density belongs at the bottom of Pope's quivering bog, and his attempt to prove that Hill can write about Auschwitz without 'poetic self-regard' is doomed by his ignorance of the poetry of Różewicz and Zbigniew Herbert. He quotes from 'Of Commerce and Society, IV':

> Many have died. Auschwitz,
> Its furnace chambers and lime pits
> Half-erased, is half-dead; a fable
> Unbelievable in fatted marble.

Hooker recommends 'the quality of Geoffrey Hill's moral intelligence', but that questionable intelligence does not stand up to a comparison with these lines from Różewicz's 'Massacre of the Boys', a poem dated 'The Museum, Auschwitz, 1948':

> A great plain closed
> like a figure of geometry
> and a tree of black smoke
> a vertical
> dead tree
> with no star in its crown.
> (trans. Adam Czerniawski)

Różewicz has developed an austere, transparent anti-style in order to approach the subject of absolute evil and horror. Hill relies on a plushy series of mannered pentameters, and the result is a grisly historical voyeurism which – despite Hooker's insistence to the contrary – sounds both insular and complacent.

Hooker is convinced that Hill is the equal of Wallace Stevens, but he is incapable of distinguishing a literary pastiche from a poem which can honour its influences. Quoting Hill's lines, 'Each day the tide withdraws; chills us; pastes/The sands with dead gulls, oranges, dead men', he fails to point out that they are ripped off from Eliot's description of the Mississippi's 'cargo of dead negroes, cows and chicken coops'. Hill is a parasite upon Eliot's imagination, and any account of his work must face this frankly in order to argue the ultimate authenticity of the style.

Take 'Idylls of the King' from *Tenebrae*:

> The pigeon purrs in the wood; the wood has gone;
> dark leaves that flick to silver in the gust,
> and the marsh-orchids and the heron's nest,
> goldgrimy shafts and pillars of the sun.
>
> Weightless magnificence upholds the past.
> Cement recesses smell of fur and bone
> and berries wrinkle in the badger-run
> and wiry heath-fern scatters its fresh rust.
>
> 'O clap your hands' so that the dove takes flight,
> bursts through the leaves with an untidy sound,
> plunges its wings into the green twilight
>
> above this long-sought and forsaken ground,
> the half-built ruins of the new estate,
> warheads of mushrooms round the filter-pond.

Hill's title is straightforwardly Tennysonian, and so is the poem's dank, mossy texture, its stagnant vowel-music. The imperative ' "O clap your hands" ' is Yeatsian: 'Soul clap its hands, and louder sing' ('Sailing to Byzantium'); while the 'wiry heath-fern' echoes Hopkins's 'Wiry heathpacks, flitches of fern' ('Inversnaid'). The berries and the pigeon/dove with its 'untidy sound' echo the last section in Stevens's 'Sunday Morning':

Sweet berries ripen in the wilderness;
And, in the isolation of the sky,
At evening, casual flocks of pigeons make
Ambiguous undulations as they sink,
Downward to darkness, on extended wings.

Like Stevens, Hill is playing a secular against a religious landscape, though they differ in that Hill would have us embrace what Stevens terms 'any old chimera of the grave'.

Hill labours to produce an image of ye olde England covered by the secular ruins of the welfare state. At times his evocation of the past's 'weightless magnificence' wobbles slightly as Hill's less-than-perfect ear skews the rhythm of the lines. Thus the rhyme 'flight/twilight' wrenches the natural vernacular spondee, '*twilight*', into a fast, freakish iamb, 'twi*light*' in order to complete the full rhyme with 'flight'. The pentameters are too monotonously definite to allow any rhythmic leeway, and the result is a false, flat note. Even so, these lines retain a certain gravid power, though in saying this I'm aware that the buried Anglican in me has a soft spot for this type of visionary mustiness.

Although Hill is endorsing the natural threat posed to collectivist society by the 'warheads of mushrooms', the image carries a contradictory suggestion of missile silos, of England as a nuclear province of the United States. Here it would be tempting to detect a Powellite strain in Hill's conservatism, and it is interesting to note that Peter Robinson connects the visionary poet with the prophetic politician when he compares 'He set in motion the furtherance of his journey. To watch the Tiber foaming out much blood', in *Mercian Hymns*, with Enoch Powell's notorious: 'As I look ahead, I am filled with foreboding. Like the Roman, I seem to see "the River Tiber foaming with much blood". That tragic and intractable phenomenon which we watch with horror on the other side of the Atlantic but which there is interwoven with the history and existence of the States itself, is coming upon us here by our own volition and our own neglect.' Robinson shows that Hill began his poem in the year Powell made his speech, and he adds that the speech was delivered to the Conservative Political Centre 'at the Midland Hotel, Birmingham; that is to say, in the modern-day regional capital of Offa's Mercia'. Though Robinson deserves credit for tracing Offa's spoor back to the Midland Hotel, he baulks at drawing any conclusions from this conjunction of Black Country powers.

Robinson, like the other essayists, is an old-fashioned, sacerdotal critic, and it is unsettling to read in a book published by the Open University a critic who speaks of 'a witness to the truth, not of God but of our unwillingness for God': reading Michael Edwards's statement in multi-racial Britain in 1985, I wonder at its exclusive, ethnically biased use of 'our' and 'God'. Edwards employs the words in a manner that assumes the existence of a white Christian monoculture ('that spirit of obedience so dear' etc.), rather than a pluralist society composed of many different religious and non-religious cultures. Does Edwards never switch on Channel 4? Clearly not, or he would realize that British society is not just composed of those neo-Christians Empson so despised.

Fortunately, there is one contributor to this collection – the gifted and intelligent Hugh Haughton – who puts the case against Hill very forcefully. Although Haughton appears not to have entirely lost his faith in the work, he lacks that reverential gullibility which so mars the other essays, and he rightly detects something 'obstinately archaic about Hill's poetry'. He asserts that all the poems, even the most original, contain an element of 'historical pastiche', and he describes their 'fraught anachronism', their lack of common humanity, their reductively Hobbesian identification of memory and imagination, and their disabling evocations of a contradictory 'lost kingdom'. Noting Hill's 'temperamental conservatism' and archaic monarchism, Haughton points to his cunning 'book-making' and suggests that Hill's titles 'have a smack of a holy Madame Tussaud's about them'. Shrewdly, he demonstrates how Hill's 'mannered sonnets re-enact and petrify a language of the past largely invented by the Victorians'. Hill's sense of tradition is revealed as bogus because his poetic language originates with the Victorians and 'can be said to be less their inheritance than their legacy'. He accuses Hill of creating a 'stilted international baroque' and cites many examples of glutted rhetoric.

Surprisingly, Haughton concludes by suggesting that if the work's 'own authority' strikes us as anachronistic, 'it may be that that will help to liberate us from anachronistic authority'. It seems to me that this critical enterprise aims to prop up a shabby and reactionary hegemony, and that Haughton – he is clearly radical and egalitarian – ought to have refused to participate in it. Still, he has signalled a wish to defect from Offa's camp, and is clearly troubled by the authoritarian imagination Hill's admirers celebrate.

Junk Britain: Peter Reading

In the late 1950s, Philip Larkin wrote a poem celebrating a journey by train from the remote city of Hull, in Yorkshire, to London. Larkin's vision of provincial lives has achieved canonical status:

> All afternoon, through the tall heat that slept
>   For miles inland,
> A slow and stopping curve southwards we kept.
> Wide farms went by, short-shadowed cattle, and
> Canals with floatings of industrial froth;
> A hothouse flashed, uniquely: hedges dipped
> And rose: and now and then a smell of grass
> Displaced the reek of buttoned carriage-cloth
> Until the next town, new and nondescript,
> Approached with acres of dismantled cars.

Drawing on the imagery of the Georgian poets and on the industrial landscapes of the 1930s writers, 'The Whitsun Weddings' lyrically documents a shabbily decent England before rising in its final stanza to a sacramental image of newly married love, fertility and disappointment. The random travellers:

> Stood ready to be loosed with all the power
> That being changed can give. We slowed again,
> And as the tightened brakes took hold, there swelled
> A sense of falling, like an arrow-shower
> Sent out of sight, somewhere becoming rain.

Through the Pauline idea of 'being changed', with its connotations of immortality, the secular urban landscape is imbued with both religious and patriotic values (the arrow-shower carries a resurgent nationalist energy and emotion). Very deftly, Larkin combines a Yeatsian big-bang effect of magisterial visionary power with an undermining sadness whose dying fall and sense of diminished horizons is lyrical and deeply English. This 'melancholy note' pervades the poetry of Thomas Hardy and Edward Thomas, and Larkin's democratic epithalamion also belongs, with Thomas's 'Adlestrop', to a genre that might be termed the 'England from a train' poem. It reflects that diminished sense of national pride which still haunts Larkin's generation, but it finally refuses to relinquish a shared sense of purpose and future commitment. It is a poem of mass observation imbued with the communal solidarity of Britain in the 1940s and 1950s. In a manner that is both anonymously documentary and idealistically self-conscious, it draws a moving frame across a landscape of cinemas, cooling towers, scrapyards and country cricket matches in order to reveal an altered country that is also somehow timeless.

The evaporating sense of purpose which may be glimpsed in the final image is parched and embittered in Larkin's 1969 poem, 'Homage to a Government':

> Next year we are to bring the soldiers home
> For lack of money, and it is all right.
> Places they guarded, or kept orderly,
> Must guard themselves, and keep themselves orderly.
> We want the money for ourselves at home
> Instead of working. And this is all right.

These lines were prompted by Britain's withdrawal from Aden under the Labour government of Harold Wilson, and they show how Larkin spoke for England in everything he wrote. His conservative nationalism deepened in later years, and metropolitan journalists would travel up to Hull to record his support for Margaret Thatcher. The Prime Minister responded in private conversation by inviting him to become Poet Laureate. 'I haven't written a poem for years,' he replied. 'Oh you must,' she said bravely and passed on. Always witty and courteous in company, and a poet of unassailable talent, Larkin's private conversation was often laced with savagely racist remarks, and, like his friend the novelist Kingsley Amis, he was outraged by the numbers of black immigrants who came to Britain during the prosperous 1950s and 1960s.

Reflecting on Peter Reading's poetry after a prolonged study of his satiric accounts of England in the 1970s and 1980s, I find an imagination rooted somewhere far back in that mythic arcadia which Larkin occupied long after it had been vacated by the Georgian poets. In an early poem, 'Embarkation', Reading draws on Edward Thomas's carefully faltering syntax to evoke 'a summer ending and a country halt'. Like Larkin, he mixes the smell of carriage-cloth (the upholstery on the seats of obsolete steam trains) with images of decay: 'Weeds prised the platform, where you waved, oblique./The day was hot and stewed grass filled our lungs.' Mortality is the ostensible subject of this poem, but its deep imaginative focus is the regimented banality of life in a declining industrial society. Despite its faintly classical aroma – a kind of unsure translationese – the poem sounds like an ersatz cento of lines from Edward Thomas and Larkin. Yet it points towards Reading's amazed and unflinching discovery of a subject few English poets have been able to confront – Junk Britain. In *Stet* (1986), he writes England from a train, but his acknowledgement of his debt to Larkin modulates into a disgusted image of loutish army cadets which implies a different politics to Larkin's:

> A cooling tower, scrap cars bashed into cubes,
> a preternaturally mauve canal.
> . . . Cropped boys
> aged about sixteen, manifest recruits
> (numbers and names and barracks stencilled white
> on khaki kit bags), smoke, guffaw and swig.

For many years Larkin was England's uncrowned poet laureate; now Reading has made himself into the unofficial laureate of a decaying nation. He writes with a journalistic commitment to the present social moment and scorns an aesthetic idea that prizes the lapidary and the fixed.

His first volume, *For the Municipality's Elderly* (1974), is a shaky recuperation of deeply exhausted, traditional English images –

graves, castles, cottage hospitals, pleached hedges, alabaster knights. However, Reading litters Deepwood Lane with some of those ephemeral consumer items which also fascinated Larkin – Kleenex and Lucozade, for example – though these contemporary markers are too obviously strategic and fail to redress the pre-First World War ruralism of the poems. The language is sometimes innocently archaic ('I awake/to you already arisen'), and this increases the reactionary and nostalgic effect. These poems appear to be insulated from a society which was in deepening economic crisis (in 1973 a miners' strike brought down Edward Heath's Conservative government, which was replaced by a shaky series of Labour governments until what now looks like the final defeat of British socialism in 1979).

At a deep level, though, Reading's imagination responded to that lacklustre, blank decade, the 1970s, and his poetry began to change radically. The early bucolicism disappeared as a new demotic voice – driven and anguished – ripped the poems apart. The new style was a form of satiric prophecy which ten years on from its first appearance seems tensely able to ride the currents of an analytic desperation. Writing in the mid-1970s, Reading mixes hooligan graffiti – 'HEADBUTTS AND BOOTS IS OUR BIZNUSS' – with high cultural references in order to conclude: 'Never let it be said that *we*/ever stood in the way of regress.' And as Britain regressed more and more into a nasty and brutal form of populism, Reading observed the national sickness and chucked torn gobbets of verse at his readers.

Soccer violence is now a permanent feature of British culture, and British football fans are feared and hated throughout Europe (at the time of writing twenty-nine supporters of Liverpool's football team are awaiting trial in Brussels for causing many deaths and injuries in a riot there two years back). A report in the *Guardian* newspaper vividly catches this rebarbative society in its description of the behaviour of British football fans in a German bar:

Spud, a Spurs fan, had been in the bar for three hours and wanted some 'proper beer'; he was still there an hour later, tolerating the local brew. He had bleary eyes, hefty tattooed forearms, and a very substantial figure. With a slobber he asked the blonde waitress to marry him and come and live in

Harlow. She declined, and Spud and his mates struck a chorus to the tune of Bread of Heaven: 'Get yer tits out for the lads, get your tits out for the lads.'

The British abroad are notoriously unpopular, and British visitors to Europe now find themselves strangers in a continent where they were used to win battles with clothyard arrows and other weapons. No one living in Britain now can fail to observe the jeering brutalism and demoralized separatism with which large sections of the island's white population confront the various ethnic minority groups within the country.

Many English people find foreigners comic, and Reading vulnerably reveals that insular sense of superiority when he makes fun of the linguistic solecisms of non-native speakers. Yet because he has the gift of making his contemporary English usage sometimes sound like a calque from Greek or Latin, he can 'make strange' and write as if he is a foreign observer:

> Over Michael in the kitchen clambered
> nude and T-shirted malicious infants
> (sired by the psychologist, of both his wife
> and his mistress)

The trochees shift into syncopated dactyls, and in breaking with the predominantly iambic mode of English verse Reading signals his dissidence from the state. His classicism has a displacing effect and it runs against the Anglo-Saxon grain of the native culture. He has an exact ear for provincial demotic, and unlike Larkin in 'The Whitsun Weddings' would never rhyme 'cars' with 'grass' (*cahs* and *grahs* in polite English speech). Larkin was hostile to classical literature and myth, and his work is never ghosted by quantitative metre as Reading's is.

If Reading's persona is sometimes that of a patrician classicist surveying the wreckage that is post-industrial England, he can also write in the manner of a contemporary John Clare and observe rural life from the inside. He delights in the cadences of rural speech, but often he caricatures it rather in the manner of the farming accents employed in *The Archers*, now a cult article for professional Englishmen such as the novelist A. N. Wilson. Reading's ear for speech rhythms is accurate and sensitive, though they can come across as a form of shallow mimicry which reduces the speakers to the status of dim-witted clowns – the eighteenth-century term for peasants which Clare's readers expected him to employ in his poems.

The scrambled literary heritage that Reading draws on is consciously gapped; this is one of his most effective deconstructive strategies, a mode of irony which subverts T. S. Eliot's idea of tradition. Eliot's tradition – an artificial and polemical construct that pretends to be natural – still weighs like a nightmare on English literary studies, but Reading is intent on bulldozing it. His dissent, though, has a conservative base – an unstable foundation which enables him to write within the wildly exciting vibrations that afflict the imaginations of all pessimistic anarchists. Like Swift, he is outraged by personal cruelty and the abuse of power, and like Swift he delights in parody and officialese. In a pseudo-translation from the Spanish, he jibes at the reactionary preciosity of England's leading conservative poet, Geoffrey Hill. This is implicitly radical, yet Reading's hatred of technology and commercial jargon points to a nostalgia for an 'organic' culture buried under acres of light industry on the fringes of Britain's towns and cities.

Playing on his ironic gift of a surname, Reading is a type of reader-response writer who makes the textures of his poems deliberately user-hostile. He throws the comments of his critics back in our faces and insists that he does not 'transcend pain with Poetry' and is 'drab rhythmless demotic':

> I am all very amusing in my way, maybe,
> (and definitely mordant)
> *but am I Art?*

His manic self-consciousness designs a poetry of extreme risk, and this is appropriate to the crazed astringency and philistinism of the present social moment. The new Right which dominates politics and the press is typified by the simple-minded conservative intellectual Roger Scruton, though it finds its most bizarre expression in the journalism of John Vincent, a leading professional historian at the

University of Bristol who writes coarse propaganda for Britain's most popular junk newspaper, the *Sun*.

Responding to the new populism, Reading demonstrates in 'Stedman's' that cultural life in Britain is now a form of choreophrasia, the continual repetition of meaningless phrases. 'Stedman's serendipitously begins as a poem about writing a poem about Huntington's Chorea, but it is soon deflected into a parody of ye olde English poetic refrains to become a small-scale assault on that cultural totem, the canon of English literature. This is the poetry of deconstruction, and it is necessarily based on a repudiation of poetry itself. Reading's work has affinities with the anti-poetry of Eastern Europe, though at some level it is too cosily insular ever to approach the icy despair of that imagination. His attempt to write directly about death in *C* (1984) exudes an adolescent self-consciousness and voyeuristic relish which makes it a failed exercise in that deliberate bad taste Reading deploys so carefully elsewhere: 'The huge firm 18-year-old malleable boobs she had let him enjoy were defiled at 42 by surgeon's scalpel and radium treatment. This, rendered into catalectic tetrameters, might do for the *TLS* or other reputable literary periodical.' The problem with this type of writing is that the writer identifies his own *gravitas* with the opacity of death itself, and suggests to his audience that only he understands the terrors of terminal disease.

In his most brilliant and assured volume, *Ukulele Music* (1985), Reading blasts the national consciousness into tacky fragments and exposes the insane ugliness of British life. One of the effects of high unemployment and a declining economy has been a sharp rise in child abuse: Reading's angry compassion insists on making us recognize the cruelty and squalor which afflict increasing numbers of British children. In these poems (or 'material' as Reading terms them on his acknowledgements page), muggers, skinheads, child abusers, bland reviewers rub shoulders with 'beetrooty colonels' nostalgic for another war that will 'get this Great Country back on its feet, sir'. The poems are interleaved with a series of wonderfully 'oral' notes from Viv, the poet's cleaning lady: 'Dear sir, have done some hoover of the front room. but am going now be back tomorrow morning if you can oblige with next week money same as last time.' Viv's long rambling notes are in 'prose', but gradually they turn into 'verse' – Reading is no respecter of literary categories and he doubts the idea of literariness, preferring to cast his *écriture* on the waters and watch the critics swipe at it. Viv's first poem is for me the volume's peak of ironic wit and tenderness:

> Who would have thought it Sir, actually putting ME in a WRITING!
> me and the Capting and ALL. What a turn up for the books.
>
> Only, I must say I do not know HOW them people in poems
> manage to say what they want – you know, in funny short lines.

These lines fuse English proletarian demotic with classical hexameters and draw subtly on Clough's democratic and revolutionary vision of working-class life in *The Bothie of Tober-Na-Vuolich*:

> Little child bringing breakfast to 'father' that sits on the timber
> There by the scaffolding; see, she waits for the can beside him;
> Meantime above purer air untarnished of new-lit fires.

This is an English anticipation of *Leaves of Grass*, and Viv's verse letter belongs in the 'purer air' of a new democratic writing.

Through the figure of Viv, Reading is able to answer those critics who disliked his earlier use of working-class speech – poet and cleaning lady here unite against the powerful metropolitan world which oppresses them. This suggests that by some miraculous movement of the spirit the British working class might suddenly take power from those who divide and manipulate it. This is the pastoral poet's dream of stealing a march on his exploitative urban readership and seizing real power.

Reading's idealism challenges conventional literary discourse and insists on his right to 'go over the top' and refuse to submit to the idea of decorum. Scorning the 'Plashy Fen School' of English verse, and mocking 'Grub St. reviewing its own lame valedictory bunk', he plunges his imagination into a mad, unrestrained mix of violence and loony tunes. Look at this culture, he cries, and details its absurdities in modified elegiac distichs:

> . . . page after page of trite news reports
> rehashed, vomiting squalor.
>   Over-exposure to vile
>   madness (from verse or the box)

And, very daringly, he crosses his satire with a narrative that is referred to in Viv's mention of 'the Capting'.

This Victorian maritime story is central to the construction of *Ukulele Music*, and in it Reading draws on the powerful ideological values which are enshrined in the British fascination with the sea, a colonial obsession that is often reflected in children's literature. Writing inside a stranded Leviathan, he imagines the emaciated survivors of a shipwreck off Patagonia and a mad captain who sleeps on a bag of stinking seal meat. The poem is also an oblique prophecy of nuclear holocaust and shows that Reading is capable of looking beyond his delimited subject, the condition of England, towards a more global sense of threat and imminent disaster. The conclusion of his untitled narrative employs a gnarled nautical lingo – the poem's language is repro archaic throughout – in order to launch this poignant question:

> And shall it, now, be counted
> as ye dignified defiance
> in us towards our fateful
> merciless element,
> or gull naïveté,
> cousin to recklessness,
> that, e'en in pitching Gulphward,
> our salt kind brings forth chanteys?

Like the dying fall at the end of 'The Whitsun Weddings', these lines carry a patriotic pulse as well as performing a kind of ritual absolution. In them we witness the isolated, scarred and diminished soul of a great seafaring nation asking forgiveness after centuries of reckless imperialism. It's a hard request to answer and it perhaps betrays a sentimental softness for the imperial past. We may be grateful, though, that the nation has found such a prolific laureate in

Peter Reading. The imaginative risks he takes in confronting the state have a witty desperation and a strange but essentially confident poignancy that speaks in that phrase 'our salt kind'. It reminds me of Churchill's remark in May 1940 that the nation was as 'sound as the salt in the sea'.

Acknowledgements

Acknowledgements are due to the editors of the following publications in which versions of some of these essays first appeared: *Critical Approaches to Anglo-Irish Literature*, ed. Michael Allen and Angela Wilcox, Colin Smythe, 1989 ('Southey Landing'); *D. H. Lawrence in the Modern World*, ed. Peter Preston and Peter Hoare, Macmillan, 1989 ('Hibiscus and Salvia Flowers: D. H. Lawrence'); *Essays on Zbigniew Herbert*, ed. Adam Czerniawski, Serena Books, 1991 ('Zbigniew Herbert: Elegy of Fortinbras'); *Times Literary Supplement* ('John Clare in Babylon', 20 June 1986, review of *The Letters of John Clare*, ed. Mark Storey; 'Hopkins on the Rampage', 14 August 1987, review of *Gerard Manley Hopkins: The Critical Heritage*, ed. Gerald Roberts, and *Gerard Manley Hopkins*, ed. Catherine Phillips; 'She Did Not Change: Philip Larkin', 20 July 1990, review of *Philip Larkin: His Life's Work* by Janice Rossen; 'Polemics in Paradise: The Republican Epic of John Milton', 12 July 1991, review of *Milton and the Drama of History* by David Loewenstein and *Politics, Poetics and Hermeneutics in Milton's Prose*, ed. David Loewenstein and Grantham Turner); *London Review of Books* ('Salid Oil and Alexindrines', 3 April 1986, review of *The Collected Letters of W. B. Yeats: Volume I, 1865–1895*, ed. John Kelly in association with Eric Domville; 'Writing beyond Writing', 29 October 1987, review of *Emily Dickinson* by Helen McNeil, *Emily Dickinson: Looking to Canaan* by John Robinson, *Emily Dickinson: A Poet's Grammar* by Christanne Miller, and *Emily Dickinson: The Poet on the Second Storey* by Jerome Loving; 'A Visionary Nationalist: Geoffrey Hill', 4 April 1985, review of *Geoffrey Hill: Essays on his Work*, ed. Peter Robinson); *Grand Street* ('Junk Britain: Peter Reading', 1988; 'Dwelling without Roots: Elizabeth Bishop', 1990); *Independent on Sunday* ('Miroslav Holub', 13 May 1990, review of *Vanishing Lung Syndrome* by Miroslav Holub, trans. David Young and Dana Hábová, *The Dimension of the Present and Other Essays* by Miroslav Holub, trans. David Young, and *Poems Before and After* by Miroslav Holub, trans. Ian and Jarmila Milner, Ewald Osers and George Theiner). I have reshaped and tried to improve the original essays, but in the case of my discussion of Geoffrey Hill have retained the error which provoked a lengthy correspondence in the *London Review of Books*.

'Yeats's Hunger-Strike Poem' was given as a lecture at the Yeats

International Summer School in August 1985. 'The Great Horn-Handled Jack-Knife: *Great Expectations* as Epic Poem' was given as a lecture at the Open University Literature Summer School at York University in July 1987. 'Poetry and Power: Robert Frost' was given as a paper at a conference on 'The Nation and its Cultural Borders' at the University of Southampton in July 1990 and was later published in *Grand Street*. 'Ted Hughes: Laureate of the Free Market?' was given as the Kenneth Allott Memorial Lecture at the University of Liverpool in November 1990.

T.P.

For permission to reprint copyright material the author and publishers gratefully acknowledge the following: ELIZABETH BISHOP: lines from 'Crusoe in England', 'Jerónimo's House', 'Brazil, January 1, 1502', 'Electrical Storm', 'Seascape', 'Santarém', 'The Bight', 'A Cold Spring', 'The Moose', 'Filling Station' and 'The Hanging of the Mouse' from *Elizabeth Bishop: The Complete Poems 1927–1979* (Farrar, Straus & Giroux 1983/ Hogarth, 1984) Copyright © 1983 by Alice Helen Methfessel, by permission of Farrar, Straus & Giroux Inc.; letter to Robert Lowell (1965) from *Becoming a Poet* by David Kalstone (Hogarth, 1989), by permission of The Estate of Elizabeth Bishop, Copyright © 1989 by Alice Helen Methfessel; JOHN CLARE: extract from letter to Octavius Gilchrist, 21 January 1820, from *The Letters of John Clare*, edited by Mark Storey (Oxford, Clarendon Press, 1985) Copyright © by Eric Robinson 1985; extract from *John Clare's Autobiographical Writings*, edited by Eric Robinson (Oxford, Clarendon Press, 1983) Copyright © by Eric Robinson 1983, by permission of Curtis Brown Limited, London; SAMUEL TAYLOR COLERIDGE: extract from letter to Sir George and Lady Beaumont, 1 October 1803, from *The Collected Letters of Samuel Taylor Coleridge*, edited by Earl Leslie Griggs, Vol. II, 1801–1806 (Oxford, Clarendon Press, 1956), by permission of Oxford University Press; EMILY DICKINSON: 'He fumbles at your Soul', 'Our lives are Swiss – ', 'A word is dead' and 'There came a Wind like a Bugle' from *The Complete Poems of Emily Dickinson*, edited by Thomas H. Johnson, Copyright 1935 by Martha Dickinson Bianchi, Copyright © renewed 1963 by Mary L. Hampson (Cambridge, Mass.: The Belknap Press of Harvard University), by permission of Little, Brown and Company; ROBERT FROST: lines from 'Trespass', 'New Hampshire', 'Cliff Dwelling', 'The Vanishing Red', 'In the Home Stretch', 'The Wood Pile', 'The Most of It', and 'Putting in the Seed', from *The Poetry of Robert Frost*, edited by Edward Connery Latham (Cape, 1971/Holt, Rinehard & Winston, 1969), by permission of The Estate of Robert Frost, Jonathan Cape Ltd. and Henry Holt & Co. Ltd.; extract from 'Genealogy' from *Selected Letters of Robert Frost*, edited by Lawrence Thompson

(Cape, 1965), by permission of The Estate of Robert Frost, Jonathan Cape Ltd. and Lawrence Thompson; SEAMUS HEANEY: lines from *Sweeney Astray* (Faber, 1984) and from 'Churning Day' from *Death of a Naturalist* (Faber, 1966)/*Poems 1965–1975* (Farrar, Straus & Giroux, 1980), by permission of Faber and Faber Ltd. and Farrar, Straus & Giroux Inc.; ZBIGNIEW HERBERT: 'Elegy of Fortinbras' and lines from 'Mona Lisa' from *Selected Poems* (1985), by permission of Carcanet Press Limited; lines from 'What I Saw', 'Old Masters' and 'The Power of Taste' from *Report from the Besieged City and Other Poems*, translated by John and Bogdana Carpenter (1987), by permission of Oxford University Press; GEOFFREY HILL: lines from 'Of Commerce and Society, IV' and 'Idylls of the King' from *Collected Poems* (1986), by permission of André Deutsch Ltd; MIROSLAV HOLUB: lines from 'The Minotaur's Thoughts on Poetry', 'Distant Howling', 'Napoleon', 'Brief Reflections on killing the Christmas Carp' and 'Although' from *Poems Before and After: Collected English Translations 1958–1990* (1990), by permission of Bloodaxe Books Ltd.; lines from 'Vanishing Lung Syndrome' and 'Heart Transplant' from *Vanishing Lung Syndrome*, translated by David Young and Dana Habova (1990), by permission of Faber and Faber Limited; TED HUGHES: lines from 'Mill Ruins' and 'The Trance of Light' from *Remains of Elmet* (1979); from 'Dust As We Are' from *Wolfwatching* (1989); from 'October Dawn', 'A Modest Proposal', 'September' and 'The Horses' from *The Hawk in the Rain* (1957); from 'The Retired Colonel' and 'Hawk Roosting' from *Lupercal* (1960); from 'Thistles', 'The Warriors of the North' and 'Wodwo' from *Wodwo* (1967); from 'A Motorbike' from *Moortown* (1979); from 'Feeding out-wintering cattle at twilight', 'February 17th' and 'The Tractor' from *Moortown Diary* (1989); from 'The Honey Bee and the Thistle' from *Rain-Charm for the Duchy* (1992), by permission of Faber and Faber Limited; JAMES JOYCE: extract from 'The Right Heart in the Wrong Place' in letter to Stanislaus Joyce, 27 August 1920, from *Letters of James Joyce*, edited by Richard Ellmann, Vol. II (1966), by permission of Faber and Faber Limited; PHILIP LARKIN: lines from 'The Whitsun Weddings' from *The Whitsun Weddings* (1964) and from 'XII' from *The North Ship* (1966), by permission of Faber and Faber Limited; from 'Homage to a Government', 'Afternoons', 'The March Past', 'At Grass', 'Counting', 'Poetry of Departure', 'Best Society', 'Vers de Société', 'Livings II', 'Friday Night in the Royal Station Hotel', 'Bridge for the Living', 'Here' and 'Deceptions', and the stanzas 'In times when nothing stood' and 'By day, a listed study storehouse', from *Collected Poems* (1988), by permission of Faber and Faber Limited and Farrar, Straus & Giroux Inc.; OSIP MANDELSTAM: lines from 'The Stalin Epigram' from *Selected Poems*, translated by Clarence Brown and W. S. Merwin (OUP, 1973; Penguin Books, 1977) by permission of

Oxford University Press; PETER READING: lines from *Ukelele Music* (Secker & Warburg, 1985) by permission of the author; and from *STET* (1986) by permission of Martin Secker & Warburg Ltd, a division of Octopus Publishing Group plc; TADEUSZ ROZEWICZ: lines from 'Mound', 'Et in Arcadia Ego', 'Green Rose', 'Grass', 'From a Biography', 'Warmth' and 'Massacre of the Boys' from *They Came To See a Poet*, translated and introduced by Adam Czerniawski (1991), by permission of Anvil Press Poetry Ltd.; WALLACE STEVENS: lines from 'Sunday Morning' from *The Collected Poems of Wallace Stevens* (1955), by permission of Faber and Faber Limited and Alfred A. Knopf Inc.; W. B. YEATS: extracts from letters of W. B. Yeats from *The Collected Letters of W. B. Yeats*, edited by John Kelly and Eric Domville (Oxford, Clarendon Press, 1986), by permission of Oxford University Press.